Death in the Tenderloin

Just because
No one can see a face
Doesn't mean
It's gone.

❝ It's never over while one person remembers you. ❞

PHOTO BY BRIAN RINKER

DEATH IN THE TENDERLOIN

© 2012, Study Center Press
ISBN Number 978-1-888956-18-4
Library of Congress Control Number 212938791

Study Center Press is an imprint
of San Francisco Study Center Inc.

Cover design by Lenny Limjoco

Interior design by Beth Renneisen

Previous page: "Dawn Over Taylor Street."
Photo by Mark Ellinger

DEATH
IN THE TENDERLOIN

A slice of life from the heart of San Francisco

by Tom Carter, Marjorie Beggs and Others
Edited by Geoff Link

A CENTRAL CITY EXTRA
STUDY CENTER PRESS

Residential Hotels and Apartments

1. 990 Polk Street Apartments
2. Pacific Bay Inn - 520 Jones
3. Coast Hotel - 516 O'Farrell
4. Iroquois Hotel - 835 O'Farrell
5. Essex Hotel - 684 Ellis
6. 555 Ellis Street Family Apartments
7. Senator Hotel - 519 Ellis
8. Cambridge Hotel - 473 Ellis
9. Coronado Hotel - 373 Ellis
10. Jefferson Hotel - 440 Eddy
11. Hamlin Hotel - 385 Eddy
12. Elm Hotel - 364 Eddy
13. Padre Apartments - 241 Jones
14. Alexander Residence - 230 Eddy
15. Ritz Hotel - 216 Eddy
16. Franciscan Towers - 217 Eddy
17. William Penn Hotel - 160 Eddy
18. Empress Hotel - 144 Eddy
19. West Hotel - 141 Eddy
20. Ambassador Hotel - 55 Mason
21. Turk-Eddy Preservation Apartments - 165 Turk
22. Camelot Residence - 124 Turk
23. Aranda Residence - 64 Turk
24. Dalt Hotel - 34 Turk
25. San Cristina Residence - 1010 Market
26. Civic Center Residence - 44 McAllister

Other Locations

1. St. Francis Memorial Hospital - 900 Hyde
2. Hilton Hotel - 333 O'Farrell
3. Tenderloin Recreation Center - 570 Ellis
4. San Francisco Network Ministries - 559 Ellis
5. Glide Memorial United Methodist Church - 330 Ellis
6. Father Alfred E. Boeddeker Park - Eddy and Jones streets
7. Tenderloin Neighborhood Development Corp. - 201 Eddy
8. EXIT Theatre - 156 Eddy
9. Tenderloin Police Station - 301 Eddy
10. Central City Hospitality House - 290 Turk
11. 21 Club - 98 Turk
12. Central City Extra - 944 Market
13. Golden Gate Theatre - 1 Taylor
14. St. Boniface Church - 133 Golden Gate
15. St. Anthony Foundation Free Medical Clinic - 150 Golden Gate
16. Tenderloin Health - 255 Golden Gate
17. Community Housing Partnership - 20 Jones
18. UC Hastings College of the Law - 200 McAllister
19. Asian Art Museum - 200 Larkin
20. Civic Center Plaza
21. San Francisco City Hall - 1 Dr. Carlton B. Goodlett Place
22. San Francisco Public Library - 100 Larkin
23. United Nations Plaza

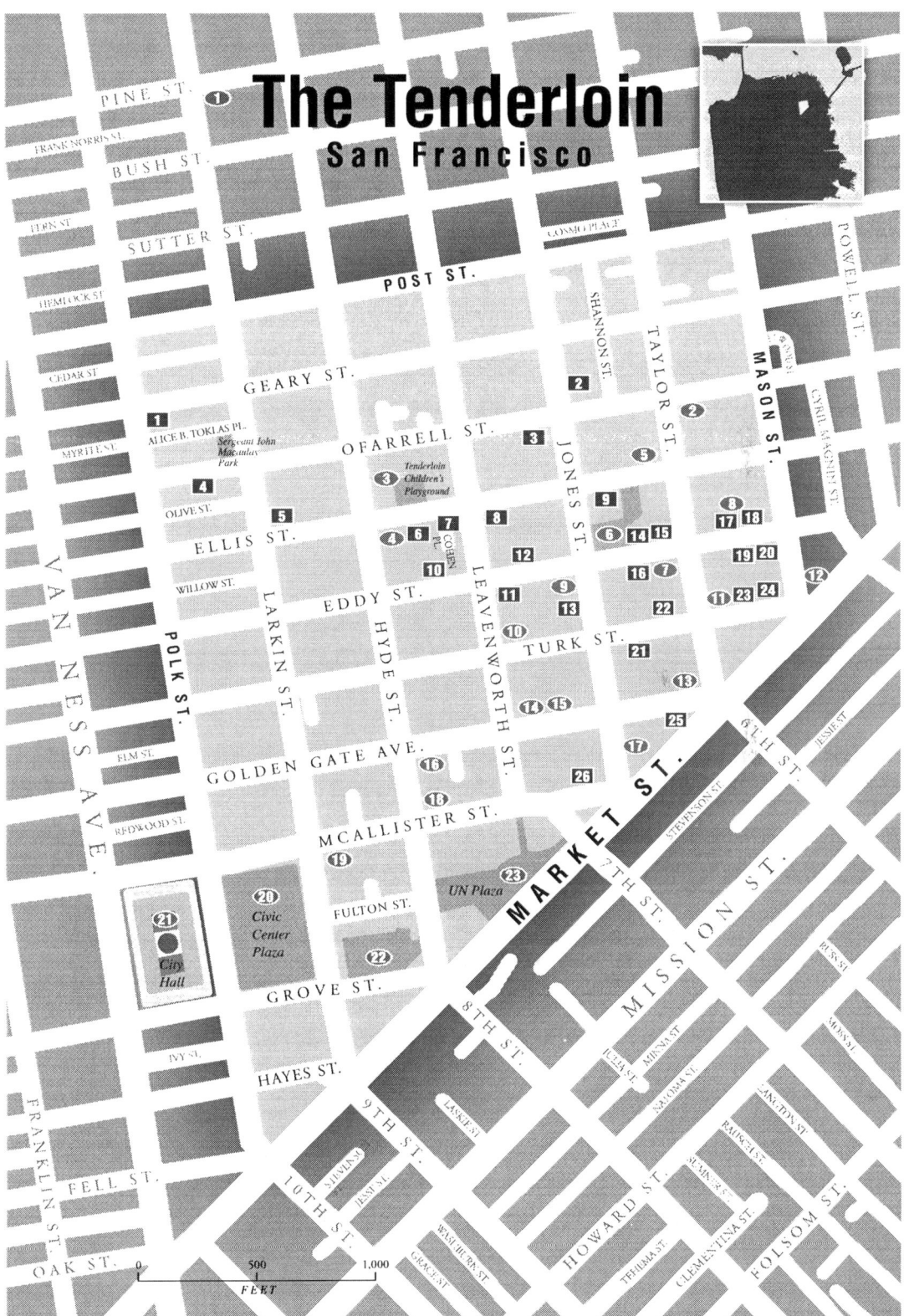

In This Book

Map of the Tenderloin vi
Acknowledgements 1

Part 1: Faces of Death

Foreword 3
Everyone's Friend at the Senator 5
Batman 6
Activist Wife of an Activist 7
One Body, Two People 8
A Troubled Man 9
Died Quietly Among Friends 10
Godfather of the Empress 11
Excelled at Kindness 12
The Elm's Happiest Resident 13
Voice of the People 14
The Man in the Red Wheelchair 17
Marched to His Own Drummer 17
Not What He Seemed 18
Jokester With Style 19
Tenderloin's Oldest Resident 20
A Long Life With Doting Daughters 21
Loved His Cats 22
A Craftsman, Not an Artist 23
Lives on in Memory 24
Kindly Gentleman Lived 101 Years 25
A Special Loved One 25

Part 2: Causes of Death

AIDS Is Foremost, Cancers Next 27
Had Rarest of Rare Diseases 31

Esteemed Black Brother 33
Original Molotov Mouth 34
Lady With a Lot of Class, Even in Pain 35
Architect, Artist, Musician 36
Restaurateur's Reversal of Fortune 37
Vietnam War Vet Who Rewarded Kindness .. 38
Fought for His Peers 39
The Gentle Giant 40
He Didn't Die on the Street 41
Celebrating the Survivors 42
A Merry Prankster 43
On Oxygen, Smoked Anyway 44
Thumbed His Nose at Pain 44
Desk Clerk Was Brutalized 45
Handled Intense Pain Well 46
Owned Top Mom-and-Pop 46
Popular Cook at Iroquois 48
Got His Wish 48
Someone Else in a Previous Life 49
Faced Adversity With Strength 49
A Very Caring Nurse 50
Bicycle Maker Who Gave Them Away 51
Clift Hotel Cook Loved the Tenderloin 52
A Man of Lightning Wit 52

Part 3: The Closer

Rev. Hope Gives a Caring Sendoff 55
Linked In: Born in June, Died in April 60
Open to the Truth 61
Survived Wild '90s at the Ambassador 62

Touched People Deeply 62	'Blew Hot and Cold' 97
Beautiful Spirit, She Only Wanted Love 63	A Diva's Ill-Timed Death 97
The Man on the Cover 64	Badass Vietnam Vet 98
Sports Talk Show Regular 64	Vietnam Vet With an Affinity for Heroin ... 100
Gone With the Wind 66	Budding Rock Star Takes His Own Life 101
Constant Advocate for Alcoholics, Addicts .. 66	
Janitor, Union Man 68	**Part 5: Analysis**
Hospitality House Icon 69	Those Who Died 107
A Tireless Force for Seniors 70	Troubadour Touched People 111
Lives on as a Garden 72	Musician Who Almost Made It 112
Activist With a Radio Voice 73	One of a Kind 113
4 Who Died Days Apart 73	Desk Clerk Like a Professor 114
A Man of Many Parts, All Good 75	Onetime Investment Banker 115
Security Guard With Good Friends 76	Essex Hotel Favorites 115
Gospel Singer Has Caring Neighbors 77	Didn't Want to Be a Burden 117
Loner Who Didn't Die Alone 78	Married for 54 Years, Still in Love 118
A Candle and a Prayer 78	Full-Throated Voice for the Homeless 118
Teresa of the Tenderloin 79	3 Die Days Apart 119
	Vietnam Vet and the Flower Peddler 120
Part 4: Murder in the Tenderloin	They Called Him 'Hollywood' 121
Commuter Criminals Do Most of the Killing .. 85	The Model Tenant 122
Sidewalk Memorial 89	Hard-Drinking Baseball Buff 123
Shocking Death of a Young Grandmother 90	Vietnam War Hero With Mystery Legacy ... 123
A Good Boy Who Got Gunned Down 91	Died One After the Other 124
Former Probation Officer 92	A Well-Regarded Man 125
Such a Spirit 93	Pioneer of Supportive Housing 126
Night Dispatcher of the Help Van 94	I Remember Hiram 129
Soul and Sunlight 95	
Loved Rock 'n' Roll and NASCAR 96	**San Francisco Study Center** 131
Transgender Artist 96	**Index of the Deceased** 133

" A sweetheart of a person, a gentle person with no pretensions, no meanness in him. "

"The Joy of Life" behind the Crystal Hotel at 128 Eddy St. now is mostly hidden by a new building of affordable housing. Photo by Mark Ellinger

ACKNOWLEDGEMENTS

Death in the Tenderloin *is dedicated to Lenny Limjoco,
for 35 years our friend and fellow artist
whose cover design graces the text and whose photos are found throughout.*

*Mark Hedin, Heidi Swillinger, Leah Garchik, Ed Bowers,
Brian Rinker and Karen Datangel are the other authors.
Their contributions enrich the volume, as do the photographs
of Mark Ellinger.*

*The San Francisco Chronicle generously allowed Study Center Press
to use photographer Brant Ward's evocative portrait of Michael Dick.*

*Many photographs accompanying the stories are courtesy
of the deceased's families and friends.
A number were taken from California driver's licenses and IDs.*

*We also acknowledge Rev. Glenda Hope's
significant personal and professional contributions
toward making the Tenderloin a compassionate community.*

> Today is a gift, that's why it's called the present.

The food line at Glide Memorial Methodist Church at Taylor and Ellis streets. Photo by Tom Carter

Part 1: Faces of Death

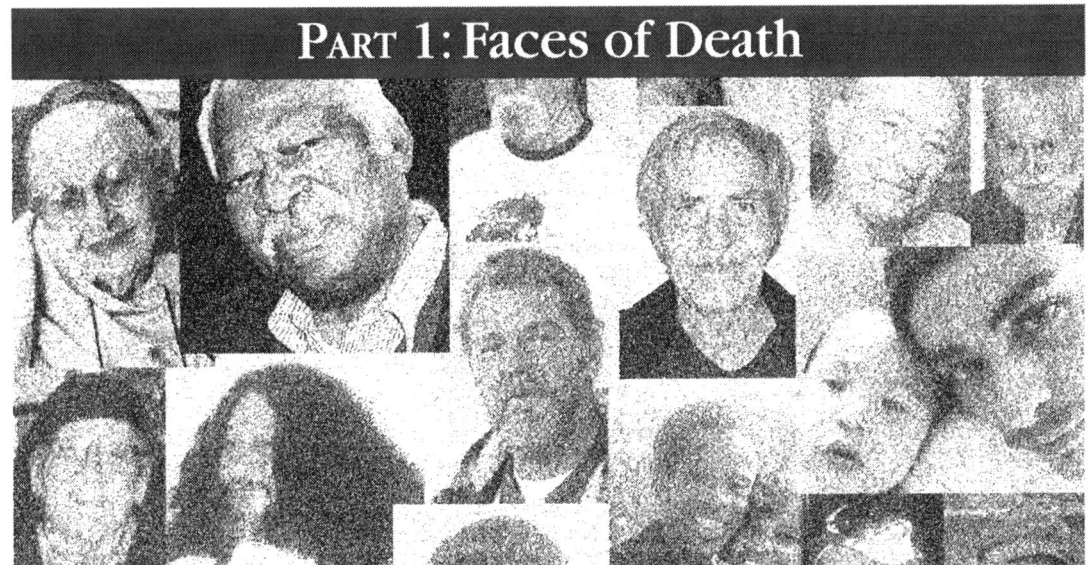

PHOTO ILLUSTRATION BY LENNY LIMJOCO

Foreword

BY GEOFF LINK

THIS BOOK celebrates the Tenderloin at its most tender. It was inspired by the obituaries published in the Central City Extra — monthly newspaper for the neighborhood's fixed-income and no-income populace. This is a hardscrabble script.

The Tenderloin is San Francisco's poorest neighborhood, a high-density, human services ghetto where hundreds of nonprofit and public providers serve a citywide caseload of homeless people in addition to treating the tribulations of the area's 30,000 residents.

Our hood is a mere few dozen square blocks cemented between downtown and Civic Center. Nob Hill is above, Skid Row below. *Death in the Tenderloin* is our eulogy to this historic, notorious neighborhood and its medley of people, absolutely the most diverse community in San Francisco, the heart of the city in more ways than one. We want you to come away with a sense of how difficult life is out here on the edge.

This book encourages us to think about death, next to birth the most important part of life. Yet these stories are not all somber, they brim with optimism. The obituaries are about people whose death, mostly quiet and independent, is dignified by their memorials, the setting for the ensuing narratives. Memorials mostly are conducted in the SRO or apartment building where the person lived. Typically they are officiated by Rev. Glenda Hope, the Tenderloin closer, who invites The Extra to attend to let the community know of the person's passing and what they meant to those left behind.

We edited the published obituaries, deleting courtesy titles and most dates, occasionally adding landscape details to sharpen the image of the Tenderloin and the people who live here. Most who are portrayed battled addictions, exorcising personal demons — or not. Quite a few had been recently homeless and, with what seemed like a sixth sense, came in from the cold to die in relative comfort with a roof over their head.

Most of these people are unknowns, some are known beyond the Tenderloin, a very few even farther. Certain readers might regret that all important dates aren't provided. But this is not a history book. It is an anthology of short stories that deal with death and dying in a rarefied setting. Each character is unique. The companion essays — three of them are edited features that were published in The Extra — offer a journalistic context.

The stories are largely composed of the facts of the dead person's life as their survivors and mourners recalled them, impressions and candid reminiscences of friends, family, neighbors and caregivers. In this culture, where last names are not important, shared experiences make people tight.

Each story helps etch a feeling for life in San Francisco's Tenderloin — a neighborhood and a state of mind. ●

> **All of us have a lot of grief in the Tenderloin.**

Popular corner of Jones and McAllister streets in front of once-majestic, abandoned Hibernia Bank.
Photo by Lenny Limjoco

Everyone's Friend at the Senator
PATRICIA CARLOS

IT WAS FITTING that Patricia Carlos ended up at the Senator Hotel, famed as a harbor for American Indians. Carlos grew up on the Salt River Pima Maricopa reservation near Scottsdale, Ariz. Then fate brought her to the SRO on Ellis Street when she was 32.

In 1971, the hotel welcomed the Indians from various tribes that federal marshals had evicted from Alcatraz after their 19-month occupation of the island. The hotel furnished them all rooms that night, plus use of the lobby for news conferences.

Carlos was at the hotel's 2006 "Remembrance and Resistance" ceremony commemorating the 35th anniversary of the Indians' "last stay among the residents of the Tenderloin," reads a wall plaque near the front door.

In her second-floor room, Carlos kept her heritage close. A flag showing the "End of the Trail" solitary horseman — sculptor James Earle Fraser's famous image — dominated one wall and pictures of proud, handsome chiefs decorated other walls.

But the 20 mourners who jammed her memorial in the small hotel community room cared first and foremost that she was a friend. Men and women passionately described the short, stout Pima as a cheerful spirit among them, someone who brought joy to their daily lives and who listened.

Her health had been declining for a couple of weeks, and when she died at 51 at UCSF Medical Center it was of cirrhosis of the liver.

Carlos had lived at the hotel the longest. The Senator, previously a tourist hotel with restaurant and parking lot, a popular haven for visiting vaudeville performers in the 1920s, closed briefly, then reopened in 1992 as a low-income SRO for the formerly homeless after renovation by a new owner, the nonprofit Community Housing Partnership. Her next-door neighbor, William Donlon, 72, remembers Carlos was already there for several months before he moved in, summer 1991.

Patricia Carlos with Dan O'Connell. Carlos died Aug. 26, 2009

A gray-bearded man in a wheelchair struggled for words, remembering her sense of humor. Black-bearded Jessie recalled their easy friendship and said her loss felt like getting "shot in the back." Tony Davidson, a large black man, was grateful he'd known Carlos for eight years. He said her upbeat personality brought the hotel's community closer. She often told him a "turtle story," of which she had many, to remind him to slow down.

Then a young black woman stood to sing "How Great Thou Art." A tall, white man walked in with a small black dog. "My dog bit 14 people," he said, "especially alcoholics. If the dog didn't bite her, well, she had good qualities."

"She was the best friend I ever had," said a man in front, facing the crowd. "I'm separated from my family in Alabama and I'm happy to have had a friend who was nurturing and supportive. It breaks my heart to lose a friend like that."

Carlos subscribed to the Pima reservation's fortnightly newspaper, AU-AUTHM Action News. Periodically, she returned to her roots and sometimes her father visited. A few years ago, they took neighbor Donlon to Muir Woods.

"She loved to travel," said Donlon, who helped clean her room. "We were going to go to Disneyland, but we never made it. "They sent her body back to the reservation. She was proud she was Indian." ●

— TOM CARTER

Batman

LONDEVETTE MORGAN

LONDEVETTE Morgan earned his "Batman" nickname by keeping a vigil over the neighborhood while seated at the window of his fifth-floor Elm Hotel room.

The self-appointed street savior claimed to know many of the shopkeepers below, and would tip Elm staff to any untoward activity in their vicinity.

"He saw himself as a peacekeeper," said case worker Adam Decker.

Morgan, a garrulous teller of tall tales, often would get lost in his random thoughts until someone pulled him back to his story line. He was prominent and entertaining at the SRO's Wednesday breakfast group discussions in the lobby, where his memorial was held.

Londevette Morgan died Dec. 22, 2009

Morgan, from Oakland, was among the city's original Care Not Cash beneficiaries. He became an Elm tenant five years ago right after the hotel was renovated. He quickly earned a reputation as humorous, friendly and generous.

"I saw him Monday, the day before he passed," said Ricky. "He came by and gave me a dollar, sometimes it was $2. He had a good heart. You don't see many like him."

Roz, the only woman among the eight mourners, said Morgan wanted her to be his girlfriend and told her he was going to marry her. But it was hard to know when Morgan was kidding or on the level, she said.

Scott Ecker, Elm services manager, recalled that once, as he was trying to catch a taxi in pouring rain, Morgan came outside and held an umbrella over him for half an hour, as a simple kindness, talking the whole time.

"His storytelling was crazy, and it was hard to know what was factual," Ecker said. "But I was fond of him."

Other mourners said Morgan had told them he had played bass in a band and had been a boxer.

A man who lived across the hall said he had had "thousands" of encounters with Morgan and "75% of them were unhappy. He could be a monster, too," he said, without elaborating. "He was very sick at the end. I think he drank himself to death."

Joseph Davis, an elderly, 24-year Elm resident, had many discussions over the years with Morgan, mostly in the lobby where residents gather to watch television.

"We always got along," Davis told the assembled. "He had a lot of imagination. Every month he was getting married to somebody. And he said he had a job at the ballpark. But he never went to the ballpark."

In Morgan's last weeks, Davis and others noticed that he'd lost a lot of weight. Yet he kept drinking.

"I don't know if he was afraid to go to the doctor," Davis said, "but I never saw him go."

Batman, apparently ignoring his failing health, died in bed reading his newspaper. He was 53. ●

— TOM CARTER

Activist Wife of an Activist

LORETTA FLORENCE PHILLIPS

LORETTA Florence Phillips overcame a crippling childhood and as an adult conquered alcoholism to eventually find peace and stability in the Tenderloin.

Phillips began life in New Orleans in 1922 with two strikes against her. She was born with polio and her mother died in childbirth. The devastating viral infection that put people in leg braces and iron lungs knew no class. It also inflicted opera star Renata Tibaldi in 1922 and Franklin Delano Roosevelt the year before.

"Her father gave her up to a convent," said her husband, Marvis Phillips, after her memorial at the Alexander Residence where she lived for more than 30 years. "But she was determined to walk as a little girl — and she did. She never had to have leg braces."

The plucky Loretta Phillips rebounded from other childhood misfortunes.

Marvis Phillips said the father reclaimed her at age 6 and moved to Chicago.

"Her father raped her when she was 13, and she had a child," Phillips said. "Then the father kicked her out when she was 18, and she was homeless in Chicago before they had adequate welfare. The authorities took her child away, and she never saw her child again."

Loretta Phillips died Nov. 6, 2009

No details of Loretta Phillips' life came to light during the memorial conducted by Father Armando Lopez of St. Boniface Catholic Church. More than 60 attended. Songs were sung and prayers said, but mourners weren't offered the opportunity to speak of their affection for Phillips, who died at California Pacific Medical Center after a long illness. She was 87.

Phillips had been active in the North of Market Planning Coalition, the Alexander Tenants Association and she was a charter member of Central City Democrats and a founding member of Alliance for a Better District 6. At meetings, she was a familiar sight at her activist husband's side. Once homeless, she was avidly interested in the Tenderloin Homeless Caucus.

Marvis Phillips doesn't know when Loretta arrived in California. He knew that when he met her she had been married three times and was an alcoholic. He believes her wake-up call came while doing six months in jail for being drunk and kicking a policeman in the groin. In her early 60s, she quit through Alcoholics Anonymous. She was sober for 25 years until she died.

Phillips met her in the Alexander lobby in 1992 when he was a new resident. The older woman came over and sat next to him and they struck up a conversation. It became a daily routine. Over months, they grew closer. Phillips asked her to help him kick his drug habit, and she did.

"She was a certified drug rehabilitation counselor through AA," Phillips said. "She showed me there was another way."

In March 1996, Phillips went downstairs to the lobby and tapped Loretta on the shoulder. When she turned around, he got down on one knee and proposed.

"She was Mrs. Herron then," Phillips said. "She said yes."

They were married two weeks later, March 19, 1966, in City Hall. The late Tenderloin police Sgt. Kenneth Sugrue, for whom the Civic Center children's park is named, was best man. Phillips was with his wife when she died at the hospital. She was on a respirator and could not speak, but her eyes fluttered open when he was at her side.

"I held her hand," Phillips said. "She looked at me and she mouthed the words, 'I love you.' Then she was gone." ●

— TOM CARTER

One Body, Two People
STEVEN ALEXXIS SILVA JR.

STEVEN ALEXXIS SILVA'S parents knew about their child's life in San Francisco, but had never visited her here. When they arrived, it was to attend her memorial at San Francisco Network Ministries, a celebration of her short life.

Silva was driving in Kern County, lost control of her car and died in the crash. She was carrying no ID, so it was many days before the county coroner identified her from her fingerprints and faxed her father about her death.

At the memorial, Steven Silva Sr. shook his head in disbelief. "The fax just was there one day," he said, "in with a stack of other faxes."

Steven Silva Jr. died Sept. 19, 2005   *Alexxis Silva*

Silva was 30. She had lived most of her adult life as a transgender in San Francisco, known to her friends as Alexxis. At the front of the room on a small table were candles, flowers and pictures of her; one photo leaned against a box covered in maroon velvet.

"The last time we saw Steven was at Christmas," said his mother, Sherri Silva. "We've never seen pictures of him like this — he was very respectful when he came home."

Home is Manteca, on the way to Yosemite. Silva, who was born in Reno, went there often to visit her parents, brother, sister and their children; another brother lives in Antioch.

Many who gathered for Silva's memorial shared stories.

"Alexxis was my good friend for two years," said Peter Hudson, "and she taught me a lot. She stayed with me for a while before the accident." Hudson wasn't surprised she was driving without an ID. "That was just so like her — she was fearless."

Kyle Simmons said he had known Silva since she was 18. "She had the most hilarious sense of humor, always doing impressions and making funny noises. Even thinking about it now makes me laugh."

Yet another friend recalled Silva sneaking out of her grandmother's house at night: "I met Alexxis when we were both 16. We started out together, and we'd comfort each other. It's very sad to know that she's gone. I will really miss her."

Sherri Silva rose and, turning to the 15 people in the room, said, "This is where she would have liked a memorial to be. Thank you all so much for coming — you were her friends."

Rev. Glenda Hope in turn thanked Silva's parents for being there. "We so rarely have parents at the memorials here in the Tenderloin, and I know coming was an act of courage for you."

"Alexxis always talked about you, about her family, about the joy and the good food and the children," added Simmons. "She loved you all so much."

Silva's parents stayed afterward to chat, asking how she had spent her time and where she had lived. They got no specific address, but were assured that Silva had stayed out of trouble, been careful and was happy.

An obituary in the online Bay Area Reporter said, "Alexxis was a true Diva who for many years kept us on the edge of our feet."

Before Steven Sr. and Sherri Silva left, Hope handed them the maroon velvet box, which contained Silva's ashes. ●

— MARJORIE BEGGS

A Troubled Man

LOUIS O. GUZMAN

TEMPERAMENTAL Louis O. Guzman likely got more respect at his memorial than he got in his 14 years living in the Turk Eddy Preservation Apartments. Cantankerous and combative, he was difficult to be around. He constantly complained and swore, and tried to hustle his fellow residents for money.

"I told him once, 'Mr. Guzman you can't go out on the street talking that way to people — you'll get beat up or killed,'" said manager Patsy Gardner. She said he shot back, "That's why I've got this cane!"

Guzman died at St. Francis Hospital two weeks before his 84th birthday. In declining health for a year, he shed weight his slim, 5-foot-6 frame could ill afford. But he had refused to see a doctor and began to eat less and less, then only sweets. When he was too weak to leave his room, an ambulance came and the crew carefully lifted him out of bed. "Maybe he weighed 70 pounds," Gardner said.

Louis O. Guzman died Nov. 1, 2009

Seven residents from the 20 occupied apartments in the building paid their respects at Guzman's memorial. A few recalled he had asked them for cash, others said he wanted to sell them things they didn't want, like the two old bicycles in his room. He was always trying to make money, they said.

Ten years ago he introduced himself to Betty Dominguez, a 24-year resident, as "Antonio." "So that's what I called him — it was my husband's name," Dominguez said. "I just learned he was Louis. He was a handsome man. But when I last saw him, one side of his face had atrophied."

Gardner spent more time with Guzman than anyone because of his complaining and the problem his filthy room became. He constantly ranted that people knocked on his door. But "no one did," Gardner said. "We had our fights." No matter which room he occupied, she said, he had trouble with his neighbors.

He irritably nagged Gardner about when rent was due — "It's always the first, Mr. Guzman," she'd say. "Once he got three months ahead with payments. I had to tell him to stop (paying)."

Guzman left Hawaii 59 years ago. He has a sister there and a brother in the East Bay. It's believed Guzman worked in construction at one time. He railed against government and disliked handouts, yet drew SSI and Social Security, totaling barely $900 monthly. Still, on a few occasions, he sent his sister $75 money orders, Gardner said.

> **"Sometimes he'd buy me little cakes, because he had a sweet tooth. I'd accept them, but later I gave them away. I don't eat sugar."**

"Not many saw that side of him," said Rev. Glenda Hope, who conducted the memorial.

"He used to call me the Queen of Sheba," Gardner said, "And sometimes he'd buy me little cakes, because he had a sweet tooth. I'd accept them, but later I gave them away. I don't eat sugar."

Guzman's filthy room got out of control and was grounds for eviction. And the new rug he was given showed burn holes right away from his smoking. Gardner knew the only way he could get assistance was if he was declared too frail to clean the room himself. So she took him, reluctant, to a doctor.

"He cursed me the whole way," she said, "but I just ignored him. Then, when we got inside the office he cursed the doctor, and we got thrown out.

"But on the way out, a nurse said to me maybe she could help. And she did. And Mr. Guzman got a house cleaner. I didn't want to evict him." ●

— TOM CARTER

Died Quietly Among Friends
MICHAEL DICK

HOMELESS off and on — mostly on — for the past 24 years, Michael Dick gained some notice when Chronicle reporter Kevin Fagan followed his scavenging activities in a three-part "Shame of the City" series on San Francisco's homeless in October 2006. Dick's story appeared shortly after he found permanent housing at the Coast Hotel.

The previous summer, Fagan and photographer Brant Ward followed Dick on his daily 2-mile shopping cart trek from Kearny and Sutter streets up Market Street to the Duboce Avenue recycling center. He'd been doing that for three years, since he lost his delivery job at a downtown florist.

PHOTO BY BRANT WARD/S.F. CHRONICLE
Michael Dick died Dec. 29, 2007

Life on the street was hard for Dick. "What he wanted more than anything was a home," Fagan wrote.

Dick had emphysema. He was 53 when he died in the lobby of the hotel where he had lived for 15 months. He'd been sitting quietly, so quiet that his passing went unnoticed for two hours.

"I was sitting right next to him, us just watching the TV, him just looking like he was asleep, until someone noticed he looked really pale," said fellow resident Steven White, still shaken by the experience. "If we'd have called [the paramedics] earlier, he might be here today."

Everyone at Dick's memorial remembered him as polite, self-reliant, quiet, intelligent — someone who was beginning to successfully make the transition from the streets to the hotel community.

"I could see the adjustments he was making in his life," said Rodney Mitchell, the Coast's assistant support services manager. "That's challenging, going from homeless to housing, but I saw him spending more time with the other residents. I'm glad we could provide for him."

While working on the "Shame" series, Fagan and Ward developed a strong attachment to Dick, and they visited him regularly at the Coast.

"He was a kind person, always told it like it was," Fagan told The Extra. "I remember that when we were doing the story, he seemed genuinely ready to get off the streets." The last time he saw Dick was several months before he died. "He seemed frail, but I was always amazed that he just kept going — he had that homeless look, thin and tough."

Ward said that the last time he stopped by the hotel to take Dick out for coffee, a monthly ritual, he learned that he had died. "Mike was a sweetheart of a person," Ward said, "a gentle person with no pretensions, no meanness in him."

Coast Case Manager Brady Skinner recalled how Dick had attended hotel meetings and coffee hours, even helped decorate the lobby for the Christmas holidays.

"We'd nod, but I didn't really know Michael well," said Joe Jackson, a Coast resident for 20 years who's seen the hotel change for the better. "Ten years ago, when someone died, the fact was ignored — they'd change the bedding and turn over the room. Now we have social support staff, social hours, a community room, memorials like this. We're becoming a community here." ●

— MARJORIE BEGGS

Godfather of the Empress
RAYMOND PUGLIESI

RAYMOND "TONY" PUGLIESI was a lot of things — a motorcycle gang member, bodybuilder, fix-it man, entrepreneur, drug addict and alcohol abuser — but to a special few he was "the godfather" of the Empress Hotel.

When someone he knew told him they had a need, Pugliesi invited them to his fourth-floor room for an appointment. The room was cluttered with nuts, bolts, little tools and crates of gadgets, plus a dozen cell phones and land line phones for his "businesses," as he called his jack-of-all-trades enterprise.

Pugliesi had a sharp mathematical mind and could fix anything electronic, charging from $1 to $3, said his social worker, Phillip Allen Jr. He sold broken things he had found and fixed, batteries he recharged, too. He always had projects going. The phones linked up his "networks" of people who sought his advice and knowledge.

Pugliesi, the godfather, sat in the middle of the room in his elaborate, jerry-rigged wheelchair wearing a yellow hard hat. He'd have Allen sit quietly in the corner like a consiglieri. Then he'd beckon the petitioner: "Come and sit."

"He'd listen," Allen said, "then make a decision and usually give them what they asked for — money, a phone, a drink of expensive stuff, or just help them if they wanted to start a little business. And he'd give them advice. He'd look over at me to make sure I saw and heard everything, like he wanted me to tell the story someday."

Some, as if they were children he'd adopted, returned three and four times.

"He never expected anything in return," Allen said. "He told me he was trying to salvage the last vestige of good in them. Some took advantage of him. They ought to be here today and aren't."

Pugliesi, once a robust weightlifter, looked mean on a hog and wouldn't shun a fair fight. Most details of his life before he moved into the Empress four years ago remained unknown, but word was he had family in Brooklyn and Illinois.

Raymond Pugliesi died Nov. 2, 2009

In recent months, drugs, alcohol and AIDS apparently took a toll. His health began to fail, he lost weight and suffered pain that he ignored. Nine days before he died, Allen said, Pugliesi got clean and he was full of life and optimism.

"I was really proud of him," Allen said. "Then Murphy's Law took over. He got despondent and wasn't eating right. I couldn't get him out of it."

When Pugliesi didn't answer calls for a couple of days, Allen and two staff members entered his room and found him dead. Cause of his death at 47 was pending, the medical examiner said.

At his memorial, a few of Pugliesi's favorite things were on a table pushed against the wall: a baseball cap with an embroidered marijuana leaf, a picture of a handsome white dog framed in gold, a plastic three-wheel motorcycle toy and on it a buff rider with silver helmet and sunglasses, a small wooden box with a collage of tiny race car pictures, a thick silver key chain with a marijuana leaf on the end. Behind these items was a bouquet of white mums, roses and carnations. On the wall were two pictures of the Brooklyn Bridge and a map of Brooklyn's neighborhoods.

Thirteen mourners attended Pugliesi's memorial. Several said they admired his generosity and craziness, which outweighed his sometimes "hard-ass" behavior.

A staff member distributed a printed tribute to Pugliesi with his picture on the sheet. Allen read aloud from it: "He lived his life like a roller coaster, a wild unstoppable ride and a surprise at every turn. Unconventional, controversial, spirited, uniquely generous and stubborn, Raymond would never take no for an answer."

"All that is true," Allen agreed.

One neighbor recalled the time Pugliesi got a squad of police to come charging up to his room, guns drawn, expecting real trouble. "Tony was holed up in his room," laughing maniacally, the neighbor said gleefully. He'd "glued his door shut" and covered the windows with black paper.

"Yeah," the neighbor said, "he was really enjoying himself."

"He was hard," said another man who used to get "blitzed" with Pugliesi and could also call him by his nickname "Tony" with impunity. "But he wasn't hard. Someone in his presence that he liked, it was different. But he could make your life miserable if he was hard."

"He was generous from the heart," added another, "a cool dude with many characters."

A woman who once pushed him around the block said his wheelchair was "his spaceship." It had bells and whistles even "hidden daggers," Allen said, "in case he got caught in the red light district with his pants down."

"He was comfortable in his own skin," the woman said. "He had no conscience to worry about."

"And when he was the godfather," Allen said, "the only thing missing was the theme song." ●

— TOM CARTER

Excelled at Kindness

JOHN McHALE

JOHN MCHALE lived Aesop's famed proverb, "No act of kindness, however small, is ever wasted," and the big turnout at McHale's service proved it.

"This is the most I've ever seen at a memorial," said Rev. Glenda Hope, who has been conducting sendoff services in the Tenderloin since 1977. Usually, a handful of mourners attend.

More than 30 residents and neighborhood friends showed up at McHale's memorial in the Ambassador Hotel where he lived for 16 years. Seated on chairs in a large circle in the second-floor community room, they bade farewell and recalled the life and times of the flamboyant man who had touched their hearts.

McHale was 46 when discovered dead in his room. The medical examiner's office had no immediate cause of death.

In a harsh neighborhood where residents often have no family and keep to themselves, some choosing isolation in their rooms, McHale was the opposite. With shoulder-length hair and mustache, and a penchant for wild clothes, he could have been a 1960s hippie. He was open and caring and treated each person like a dear old friend. "Compassionate," his friends said, "he accepted everyone for who they were."

"He was the first tenant to be nice to me," said an elderly Asian woman, dabbing her eyes as she recalled when she moved in. "He was so cheerful, a wonderful person."

Mike, who uses a walker but was unable to stand to speak, said McHale would sit and talk at length with him about his debilitating neuropathy "when I first came down with it."

"He was my neighbor," said a man named John. "He said hello every day, and every day he was so nice."

"We were tight," said Theresa. "When I couldn't walk he got me a wheelchair from Shorty. Every night he gave me a kiss on my forehead."

"He always gave me his arm," said a blind woman. "And when I was locked out of my room and sitting on the floor, he sat down to wait with me. He was a very kind person."

"He would always lend me a helping hand," said a tiny woman.

"He was just so cool," said a short black man.

"I didn't even know his name until now," said a woman from the Bristol Hotel across the street, "but I saw him all the time and felt he was my friend."

Ron Williams, also from the Bristol, was a good friend. He brought two dozen donuts to the memorial. "He was real," Williams said, fighting back tears, "and the Ambassador was his family."

John McHale died Sept. 15, 2010

The Ambassador's Gerry Kirby thought that growing up in the school of hard knocks made McHale the man he was. Kirby said McHale was from Natchez, Miss., and was on his own at 10, forced to survive any way he could.

McHale was addicted to heroin for more than 20 years, Kirby said. Then, three years ago, he "had had enough" and kicked.

"He had the courage and nerve to turn his life around — to do what he wanted, and to dress the way he did." Kirby said. "You know, scarves flying, boots clicking. On a cold day he might wear short shorts, and maybe a touch of makeup."

Everyone knew McHale was crazy about decorating cardboard stars. Kirby passed one around the circle. It was a five-point, 7-inch star that McHale had painted red and gray and doused with silver sparkles. The flip side had a bunch of little arrows on a gray background.

Scores of these stars, along with necklaces, hung by strings from the ceiling of his room. "It was like Christmas in there," said one mourner. "And he'd leave the door wide open so people could see. And others started really decorating their rooms, too."

"He'll be a permanent part of my heart," said another mourner. Everyone nodded in agreement. ●

— TOM CARTER

The Elm's Happiest Resident

LUKE SMITH

LUKE SMITH'S daughter broke into tears two years ago when, while walking near Boeddeker Park, she chanced upon her father, who she hadn't seen since she was 11 years old.

At 28, Gloria Smith got her father back. And Smith, as his health later deteriorated, got a loving caretaker for months — until his death.

It was hard to say, by looking at him, whether Smith was any happier after their chance meeting. He always looked upbeat. He was forever smiling, a rare one blessed with the gift of happiness.

Gloria Smith said at her father's memorial that he had up and left his family of six, all living together in the Tenderloin, in the early 1980s. There had been no contact with him since, and his whereabouts were unknown to the family.

After the reunion, the father and daughter saw each other "off and on," Gloria Smith said. Only after her father's health seriously declined, when he was making three trips a week to the hospital for dialysis, that she began to care for him, and they grew closer.

It was a role reversal from what she remembered best of their former life.

"He took care of our hair back then," she said. "And he tried to weave his hair, even if he didn't have enough."

Smith died at age 55 in his third-floor Elm Hotel room. Gloria Smith, his only child at the memorial, said drugs and alcohol had weakened his liver. A neighbor said he also had diabetes.

His trademark smile aside, her father's favorite hobby was watching horror movies, the daughter said. He had nearly 200 films, "too many," she said.

"They were stacked, VHS and DVDs combined," said Deandre Jones, Gloria Smith's boyfriend, who also visited Smith regularly.

Luke Smith with daughter Gloria. He died Oct. 27, 2009

The memorial's dozen mourners remembered Smith as uncommonly upbeat — always smiling, he argued and was cordial, giving advice or inviting somebody to just hang out.

"He always offered a good thought or a good feeling, no matter what your day was like," said one man.

Another resident, who met Smith a year ago, said, "He told me, 'You're always welcome to come over.' "

"He was a part of the community, and he wasn't reclusive," said Scott Ecker, the Elm's support services director. "He had a lot of friends here and was well-liked."

Kenneth Lawrence, who lived across the hall from Smith, said he still waits for his neighbor to walk out his door.

"I used to look at him like he was stuck on stupid," said Lawrence. "I couldn't understand why he was always so damn happy. Even when he went to the trash room to take out the trash, he was still smiling." ●

— KAREN DATANGEL

Voice of the People
STEVE CONLEY

IF EVER a voice could speak for the Tenderloin it was Steve Conley's.

His measured, rich baritone and his trademark dark beret were familiar at community meetings, neighborhood summits and at City Hall, where he weighed in on civil rights, quality of life and homeless issues. As an activist on many community organization boards, he interrogated or championed populist causes with polish and style. Sharply intelligent, gentle, and sometimes intense but never overbearing, he was a pro.

The multitalented Conley was in the radio business 20 years and a TL activist for a decade. And, in his colorful past, he was a musician who had backed Stevie Wonder and Patti Labelle.

With a half dozen neighborhood friends at his side, he died of cancer in Veterans Hospital. He was 58.

Ironically, at the end Conley communicated in writing because he was too devastated by his disease to speak. Retired St. Boniface priest Dan O'Conner said at Conley's memorial that when he asked him if he was religious and wanted last rites, Conley added yet another distinction to the many hats he wore in his life: "Altar boy," he wrote.

O'Connor told the story in the community room at 150 Golden Gate Ave., the new St. Anthony Foundation building where 60 residents and city officials, including District 6 Supervisor Chris Daly and Tenderloin police Capt. Gary Jimenez, paid their respects. The Board of Supervisors had adjourned in Conley's memory. The next day, as an Army veteran of the Vietnam War, Conley was buried with honor guard services at the Sacramento Valley National Cemetery.

"He had a gentle, caring voice," said Adrianne Lauby, who worked with him at KPFA. "And he led a wonderfully useful life."

Conley was known for his love of democracy and his ability to get groups and individuals to work together. A high point in his life was in October 2002 when he co-produced with community organizer Michael Nulty, and then directed and moderated, the Tenant Leadership Summit. It was a live, four-hour feed on KPFA, held at 201 Turk St., a neighborhood meeting room. It brought together 40 community organizations and attracted 125 residents who had attended a monthlong series of workshops on solving neighborhood problems. Then they spoke of them on radio at the summit. In 2004, Conley and Nulty reprised the show at the Blue Cube on Mason Street.

Steve Conley died Jan. 23, 2009

"He was the idea guy, I was the organizer," Nulty said after the memorial. "We used our connections, but it was a six-month process (to create) both. It was an idea that had to be promoted, and he was the voice of the people."

Conley co-founded with Nulty the Alliance for a Better District 6 and Central City Democrats and was a board member on both. He also served on the North of Market Planning Coalition and the Tenderloin Community Benefit District boards and was media director for Tenant Associations Coalition.

Conley also moderated the first 2007 mayoral debate. One mourner recalled how skillfully he could handle difficult guests to maintain order and decorum.

A dozen people spoke at the memorial, several from Pacifica radio, owner of KPFA in Oakland and KPFK in Los Angeles, stations where Conley worked. Chandra Hauptman read a tribute signed by 11 KPFA co-workers that summarized his career.

"He respected everyone's right to have their say," Hauptman said. "He spoke and wrote forcefully, with an air of self-confidence, and encouraged others to do the same. We will greatly miss his presence and his originality."

Conley attended Pierce Junior College in Winnetka, Calif., in the mid-1980s and Cal State Northridge 1988-90 as a journalism major with a minor in theater arts. He worked as a freelance correspondent in Asia, the Middle East and Europe covering human rights, economics, social movements and war before joining KPFK in Los Angeles in 1992 and completing its apprentice program.

KPFK made him public affairs production coordinator. He also produced and directed "Morning Magazine" and created the probing "Beneath the Surface," a popular program that's still aired. His programs ranged from a national broadcast of the second Rodney King verdict to live coverage in Germany of the fall of the Berlin Wall to a series on human rights in conjunction with Amnesty International.

> He had a gentle, caring voice, and he led a wonderfully useful life.

When Conley moved to the Bay Area in 2000, his activism and KPFA work began immediately. That year he received a commendation from the Board of Supervisors for his outreach to multiethnic communities in developing new supervisorial district boundaries. His main job at KPFA was to get the station involved in ethnic communities. He was also a computer expert who knew graphics programs and sold software for network security and storage.

At the time, he was involved with a West Oakland community performing arts venue called The Noodle Factory that had live-work studios. He divided his time between Oakland and the Tenderloin.

Conley was from Philadelphia. Before coming West after getting out of the Army,

Conley had compiled a history as a musician and actor. His resume lists nine plays and the characters he played, including Andre in "My Dinner with Andre" and Morris in Neil Simon's "God's Favorite." But no dates or sites are given. As a musician he listed the major venues where he performed — Carnegie Hall, Madison Square Garden and Radio City Music Hall among them. He also was a playwright and poet.

To the side of the community room, on a table with a bouquet and candles, some of Conley's personal effects were displayed: the American flag that Nulty, as Conley's designated executor, received from the Defense Department at the interment, a stack of Tarot cards, a harmonica and casaba — a Turkish rhythm instrument.

"He played many instruments," musician Per Marshall said before the memorial as he picked up the casaba and shook it. "I knew him in Philadelphia in the neighborhood. He was our hero. He gave me music lessons and really encouraged me. He came out to California before I did, but he went to L.A. I came here."

MARSHALL said Conley played in Patti Labelle's Brooklyn band in the 1970s and was backup for Stevie Wonder, too. On Marshall's "Night birds" CD, Conley played on "Lady Marmalade," a song about a New Orleans hooker. And Conley co-wrote "Traveler" on Marshall's "For the Journey" CD.

Marshall later played guitar for the crowd and sang Conley's composition "Love Will Lead Us," which he had often accompanied on harmonica. Jim Meko, city entertainment commissioner and chairman of the Western SoMa Advisory Task Force, read this poem by Conley:

> *One person's struggle is shared,*
> *one person's success is heartfelt,*
> *one person's kiss is our loss,*
> *one person's determination inspires us all.*
> *We must believe in the one's,*
> *we must believe in the whole,*
> *each person adds to the foundation,*
> *if for only a moment.*
> *We should all aspire*
> *with the success of the whole,*
> *then we can all succeed*
> *as one.*

"He was a friend who fought against war and homelessness," Nulty said. "He was passionate. His ego was in his heart."

Mourners were treated to pizza and beverages. An Irish wake with door prizes and entertainment was announced at the Swig Bar to celebrate Conley's lifetime achievements. Donations for his memorial fund were requested.

Soon Nulty expected Conley's marble tombstone would be set on his grave in Sacramento bearing the inscription: "A voice of the people." ●

— TOM CARTER

The Man in the Red Wheelchair
JERALD WALSH

THE "WHEELIES" Jerald "Rob" Walsh often performed when his red wheelchair zipped out of the Camelot Hotel and teetered on the Turk Street sidewalk told as much about his zest for life as the tenderness he showed for his cat, Sable.

It's the way three friends at Walsh's memorial remembered the blond-haired young man. Walsh was found in his fifth-floor room, dead of unknown causes, Sable near his side. He was 39.

No one knew how Walsh came to have a red wheelchair, or what tragedy put him in it. He arrived with it in May 2003, when the Camelot opened, and it became the signature of his free spirit as he tooled around listening to music on headphones.

Jerald Walsh died July 9, 2005

"He'd rev it up and then he'd be gone," Arnold Stringfellow said with a smile.

Shannon Hugon, services manager, said he told her he once was a dancer. She recalled how he laughed at just about everything and talked with everyone, and how he was "sweet and kind" to his cat. But he had a hard-headed side, she said, and he would only do things in his time, his way.

"He lived life on his own terms and was very effective at it," Hugon said.

A semicircle of votive candles and a floral spray with Walsh's Polaroid picture in front were on a table covered with a maroon paper tablecloth. Longtime Tenderloin minister, Rev. Glenda Hope, prayed for him and read Bible passages. Each friend lit a candle for him.

"There was a time," Hope said, "when SROs wouldn't allow pets."

Soon Sable found a home elsewhere in the Camelot. ●

— TOM CARTER

Marched to His Own Drummer
PATRICK MANN

PATRICK MANN had lived at the Bristol Hotel for only two months before he died. For five-plus years before that, he was homeless and had many friends on the street where he was well-known and well-liked.

Mann, 56 when he died, was from Oklahoma. He had nine brothers and sisters. One sister, Karen Johnston, traveled from Sacramento to attend Mann's memorial, which was held in an empty room on the Bristol's third floor. On a table were flowers, pictures and Mann's ashes.

Some people mentioned his love of animals, including hotel cats, which were generally despised.

"I remember he once brought home a bobcat when we were young," Johnston said. Mostly, she said candidly, she had few pleasant memories of her brother, who had been "in prison or on the streets, and out of my life. I came today because he was sick and alone, and I believe family have a responsibility to each other. This has given me the opportunity for the healing I needed."

Patrick Mann died May 9, 2004

She thanked everyone for coming. "I might not be grieving for him, but I feel profound sadness," she said. "He chose his life as he wanted it to be — he's always been colorful, and marched to his own drummer early on." ●

— MARJORIE BEGGS

Not What He Seemed

JAMES GOMBOS

IN THE PADRE APARTMENTS basement are a laundry room, management office, comfortable common room with a small kitchen, and, at the end of the hall, an apartment. That's where James Gombos lived for seven years and where he died at age 70.

James Gombos died Nov. 19, 2009

Ten people gathered in the common room to remember their friend and neighbor — a man, they all said, who worked hard to look and sound gruff to cover up gentleness and the sense of humor underneath.

"Like a jelly bean," is how Sister Lorna Walsh, Mercy Housing community operations manager for the 41-unit Padre, described him. "Soft and delicious inside and crackly and hard outside."

"It's strange to be down here without him, to think of him being gone," said Jennifer Fu, one of two resident services coordinators at the Padre, an apartment building on Jones Street, just below Tenderloin Police Station. "He took care of the plants out back and always checked to make sure the property was secure. He could be grumpy and harsh, but he was sweet under that tough exterior."

Charles Dobson said that every time he came down to do his laundry, Gombos, who could hear the washer running, would stop by at least twice.

"First he'd stick his head in to say hello, then come by another time to talk more," Dobson said. "If he liked you, he'd express what was ailing him — and you'd try to help him iron out his problems. I think he really liked the camaraderie of this place."

Gombos almost lost his apartment. A year ago, while frying potatoes he set the place on fire, gutting it. Walsh said she spent months "fighting for his rights" so he could return to his refurbished apartment, and she won. "Without that, he might not have made it back. He wasn't that aggressive, but we wanted him back here."

Bingo at the Padre was among Gombos' favorite activities. "He was so happy when he won and so very angry when he lost," recalled Michael Cooper, Fu's counterpart.

Cooper said that despite Gombos' increasing debility, he spent hours at the Kroc Center computer lab.

Ed Evans, who has lived at the Padre since 1992, said he was with Gombos when he died. Their relationship was special, Evans said. Gombos would just walk into his apartment to chat. If he wasn't feeling well, Evans would shop for him.

"He'd come to me and say, 'I have a problem.' Then he'd ask, 'How should I handle this sweepstakes mailer?'" Evans said. "We teased each other a lot, and I worked at getting past the gruff exterior. There'll be a hole in my life now."

For the memorial, Cooper read a passage from Seneca, the Roman philosopher and statesman:

"In the presence of death, we must continue to sing the song of life. . . . Let us not be gripped by the fear of death. If another day be added to our lives, let us joyfully receive it,

Jokester With Style
BERNARD DEFOE

THE IMPECCABLY dressed Bernard DeFoe had troubles enough with debilitating kidney dialysis treatments three times a week. But, returning from the hospital one day, he fumbled with his apartment key, fell and broke his hip.

The accident put him in a wheelchair and one step from the grave.

"I used to push him up the ramp here," said one mourner at DeFoe's memorial in the lobby of the Turk-Eddy Preservation Apartments, where a dozen friends gathered. "He was in a lot of pain but remained upbeat."

TNDC's apartment manager, Patsy Gardner, found DeFoe dead during room check. He was 57.

His friends said the affable DeFoe loved to joke and occasionally fibbed a bit to see if the person could catch on.

"He was hard to read sometimes and would throw you off to the left," said one man. "I knew him a long time. He used to run a little newsstand at Taylor and Eddy. He was a good guy. Everybody knew him."

"He was the kindest man I ever met in my life," piped up another.

Bernard DeFoe died Dec. 10, 2007

The memorial was momentarily interrupted when an ambulance arrived to take an elderly woman to the hospital. Rev. Glenda Hope, who was officiating, paused to say a prayer for her.

DeFoe was from the Bronx where his mother and sister live. He came to San Francisco 25 years ago. He moved into the Aspen in 2003 and became a tenant activist.

He worked part-time for about eight years at Pete's grocery across from Boeddeker Park, now called Downtown Grocery. His nine-year battle with kidney disease forced him to slow down, but not melt down.

"He was an immaculate dresser and very cordial," said a woman. "It's not every day you meet somebody like that. He had nice clothes, color-coordinated, tidy and neat. He was from New York — that's where we get our classy men from."

Kelvin Nance, DeFoe's social worker for 10 years, said he and his wife invited DeFoe for holiday dinners at their South San Francisco home and that he often brought presents to Nance's granddaughter.

"We were his only family," Nance said. "He liked to think he was like my father — I just let it go. I miss him already." ●

— TOM CARTER

Tenderloin's Oldest Resident

CHUI Y. TAO

CHUI Y. TAO, a devout Chinese woman with a radiant smile — believed to be the oldest person in the Tenderloin — died 12 days after celebrating her 96th birthday.

Tao, weak and cyanotic, was taken to California Pacific Medical Center by ambulance from TNDC's Turk-Eddy Preservation Apartments, coincidentally during a memorial service for Bernard DeFoe, also a resident.

Chui Y. Tao died Dec. 28, 2007

Tao had suffered a heart attack and it prevented her from swallowing food, her daughter, Anna Cheung, said later. But the old woman refused feeding tubes. A week later, she died in her sleep.

"It was like a candle burning out," Cheung said. "In the Chinese way of counting, she was 99."

Cheung had treated her mother and friends to a birthday dinner the day before her birthday, at the Tong Palace restaurant on Clement Street, as she had for the past five years. It was a festive occasion.

Tao had been in fair health until May when she started using a walker indoors and a wheelchair outdoors, aided everywhere by her faithful caregiver of 2½ years, Ming, who speaks little English. At night, Kevin Thomas, her next-door neighbor on the sixth floor, looked out for her.

A memorial for Tao was held at the apartment building. More than a dozen of her friends attended. Some went up to a table to view an undated framed color photo of her and bowed in the Chinese tradition. In conducting memorials for several decades, Rev. Glenda Hope said afterward she couldn't recall anyone as old.

"Mrs. Tao had the most beautiful smile," said building manager Patsy Gardner. "You could just feel the warmth. She came down to coffee every day and, no matter how she felt, she sent out good feelings for her fellow man. She kept a red paper cross on her door."

Her friends told how sweet she was, how she smiled and "talked nice." She read the Bible every day, they said, and prayed for everyone. Ming took her on Sundays to a Lutheran church at Anza and Ninth Avenue and to her family doctor in Chinatown and to the bank.

But for two hours every day, Cheung said, she was glued to Chinese soap operas on the TV in her apartment.

Tao left China in 1985 to live with her son in Texas. Then she moved to London and lived with her daughter for 10 years. She came to live by herself in the Aspen Apartments in 1997 and was still there when TNDC bought the building the following year. Her daughter now lives South of Market on Harrison Street.

"She was good people," said one man. "She was good to everyone. I'm glad she didn't suffer."

At the end, the Chinese women hugged Ming and each other and cried softly. Then the mourners had the hot tea and cranberry bread that Gardner set on a table. ●

— TOM CARTER

but let us not anxiously depend on our tomorrows. . . . Let us make the best of our loved ones while they are with us, and let us not bury our love with death." ●

— MARJORIE BEGGS

A Long Life With Doting Daughters
GYULLI MARTIROSYAN

GYULLI "JULIE" MARTIROSYAN, a Russian woman of remarkable health who was doted on by her daughters, died soon after the onset of a heart condition.

Martirosyan experienced chest pain and was taken to the hospital from her home at Turk-Eddy Preservation Apartments. She improved but during rehabilitation relapsed and died. She was 91.

"It was the first time she had ever been in a hospital," daughter Nina Sochilina said after the memorial at Preservation apartments. "And she had never even taken a pill before that."

Martirosyan's father died at age 105, Sochilina said, and her brother was 98.

Another Preservation resident, Chi Y. Tao, believed to have been the Tenderloin's oldest person, died the year before, also of a heart condition, 12 days after her 96th birthday.

Sochilina said her mother ate "only fresh vegetables, lots of fish, and she loved caviar, black and red."

Sochilina, who lives two blocks away on Turk Street, and another daughter living in San Francisco visited their mother every day so they were familiar faces to the Preservation residents. A third sister, in Israel, visited in February, stayed a month, spending every day with her mother, Sochilina said.

Gyulli Martirosyan died Aug. 26, 2008

The San Francisco sisters arrived at the memorial carrying two large pizzas, fresh cantaloupe and orange juice for the 13 friends and acquaintances attending.

"I knew her," said one. "She said her name in English was Julie. She couldn't speak much English and I didn't understand her. But it didn't make any difference. She'd touch my face and say, 'I love you.' And I could tell she did. I'd visit in her room and she'd show me all her family pictures."

A neighbor said he went to the grocery for her once and she kissed him on the cheek, an affection he still treasured.

Another man thanked the sisters for the "wonderful care" they gave their mother. No wonder "she was always smiling."

The mourners recalled a time Martirosyan wandered off on on Muni and ended up lost at Ocean Beach before police found her. After they brought her home she kept smiling as if nothing had happened, they said.

Martirosyan was Armenian, born in Tehran, Iran, but grew up in Azerbaijan, then part of the U.S.S.R. She was the mother of five girls and a boy. She left the country at the outbreak of the Armenian-Azerbaijan war, 1991-94. After temporarily living in Moscow, she was granted political asylum in the United States in 1994, her daughter said.

"You could tell that she loved people by her body language," said one woman. "We all miss her." ●

— TOM CARTER

Loved His Cats
SAMUEL ROBERT PIKE

CATS filled Sam Pike's life and he and his fuzzy, playful pets were an entertaining feature of life in the Coronado Hotel.

About a year ago, when both of his 14-year-old cats died, leaving Pike companionless, he became terribly depressed. He went through grief counseling. Soon, a staff member of CATS — the ironically named drug treatment program next door to the hotel — had a friend with two kittens that needed a home.

Pike took the pair and immediately introduced Crystal and Andrea, his new loves, to the Coronado's residents. It became his habit to bring them into the hallway and play with them, much to the residents' amusement.

"He loved those cats so much," said CATS Program Coordinator Kumiko Kawasaki at Pike's memorial. She had trouble finding words through her tears. "And I loved seeing him play with them."

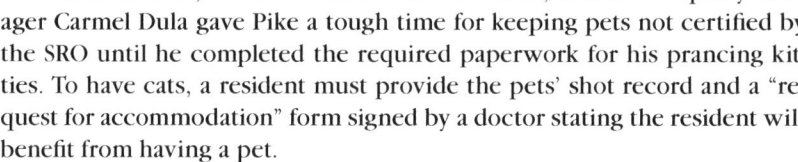

CATS (Community Awareness & Treatment Services), a nonprofit founded in 1978 to serve the poor and homeless, offers a range of help, including the Mobile Assistance Patrol, which picks up people passed out in alleys and on the street and takes them to where they can get help. CATS' Coronado Hotel program serves about 70 clients, most of them residents of the 67-room SRO.

Cuteness aside, there were hotel rules to follow, and new Property Manager Carmel Dula gave Pike a tough time for keeping pets not certified by the SRO until he completed the required paperwork for his prancing kitties. To have cats, a resident must provide the pets' shot record and a "request for accommodation" form signed by a doctor stating the resident will benefit from having a pet.

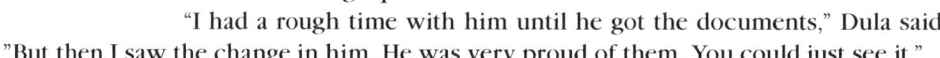

Samuel Robert Pike died Sept. 12, 2010

"I had a rough time with him until he got the documents," Dula said. "But then I saw the change in him. He was very proud of them. You could just see it."

Almost all of the dozen mourners who spoke of Pike, who was from Oklahoma, said he was a good, caring man, and that they had all been affected by the touching image of him with his pets, the only cats in the Coronado.

A new CATS staffer, Sherri Drake, began talking to Pike about her love of cats. She discovered he had a bad heart and emphysema, the conditions that had caused her mother to die of congestive heart failure.

"I became close to him," she said, "and we talked every day."

Pike walked with a cane then and appeared to be losing strength. In recent weeks, Drake noticed his breathing had become "very, very difficult." She went to his room to check on him, and found him weak and leaning against his window.

"His color had changed and he was clammy," Drake said. "I told him he had to go to the hospital and I was going to call 911. He said he didn't want to go. He said he didn't have the money to get back home. I gave him a bus token and then called 911."

An ambulance picked Pike up and took him to nearby St. Francis Hospital. He died there three days later, four days after his 54th birthday.

Desk clerk Linda Carr, who knew Pike for four years, took the 7-month-old Crystal and Andrea. She said they were a little "standoffish" now, but that she felt Pike's spirit was with her and the kittens would adjust.

The mourners afterward were treated to chicken salad that Drake brought, cookies from Dula and sodas from CATS. •

— TOM CARTER

A Craftsman, Not an Artist
JOHN 'MIKE' McKENNEY

BY ALL ACCOUNTS, Mike McKenney was a unique Tenderloin resident. He lived at the San Cristina Residence for 13 years, longer than most other tenants. His room was "a masterpiece of organization and creativity," said Yusef Shakuur, tenant services counselor. He'd built a loft for his bed, decorated his room to make it a showplace, and on his hallway door and all around it he'd mounted artwork and found objects.

McKenney owned a car — among the 1 in 5 Tenderloin residents who do. He drove to visit his mother, father, brother and sisters in Redding. He was an avid camper and fisherman, and loved to build things.

After five days in the hospital, McKenney died, essentially of alcoholism, at 50 years old.

McKenney's doorway at the San Cristina.

At his Sept. 11 memorial, his picture was flanked by two big bouquets, candles and crosses arranged on a lace-draped table.

"Having Mike's memorial on this emotional day reminds us of what a good man we've lost," neighbor Ben Wynn said of the auspicious anniversary. "He did things for this hotel all the time. You needed a bench for the kitchen? He'd build a bench. He was skilled, intelligent, and I'm going to have a hard time getting used to him not being here."

Neighbor Mark Anthony called him a "people person and a live wire." Yet another, Joseph Bolden, considered him an artist.

"But he'd argue that he was a craftsman, not an artist," said Bolden, San Cristina veteran with a year seniority on McKenney. "Sometimes in the hallway we were like two bears passing in the woods — we'd just grunt hello. Other times we'd talk."

Mike McKenney died Aug. 27, 2008.

No barriers existed between McKenney and neighbor Earl Gadsden, another car owner, though they were as different as could be, Gadsden said. "Those of us who have vehicles, we'd play hopscotch finding the few parking spots. He'd watch out for the meter people and let me know.

"Mike was a guy you could get eye-to-eye with. He listened to you; he cared about you. A week before he passed, we embraced. He was crying. I told him everything was going to be okay."

Joseph Sierra, a fellow resident, said McKenney lent him tools. "He was strong-tempered but a hard worker who tried to show others how to avoid the mistakes he'd made in his own life," Sierra said.

The stories about McKenney finally got to be too much for Lucinda Walls, tenant services supervisor. "The hardest part of this job is when you know someone is suffering and you can't do anything," she said, crying. "Mike was not a forgettable soul. And we were like his extended family." When McKenney's parents visited him at the San Cristina, his father told Walls that he finally understood why his son had wanted to live there.

"He saw that this was his family, too," Walls said. "And that's the lesson for me: You have to cherish the time you have with people. Let people help you. Today was my closure and now I have to let it go."

The 20 people in the room burst into applause. ●

— MARJORIE BEGGS

Lives on in Memory

LARRY ENTRIKEN

"COMMUNITY ACTIVIST, gentle soul, friend to all," read the flyer announcing Larry Entriken's memorial at the William Penn Hotel on Eddy Street. Thirty-five of his friends and family gathered there and bore out the claims.

"Helpful," "easy to be around," "smart," "giving," "humorous," and "very, very kind," they called him.

Entriken, who previously lived 20 years in the Haight, once had his own Tradesman construction company but fell on hard times, went homeless, then was housed by the city. He was found dead in his SRO room, apparently from liver problems, his family said. He was 51.

Larry Entriken died Dec. 30, 2010

The solid turnout was a testament to Entriken's popularity. Speaker after speaker mentioned his wit and his desire to help others. He once volunteered to write fundraising proposals for San Francisco First, a Department of Public Health program, to get homeless families and individuals into permanent housing with supportive services. A beneficiary of the program himself, he took a grant writing course. But his efforts snarled in red tape and Entriken never got the grant.

"I was always impressed that he wanted to give back," said Russell Bermann, head of Vocational Services at the South of Market Mental Health Clinic where Entriken was a client. He was also part of the Power Program, in which clients are interviewed, then selected for a team where they choose an area of work to pursue with the goal of becoming employable, possibly even leaving the mental health system.

> "It's never over while one person remembers you."

"But choosing grant writing to get money for us wasn't that simple," said Eileen Turner, who worked with Entriken. "Too many layers and glitches to get through."

Dan Entriken, his father, a professional singer from Manhattan, attended the memorial with his wife, Deegee Brandemour.

"I wanted to see the faces here today," he said. "It gives me a great deal of peace to see them."

Entriken, born in New Jersey, was "a master of humor" even as a kid, his father said. But he gave everyone a fright when he nearly drowned at age 6.

"To me, he seemed a happy child," Dan Entriken said, "but we all have struggles with life. Now, he struggles no more."

Larry Entriken came to San Francisco in 1983. His father didn't know what had become of the construction company or how his son became homeless, nor did others. But two years ago, through San Francisco First, Entriken became a William Penn resident. He called his parents regularly. His stepmother said he told her he had felt like "an outcast" when no one contacted him after his grandmother died.

"I talked to him a lot after his father's heart attack," Brandemour said, "and he said he was drinking. I told him he was always welcome (with us) and we appreciated his reports."

Entriken last saw his father in 2004 in Los Angeles. He called his dad on birthdays, Father's Day, Thanksgiving and Christmas. The Giants' World Series victory parade was the last time he called. No one was home.

"I still have his voice on my answering machine from Christmas," the father said. "He talked about a possible job. I dunno, maybe it was wishful thinking." He paused. "But it's never over while one person remembers you." ●

— TOM CARTER

Kindly Gentleman Lived 101 Years
WILLIE LEACH

Willie Leach died in May 2004

CURRY SENIOR CENTER nurse Linda Muller recalled going to care for Willie Leach at the Dalt Hotel and hearing a loud squawk.

"I turned around and there was a seagull outside his window," she said. "Willie fed a little of his lunch every day to that gull." Hers was among the many memories shared at Leach's memorial at the Dalt, his home for 10 years.

Born in Rosebud, Texas, in 1903, Leach was orphaned at 5, became a cook's assistant in Houston at 9, a Pullman cook in the 1930s and worked in Bay Area shipyards in the 1940s. When he died at 101, "he was still alert, had good mother wit, was still a gentleman," said Liz Waddell, a friend of 30 years.

Suzanne, a fellow resident, recalled Leach: "He dressed sharp — I can just imagine how he broke hearts back in the '30s and '40s." Added retired nurse Karen Hagen, "I admired his independence. He took great pride in his accomplishments, and he'd always show me his newest outfit. He was a classy person."

Leach was also admired by a Dalt construction worker who attended the memorial, hard hat in hand: "I just knew him a very short time, when I worked on his floor, but he was the most kindly gentleman I've ever met." •

— MARJORIE BEGGS

A Special Loved One
RAYMOND EVANS

Raymond Evans died Nov. 27, 2004

RAYMOND EVANS, who was 44 when he died in the hospital after a long illness, had lived at the Ritz Hotel for 10 years.

"He had family nearby, and he was a very happy person, a loving person who'd say hello to everyone," said Teresa Peace, Ritz assistant manager, at Evans' memorial. "If he went to stay overnight at his mom's house — which he did often — he'd call and let us know. He loved to cook and often helped prepare food for the hotel's special events."

"It's really hard to imagine Raymond being still," said a Ritz resident, shaking his head. "He was so active and energetic — always."

Another neighbor, who apparently had been drinking that morning, made a speech about life and how he saw it: "You know, death is as common as the cold, but we never get used to it. I lived here eight years and I loved Raymond — though there were things about him I sometimes didn't like." He turned to Rev. Glenda Hope, who was officiating. "What does the Bible mean?" he asked her, then answered: "B-I-B-L-E: Basic Instruction Before Leaving Early. We're all God's children." Peace closed the memorial by passing out the poem at right. •

— MARJORIE BEGGS

> FOR A SPECIAL
> LOVED ONE
> *To know him, was to
> love him. To miss
> him, is to
> cherish him. To lose
> him, is to
> remember him.
> Yesterday is history,
> Tomorrow is a
> mystery. Today is a
> gift, that's why it's
> called the present.*
>
> — By Alexia Gleaves,
> a friend of Evans

> **❝** I held her hand. She looked at me and she mouthed the words, 'I love you.' Then she was gone. **❞**

**Turk Street in the Tenderloin.
Photo by Lenny Limjoco**

PART 2: Causes of Death

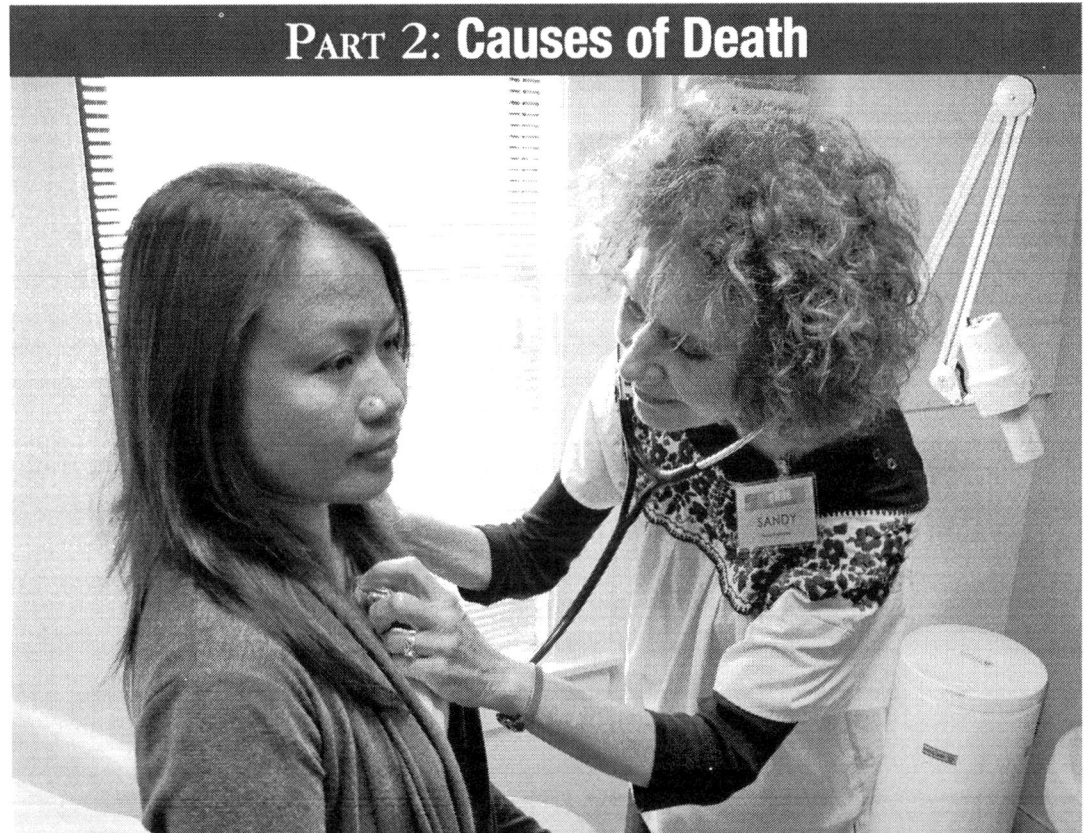

PHOTO BY LENNY LIMJOCO

Liezl Baltazer, 34, is a "lucky" one among Glide free health clinic's more than 3,000 patients per year, says nurse practitioner Sandy Prentice. The clinic helped detect a pituitary tumor, later removed at S.F. General Hospital. "The bottom line could have been death," Prentice says.

AIDS Is Foremost, Cancers Next

THE TENDERLOIN is a rough place to live and a hard place to die. Obituaries tell personal stories of many of the deceased, but this story details the neighborhood's major causes of death, and puts them in perspective with what kills people in the city as a whole.

In San Francisco, a man's life expectancy is 78 years. Women usually live at least five years longer. "It's 20 years less" in the Tenderloin, says Dr. Ana Valdes, medical director of St. Anthony Foundation's free clinic.

BY TOM CARTER

The clinic on Golden Gate Avenue is across from St. Boniface Catholic Church and near St. Anthony's Dining Room, renowned for its daily bread lines. The clinic sees nearly 300 patients a month, all are poor, 25% homeless, the majority are alcoholics. "Men are dying in their 40s and 50s," Valdes says. "For women, maybe 60s."

Four blocks away at Glide Memorial Methodist Church's 4,000-square-foot free clinic — a stone's throw from the luxury Hilton Hotel — Karen Hill agrees. "Clients die early here because of their lifestyle," says Hill, clinic manager, an R.N. She has worked at Glide seven years. "A fair amount die of self-inflicted injuries, and alcohol and drugs play a part.

Cancer is another leading cause."

The spiffy clinic, not as famous as Glide's colorful Sunday church services that sometimes attract curious celebrities, works with UCSF's School of Nursing and St. Francis Memorial Hospital, the neighborhood's only comprehensive medical center. In 2010, Glide's clinic served 3,105 clients; roughly 90% were homeless.

A block south is the Department of Public Health's Housing and Urban Health Clinic that serves up to 100 formerly homeless patients per month. All live in supportive housing, which means an SRO typically run by a nonprofit. His average patient, says Dr. Joseph Pace, has multiple diagnoses, all complicated by mental illness and addiction; diabetes and hypertension are common. Twenty-one of the clinic's patients died in 2010. Their average age was 58.

"By the time they see me they've been contending with these issues for quite some time, since young adulthood," says Pace, DPH director of Primary Care Homeless Services who works at the clinic Wednesdays and at Tom Waddell Health Center on nearby Ivy Street other weekdays. "They've been homeless and they self-medicate." That, of course, means using alcohol and illegal drugs as well as a host of prescription med possibilities.

TOP 5 KILLERS

The clinic's 2010 program review, Pace said, found that the five leading diagnoses for both men and women were: AIDS/HIV, depression, schizophrenia/psychosis, diabetes and hypertension.

1 in 15
Number of people in TL with HIV

Staff of Glide's HIV screening and referral service, one of 19 in the city, estimate 2,000 HIV carriers live in the Tenderloin. That's roughly 1 in every 15 people in the neighborhood, or 6.67%, triple the citywide rate.

While the Castro has more people with HIV, the Tenderloin leads all neighborhoods with injection drug users, as reported by clinics. Moreover, "the Tenderloin had the highest number of homeless injection drug users newly diagnosed with HIV/AIDS" in 2006-10, the Health Department report said.

Glide sometimes refers HIV/AIDS patients for treatment to S.F. General Hospital's Ward 86, the city's leading treatment center, but more often to Tom Waddell Clinic at the western edge of the Tenderloin. Pace says that among the 3,000 patients seen annually at the clinic, there's consistently a caseload of 30 to 50 AIDS patients. The leading causes of death for AIDS patients are liver disease and complications from substance abuse, he says.

DIABETES 5 TIMES CITY AVERAGE

There are five major medical clinics in the Tenderloin, two city-run, three private. Clinic staff consensus suggests that AIDS is the No. 1 killer, with the following four causes: myriad cancers, diabetes, heart disease and liver damage, not necessarily in that order. Hospitalization rates in the Tenderloin for diabetes and its complications are five times the city average with asthma yet another complication.

Outside of neighborhood clinic statistics, hard medical data and mortality rates for the Tenderloin don't exist.

The neighborhood is delineated by Polk Street to the west, Market to the south, with Post on the north side and Mason Street the eastern border. Health and mortality data, though, are available by ZIP code and the Tenderloin is part of three overlapping ZIPs. Most of the neighborhood is subsumed in 94102 along with Civic Center and Hayes Valley, which is largely middle income. ZIPs 94109 and 94103 contain small chunks of the Tenderloin. Any recitation of ZIP code data for causes of death is skewed by the relative prosperity surrounding the Tenderloin's poverty.

For the city as a whole, Health Department data show heart disease heads the men's mortality list, based on 2007 figures, the latest available in 2010, followed by lung disease, cerebrovascular disease, chronic pulmonary obstruction and hypertension. The women's list is similar with the exception of Alzheimer's disease and other dementia, which is No. 4. Citywide, AIDS/HIV was No. 7 among men and not even in the women's top 20.

The majority of the city's 501 single-room-occupancy hotels are in the Tenderloin, most built after the 1906 fire and earthquake. Some are sketchy abodes, privately owned flophouses. Others, renovated and up to code, are run or owned by nonprofits, generally in collaboration with city departments to accommodate low-income residents and formerly homeless. The 10-by-12-foot rooms can be a godsend to a single person or a harrowing cell to someone fighting depression, chronic pain and addictions.

HOUSING AFFECTS HEALTH

"Clients are impacted by where they live," Valdes says. "The bad SROs have filthy carpets, mildew, bugs and mold. It's a small space and some of those walls are blackened with mold."

In that event, people are actually better off living on the street, she says. But homelessness is a downward spiral.

St. Anthony's clinic sees a lot of drug and alcohol abuse and, as a result, often brain damage, Valdes says. Methamphetamine, for example, makes people anorexic, psychotic and suicidal; overdosing can cause heart attack and stroke.

PHOTO BY TOM CARTER

Dr. Joseph Pace at the city's Housing and Urban Health Clinic gives patients latitude in choosing their medications and treatment.

"Self-medicating against things that harm them is a lose-lose roulette that eventually takes their life — or they will escape it all with an overdose.

"Complications come on quick," Valdes says, "and require many hospitalizations. Liver disease, infections, gangrene, limbs amputated."

It's difficult enough to live on the street and maintain good health. But to recover from bad health out there is tougher.

"It's hard to stay on that path to recovery when there's so much adversity around you — people throwing up in the street, shooting up on the sidewalks," says Hill at Glide. Dope peddlers are everywhere, offering an affordable antidote to suffering.

The outlook for the average longtime-poor man or woman who seeks help at a Tenderloin medical clinic is troublesome and not hopeful. When Pace has asked about a patient's background and how he or she became homeless, many tell stories of violence from early childhood, ruthless abuse by parents or other relatives, "all sorts of violence in difficult home environments." So they try to escape their emotional succuba with feel-good or deadening substances off the street.

The clinic's doctors refer to a "dose response curve," in prescribing patients' medications. The worse the childhood experience, the heavier the dose of whatever is prescribed. Disastrous childhoods can lead to alcohol and drug abuse as adults, then to heart disease, HIV/AIDS, diabetes, cancer, lung disease from chronic stress, adrenaline surges and chronic inflammation.

"My opinion has been shifting on this over the last six months" prescribing patients' medications, Pace says, referring to what he now considers an undeniable correlation. "I think we underappreciate the patients and the true pain they carry. They do their best with what they've been dealt — and there's more to a story than we see — and their problems affect learning, too. The violence and drug trade keep fueling a fire when people are trying to survive."

LOW ESTEEM AN OBSTACLE

Glide's Hill believes her average client reads at the fifth-grade level and suspects many have been victims of violence and sexual abuse as youngsters. Such details contributing to low self-esteem are elusive. In the UC doctoral program she pursues, she has learned as a rule of thumb "you have to ask a woman client nine different times if she had been abused before the truth comes out."

A female patient Hill had seen several times dropped out of sight, then months later showed up at St. Francis Memorial Hospital emergency diagnosed with terminal cancer. "They disappear, then I get a call from the coroner that they've ODd on methadone," she says. "A lot lose their recovery during the Christmas holidays.

"It's almost a hidden population here," Hill continues. "They may go to UC and I never see them again. Or some go to other places to die, too. I've had trouble tracking my own patients. If we had a database for the whole city it would be better — and less costly."

The first question a clinic patient is asked: Have they been in S.F. General's emergency room in the past two weeks?

"It's where some of them get their health care," Hill says. "They wait until they can't stand it anymore and then go in — or are taken in. It's mental health that puts them there, or chronic pain. Sometimes it's to get out of the weather."

She's seen patients just get tired, they're lonely, and then they die.

POPEYE FINDS A PLACE TO DIE

Hill tells a story of a man called Popeye, a clinic regular who cleaned himself up, got a job at Glide and Glide put him in one of its nice apartments on Mason Street.

"He hadn't been there four months and he hanged himself," Hill says, nonplussed. "You don't know what's inside people.

"And death in the Tenderloin affects us, too. Popeye had services here by Rev. Cecil Williams. We all talked about it. We talk about the terrible things."

This case and others have changed her, she says. Before she came to Glide, she'd drive by the ragtag soup line on her way to work and wonder why those people didn't get jobs.

"So naïve," she says now, recalling circumstances that crush people and land them in the Tenderloin. Like the man from Indiana who was married, had four kids and a good job. But the whole family was killed in a car accident. He never recovered psychologically and became adrift in the neighborhood.

"They've given me empathy," she says. "I've learned the Tenderloin is a hard place to live." ●

Had Rarest of Rare Diseases

JIMMY MAI

HIS FRIENDS had a special sendoff on the street for quiet Jimmy Mai, the gutsy little guy with the bad blood and the wire in his gut. Mai was supposed to die by age 18. But he beat the odds by living 20 years, 6 months and 12 days. His sweet face made him look younger. The disease that killed him also had stunted him at 4 feet 10, not even 100 pounds. But it didn't stop him from being, by example, a moral force in the hood.

He died in the UCSF hospital where he had spent most of the year. The next day his friend Milton Mang started an informal shrine in front of the Tenderloin Recreation Center on Ellis Street. The place had been an oasis for Jimmy and many of his friends growing up.

The shrine at first was a cardboard box, some flowers in a coffee cup, and a ragged, 30- by 20-inch piece of cardboard hung on the fence so that people could write farewells. The corner grocer posted a notice giving funeral details and how to make donations to Jimmy's family. On the fence above it all hung a white T-shirt with Mai's birth and death dates and "Rest in Forever Peace" scrawled on it. Flowers were jammed into two black and red Remy Martin boxes affixed to the fence and 10 assorted empties lined the sidewalk next to the shrine.

The large, clean Recreation Center is a popular place for Tenderloin youth. Mostly for small kids, it has indoor and outdoor basketball courts. The directors called it Mai's second home. Though he got winded easily, Jimmy liked to shoot hoops and play other sports. But over-18s aren't allowed inside the center, so Mai and his buddies hung out in front.

Jimmy Mai, front and center, 11 years old in 1996, with his friends and directors of Tenderloin Recreation Center. He died Aug. 31, 2005.

"I knew Jimmy since the third grade," said Michael Ham, standing in front of the shrine one afternoon. Ham was eager to talk about his friend. "We went to Francisco Middle School together, and we'd shoot basketball and hang out. He was very quiet. And he was very friendly and very generous. You think of a nice person — he was that person." He took care of his three younger sisters and little brother and made sure his friends always had food, Ham said.

The family lived on O'Farrell, but when his parents separated, Ham said, the younger kids went with the mom and Jimmy with his dad. In January, Jimmy moved to his grandmother's house — where that was, Ham didn't know — and nobody saw him much.

Aizza Asuncion, standing next to Ham, said she had known Mai for five years. She called him "a trustworthy person with a big heart. He could share a secret with me and I could with him. We talked hours on the telephone."

Other young men Ham's age, caps on backward, arrived one by one to stand around. They nodded to each other, talked quietly to someone a while, then they faded away down the sidewalk.

Ham said the small box Mai wore at his waist under his shirt had a wire connected to his stomach, and every month Jimmy went to the hospital "to refresh his blood."

"He was in the hospital a lot this year," Ham continued. "He came back for one day about three weeks ago and saw some of us. I work the graveyard shift at UPS and sleep during the day, so it was hard to get over to see him. But when I went to the hospital, I found out he had died the day before and I didn't know it. I felt terrible. It's hard to lose a friend. He was someone you wanted to grow up with, and have your kids be friends with his kids and stuff."

Mai had beta thalassemia, a disease he inherited. It stymies hemoglobin production and the delivery of oxygen to all parts of the body. In all of North America, fewer than 1,000 people have it. Jimmy Mai's case was so severe doctors told him he likely wouldn't live to 18. The disease occurs most in Mediterranean countries, North Africa, the Middle East, India and Southeast Asia. Mai was Vietnamese. Most often, parents are carriers of the altered gene that causes beta thalassemia, but they have no symptoms.

"We drank that for him," Ham said, nodding toward the gin, brandy and cognac empties on the sidewalk. "We poured some out of each bottle for him. I set out some flowers and food, too."

HAM IS Cambodian, part of a network of 40-50 Vietnamese, Laotian, Mexican and black kids who live nearby and have grown up together on playgrounds, in schools and on the street. In front of the Children's Center is their hitch rack. Day or night, looking for friends, it's the place to go. "We call each other family," Ham said. "We all stick together — we're little brothers to each other and make sure people are taken care of. We buy food for people in the group who need it. We don't have a name, we're just TL."

Mai embodied the ethic, giving in every way he could. Tim Najjar, the Palestinian corner grocer, said, "When he brought his sisters in, he'd buy them anything they wanted. He was very nice and very, very honest. And when Jimmy ran a tab, he always paid on time." Mai would watch the store whenever Najjar went downstairs for supplies.

Najjar visited him in the hospital early in the year and intended to return and bring him some steak, Jimmy's favorite. But Najjar's helper recently got married, and Najjar couldn't leave the store. He keeps a large bottle on the counter for donations to the family.

"There were five kids in that family, and he was the second father," said Al Roberson, the playground director for 10 years. "He was the money keeper and rationed it out to everyone like he divided up boxes of Chinese food. And he made sure they all got every place where they had to be — and on time."

Mai was generally "pretty mellow," Roberson added, but if he thought someone was treating him badly, he "was in their face no matter how big they were. He wasn't intimidated by size. He was a little sparkplug." But some said that in recent years Jimmy stopped taking care of himself and started drinking more with his friends.

Mai's funeral was in Daly City at Duggan Mortuary and more than 200 people attended. It was almost like a reunion. The gathering was remarkably composed, the lack of tears was perhaps because, someone said, "everyone in the Tenderloin knew of Jimmy's disease and accepted that he didn't have long."

A Buddhist monk chanted for an hour. Little was said about Jimmy Mai. Then the crowd went to the burial in Colma. The mourners threw their flowers in the grave and most stayed to watch the bulldozer push the earth in and tamp it down.

LATER that cold, gray day, a dozen more empty booze bottles, plus a plastic-wrapped white bread sandwich, embellished the shrine. A young Asian man got out of a parked car, walked over and carefully emptied the better part of a Hennessey half-pint on the shrine, got back in the car and drove away.

The next day the shrine was gone. The bottles were in a cardboard box, everything else was in the Recreation wCenter's office. Roberson said the family had till the end of the week to claim the stuff. He said the police told him Monday to remove the shrine because some "gang might come by and debase it." But Rec and Park's Roberson got the cops to agree the cleanup could wait until after the Wednesday funeral, giving Mai's memorial two more days of life. ●

— TOM CARTER

Esteemed Black Brother
DEWAYNE BISHOP

THE DEATH of Dewayne Bishop was discovered when police found him on the floor of his room at the Ambassador Hotel. At a service in the hotel's Listening Post, about a dozen friends and fellow residents gathered to remember him.

Bishop was born April 12, 1969, perhaps the only certainty about his past. His social worker will say nothing about his roots; the medical examiner says his birth certificate will reveal nothing. At his memorial, a vase of flowers — provided by social workers, as is traditional at the TNDC-run Ambassador — sat on the windowsill. On the floor, encircled by the chairs of those who came to remember, lay a lone blossom broken from its stem.

Dewayne Bishop died Feb. 15, 2011

Bishop, with diabetes and kidney failure, had been on a transplant list, but prospects were bleak. He had missed his last six or so dialysis appointments, said his friend, Cecil Baker. Dialysis "can be painful and unpleasant," said Rev. Glenda Hope as she presided over the gathering. "I don't think anyone could judge Dewayne's choice."

Billie Cooper, who'd known Bishop for five or six years and had brought him home to the Ambassador after a recent hospitalization, said Bishop's medical problems were many, including blindness in one eye. "He wasn't taking care of himself," said Cooper, and over the past few months, physical weakening may have caused him to appear "a little standoffish. He was a troubled soul. Like most of us, he was confused."

"When a person is sick," said Henry Banks Ladd, who honored Bishop by singing a powerful version of "His Eyes Are on the Sparrow," "you think that they can do things. But they can't." Ladd had met Bishop at a group meeting. But when they played tennis together in Golden Gate Park, "He allowed me to see another side of him: vibrant and healthy."

"Some people said he was withdrawn," said Tom Laurent, "but we had lively conversations. We enjoyed talking for long periods of time. Before Christmas, he knocked on my door and handed me a stocking filled with various items he had hand-picked for me. ... He showed great respect for other people."

> **"When a person is sick you think they can do things. But they can't."**

Several of the gathered identified themselves as "fraternity brothers," fellow members of Black Brothers Esteem, a group that is part of the S.F. AIDS Foundation. Bishop had been a client, then volunteered in a variety of events around the city to help promote health. Black Brothers' Tony Bradford called Bishop "a great spirit," and the group's Micah Lubensky said Bishop had done "a lot of speaking, talking about how important HIV prevention was. He was very passionate about making a difference in the community."

When Bishop worked at a Starbucks, said Lubensky, he was "very well-organized, very clear on deadlines, on making sure he'd stay on track at work. And that's one of the reasons he was a very good volunteer for me. I asked him to speak publicly; he was very happy to do so. And he was a very sweet person, a very sweet individual."

Edmund Juicye recalled that Bishop had been working at a 7-Eleven when he was recruited by Black Brothers Esteem. "Coming to BBE was really great for him." Juicye described him dressing as a bishop — reflecting his name — at a Halloween party, and the great appetite he had for chicken pizza from Trader Joe's. "He would always eat with great appetite. ... He liked to listen close. He had people he bonded with and cared about."

"To Dewayne," said Baker, "everybody was special. He related to each of them differently." •

— LEAH GARCHIK

Original Molotov Mouth
GEORGE TIRADO

CHICANO POET and activist George Tirado was passionate about his art — spoken word — and his passion exploded on stages, on DVDs and CDs, at festivals and cultural events.

Tirado died unexpectedly at the Empress Hotel where he'd lived for a year.

It was his mother in Texas who had the idea of a spoken word memorial for him at the hotel.

George Tirado died Jan. 16, 2009

As about 30 people were gathering in the SRO's community room, a large monitor at the front of the room was playing a DVD of Tirado and other artists reading at City Lights bookstore in 2001. His piece, "509 years," was a poem that also appeared in the 2003 book "Molotov Mouths, Explosive New Writing." Tirado was a founder of the Molotov Mouths, a political word troupe with a social justice message.

On the DVD, he begins in his low, dramatic voice, "I was born into two worlds, one of the earth, my skin brown from the sun, and my heart charged with the power of the sun, and my mind able to contemplate the complexities of the gods." Like a Greek chorus, other performers on stage with him intone, "509 years, 509 years, 509 years."

Roberta Goodman, Empress property manager, brought a phone into the community room. On the speakerphone was Tirado's mother, who was able to hear what people were saying about her son.

"George was a complex fellow," Goodman began, "and for a year he graced us with his presence here at the Empress. We're all grateful to have known him."

He was part of a writing project that Goodman introduced at the hotel, an offshoot of Community Works/West, which uses the arts and education to help underserved populations such as women coming out of jail and people in recovery. Tanya Perlman coordinated the project at the Empress.

Perlman held a fat sheaf of papers. "I know George was complicated," she said, "but I got to know him through his writing. He believed there was a huge responsibility to put one's writing out there." Perlman said there are plans to publish Tirado's works, as well as others' in the program. Then she read four of his powerful pieces — about his mother, about what was in his pockets, his drug habits and about Tonia.

Others described their relationship with Tirado or read their own compositions. One who shared was photographer Nappy Chin, who lives at the Empress: "George, you pissed me off," he began. "You could have given me a hint."

Angela recalled how she and Tirado talked about their speed days: "We'd talk for hours. We were going to take a long, long trip, maybe on a boat."

Josiah Luis Alderete, one of the Molotov Mouths, said, "George had a lot of Georges inside of him — some who inspired me, some I couldn't trust. Don't make a saint of him. Remember all of him."

Alderete then read a composition by Tirado, "Poesia." An excerpt: "This guy once asked me, 'Why don't you write like Pablo Neruda?' I laughed as I found my favorite spot on 16th and Mission. … There is nothing more promising than the twinkle in the eye of an early morning score when you know everything is good. … In the corner of my eye I see Satan lurking in the shadows, he's dressed in his favorite hoodie."

Junebug, also a Molotov Mouth, said writing helps her keep her sanity. "I can't believe George is gone." Then she read a poem she said she wrote at Hospitality House in honor of Tirado, which began, "Que pasó, wassup, wassup, wassup."

The Internet is filled with references to Tirado's work, his life and his death.

Writer and comedian Bucky Sinister, a fellow performer, wrote on his blog about Tirado's art, his physical size — 400 to 500 pounds, he says — and his destructive drug use: "George and I shared a fascination with dirty, earth-bound angels as images in our work. … I always hoped he would show up at a 12 Step meeting. About a half dozen of us from the same circle, out of all of us who got high and drunk together, are 12 Steppers. But too many, like George, didn't make it past fifty. Fifty used to seem like forever away, back when 25 sounded old. George, you fat fuck, you tenderloin death star, you Oxycontin troll under a self-burned bridge. I used to be jealous of you. I've missed you for years."

Tirado is survived by his mother, one brother in Texas and another brother in Arizona. ●

— MARJORIE BEGGS

Lady With a Lot of Class, Even in Pain
RITA RESTO

"THIS IS OUR time to remember Rita — a very religious person," Pastor Mark Ferrell told Rita Resto's friends, fellow tenants at the Iroquois Hotel and Seventh Day Adventist Church members who had gathered to mourn her. "We're going to try to do things today that would have made her happy."

The memorial was held in the community room at the Iroquois, where Resto had lived for nine years. That may have been a record for her — moving around was more the norm. Born and raised in New York, she was in the military as a young woman and had been married to a military man. They spent many years in Europe, including three years in Berlin. She moved to San Francisco 17 years ago.

"After she died, her son and I went to her room," said Michael Medema, the hotel's tenant services supervisor. "There was a picture of her in Germany in a fur coat — she looked like a movie star."

Almost everyone who shared memories of Resto said how stylish she was.

"She was a lady with a lot of class who always dressed well and was a really good singer, too," said church member Marlena Dupas, who sang "What a Friend We Have in Jesus."

Rita Resto died Nov. 12, 2004

Resto's neighbor from across the hall called her "a sweetheart with a great sense of humor and beautiful clothes," and recalled how she sometimes left her door open so her singing would waft into the hall.

"She was a classy lady, a class act — she wore well," added another neighbor.

Others recalled her generosity: invitations to come to her room for tea and crackers and to smoke cigarettes, and a gallon jar of bay leaves for a neighbor who cooked her a dinner of lasagna and cannoli, Milano style.

"I was her daughter-in-law for six years when I was married to her son, but we've stayed in touch," said Andrea Witt. "She was very creative and a woman of faith. I think I fell in love with her eyes, which were just like her son's. I know she'd been hurt in her life — she's better off now."

Medema, too, remembered how, despite Resto's perfect appearance, she'd sometimes lean over and say, "But I'm in pain inside."

Last Halloween, Medema said, he invited Resto to the hotel party and she surprised him by showing up. "She was dressed all in white and she whispered to me, 'I'm an angel from the North.' I think she's an angel in the North now. She'd probably hate this gathering — she'd wonder why we all weren't dressed better."

Resto was 59 when she died of a heart attack. She got a military burial in San Joaquin Valley National Cemetery. ●

— MARJORIE BEGGS

Architect, Artist, Musician
BRUCE STURGIS

CRAIG WAUL brought his alto clarinet to the memorial for his friend, architect and artist Bruce Sturgis, who was 58 when he died.

"Bruce was a musician, too. He played a lot of instruments, and he could get way out there, but when he was serious, he was one of the best," Waul said. "He was my first friend in San Francisco, in North Beach."

Sturgis periodically fell on hard times, said another friend, John Bukur, at Sturgis' memorial at Civic Center Residence, his home for the six months before his death. "The first time I met him, he was dressed in a suit with a tie and spats, but he was on the street, homeless. Later on, I introduced him to that lady in the purple jacket," Bukur said, pointing to an elderly hotel resident seated just outside the circle of chairs.

Bruce Sturgis died Nov. 30, 2005

"I took him in, let him live with me, until he could get a room here," the woman told the small group of mourners. "I understood his problem — I've been clean from alcohol for four years and I understood him."

The hotel's social worker recalled how Sturgis once surprised her by attending a hotel crafts session. "We had a watercolor set, very simple, like for a child," she said, "and Bruce used it to paint these really beautiful sunflowers for me. I kept it on my desk, but I gave it to the family when they came to clear his room."

Sturgis spent his last week with his ex-wife and teenage daughter in Fresno, the social worker said. "It was wonderful that they were able to be together. We'll miss him here — he was very well-liked, and he knew it and was proud of it."

In memory of his friend, Waul stood and played a long, slow, haunting blues, dipping and swaying, eyes mostly closed. The music, he said afterward, was "original and it came through me to honor Bruce." ●

— MARJORIE BEGGS

Restaurateur's Reversal of Fortune

ANNA PRILL

THE EUROPA restaurant, just outside the Presidio's Lombard gate, was a popular destination for Czech and German fare in the 1970s and '80s. Besides the food and the atmosphere, a big draw was Anna Prill, "a cute waitress in her blue-and-white apron," recalled Marge Angelo, Prill's longtime friend.

Prill not only owned the restaurant with her husband, they had a house on Diamond Heights and other property in the city.

Angelo was among the 20 people who came to the Cambridge Hotel to honor Prill, who died at age 64. She had moved into the hotel a year before, directly from the shelter that housed her when homelessness became too difficult — she was in a wheelchair, one leg lost to diabetes.

Like Prill, many Tenderloin residents have had precipitous declines in their lives. Her divorce brought hard financial times that were complicated by physical ailments. She refused treatment for her infected toe; then, to save her life, the county had to get durable power of attorney to amputate her leg.

"I feel so sorry for all the reversals in her life, but it still was a blessing to know her," Angelo said. "She was my daughter's and my grandson's godmother, always a kind person and very generous."

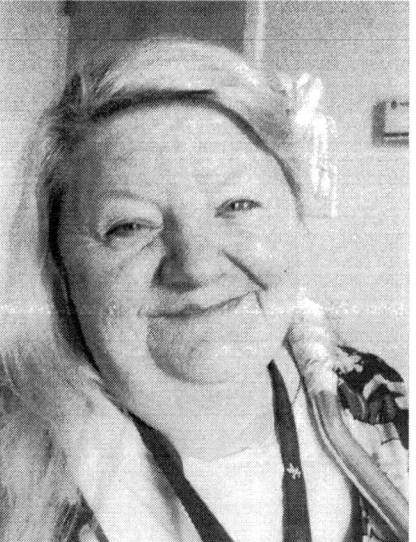

Anna Prill died May 23, 2009

Sue Eldredge, a friend for 32 years who met Prill in a Bible reading group, remembered how she "walked into a room and lighted it up — and she always had flowers in her hair."

To those who knew Prill only from her stay at the Cambridge, she was a compassionate, smiling, devilish extrovert, despite her physical disabilities.

"She spent a lot of time in this community room and was involved in all our activities and went to City Hall protests," said Natalie Swenson, the hotel's tenant services supervisor. "But she also told hilarious jokes — sometimes inappropriate — and she just loved to eat, three big meals a day."

"And more," piped up a man at the back of the room. "She sometimes pinched men's butts."

Ron Santos, 13 years at the Cambridge and president of its tenant council, recalled how Prill loved to play bingo monthly at the hotel and even cooked occasionally for fellow residents. "She cooked Slavic-style, with lots of vinegars and fermented vegetables. When I visited her in the hospital and asked what I could bring, all she wanted was pickles and sauerkraut. We tried to get her to eat more healthy food, but . . ."

Neighbor Curtis Johnson recalled how popular she was and how she always wanted a hug. And James Wagner, program director of Family Service Agency's Senior Wellness Program, joked that as a client, Prill "used to call me 'honey' and 'sweetie' — I'm jealous. I thought it was just for me! She also presented unique opportunities for services, especially around donuts and fried food."

Prill's deep faith was well-known to her friends and service providers. Her memorial ended with a spiritual, sung by resident Mama Tracy, eyes closed and swaying. ●

— MARJORIE BEGGS

Vietnam War Vet Who Rewarded Kindness
CLYDE WOOD

UNTIL HIS DEATH two weeks before his 58th birthday, Clyde Wood felt he was haunted by bad luck and the worst of it was post-traumatic stress disorder that stemmed from his Vietnam War days under fire as a young Marine.

He didn't talk much about those things, even to his caseworker. From the outset he appeared to be a crusty customer when he moved into his sixth-floor room at the Coast Hotel three years ago, finally no longer homeless.

Wood kept mostly to himself. But gradually, when he left his room using a walker, dozens of residents came in contact with him, and most reached out to him when his health began failing seven months ago. They found him to be a nice man with a penchant for giving small gifts and rewarding people for their kindnesses.

"He gave my daughter candy," said a young blonde mother at Wood's memorial at the hotel. "And when I carried his groceries upstairs for him, the next day he tried to give me a dollar. But I wouldn't accept it."

Clyde Wood died March 8, 2009

"He was really kind," said another woman. "He gave my dog treats. I'd walk around the block with him all the time."

"A friend told me he had a bad side and could raise hell," a man said. "But so many of us never saw that."

Wood was the third Coast resident to die in the past three months, making the mood in the SRO especially somber.

Dennis Reynolds, Wood's caseworker, saw him the most. Reynolds is also a Vietnam War vet who suffers from PTSD. He uses a cane now because an old leg wound flared up. Based on their common experiences, he built rapport with the reticent Wood.

"I met him two years ago when I started," Reynolds said, "and he was a distrustful, crotchety old guy. Very private about his past. He was using the walker then. When his health started failing, he said he was okay.

"He was in Vietnam about the same time I was," Reynolds said later. "There was a lot he wouldn't talk about. He was distraught about things that had happened to him in his life. He had a hard exterior. I think he was very alone. But he had a lot of friends here and in the neighborhood, and they showed up to help him downstairs. He'll be missed."

Other than his military service, little was known about Wood's past.

Despite the walker, Wood looked healthy until about December when he started to decline. Another piece of bad luck followed in January and February. The hotel elevator was out of order for 23 days. Wood struggled up and down the stairs, weak and losing weight from his 5-foot-8 frame. One resident who had helped him said it took Wood two hours to get up or down from the sixth floor.

In February, Wood was taken to the VA Hospital. When he returned three weeks later, Reynolds thought his health would improve. But it wasn't the case.

March 5, Wood summoned Reynolds to his room to check his "bugged" telephone. The caseworker was shocked at the sight of him standing at the door in his socks and underwear.

"He weighed 50 pounds if he weighed an ounce," Reynolds said. "He was a living skeleton."

That day an ambulance took Wood back to the VA Hospital. He died there three days later. The Veterans Administration would not reveal the cause of death. Wood was buried with honors at the Golden Gate National Cemetery in San Bruno. ●

— TOM CARTER

Fought for His Peers
DARWIN DIAS

DARWIN DEAN DIAS, a Latino who became an activist in many causes but was noted for fighting for the rights of the mentally ill, died of lung cancer at age 77. He died at Coming Home Hospice a week after relocating there from the Alexander Residence, where he had lived for two decades.

Sister Andrea Turbak of St. Anthony's Foundation welcomed four dozen people to the Alexander for a memorial service. Among those in attendance were Robby Cruz-DeCastro, Dias' partner of 36 years, and many friends and colleagues from their battles on behalf of the mentally disabled and other righteous causes.

The service opened with a 12-member group from St. Boniface singing "Amazing Grace." Speaker after speaker reminisced about Dias' efforts on their behalf.

"He was just one of those wonderful spirits," Fancher Bennett Larson, fellow advocate and longtime friend, recalled. "Darwin had a true vision of what self-help was about. He was imbued with something that was righteous and right and beautiful. He was able to project this, giving hope and dignity. He was a light to this community, striving for what is good."

Betty Duran, a social worker at the Alexander, and Yolanda Recania of the Salvation Army, said that, in his power wheelchair, Dias earned the nickname "Speedy." "He was always going so fast, with his hair flying," Duran said. "I used to tell him, 'Be careful, you might get a ticket for speeding!' His dream was being in a city with no homeless people."

Darwin Dias died July 24, 2011

Dias had lived in San Francisco, the city of his birth, since the mid-1950s, after growing up in Fresno. He was out as a gay man and living in the Castro "long before it became the gay mecca," Cruz-DeCastro quoted him as saying. Dias worked for Bank of America and then at Cliff's Variety Store on Castro Street, and during the Summer of Love lived in the Haight-Ashbury and worked light shows at rock concerts and for the Angels of Light.

He continued to wear his hair long and prided himself on being an original long-haired hippie, Cruz-DeCastro wrote in a biography he submitted to District 6 Supervisor Jane Kim, when she asked for something to read about Darwin at a board meeting, which was adjourned in his memory.

Dias advocated against the Vietnam War and for the civil rights of people of color, gays and the mentally ill. Cruz-DeCastro said that in a '70s demonstration outside the Examiner newspaper offices, police kicked out his front teeth but never charged him with any crime. The protest was against police entrapment of gay men at Macy's and the newspaper's publication of their names and addresses.

Cruz-DeCastro wrote that he and Dias were in the crowd outside the International Hotel in the early hours of Aug. 4, 1977, when police and ax-wielding Sheriff Richard Hongisto evicted its elderly, mostly Filipino and Chinese tenants, after almost a decade of controversy.

Otto Duffy recalled how Dias, who in the early '80s had taken to living on the sidewalk behind the Aarti Hotel on Leavenworth Street, was eventually invited in by the friars and then participated in its transformation into the first Tenderloin Neighborhood

Development Corp. building in 1981. Dias went on to serve on TNDC's Board of Directors in the 1980s and '90s.

Larson, first to speak, also prepared a printed testimonial that was distributed to the gathering. In it, she describes Dias' work with the San Francisco Network of Mental Health Clients and its Spiritmenders Community Center, a no-meds, no-shrinks, self-help drop-in center for people who felt abused by the mental health system. Spiritmenders, with Dias on its staff and board, served the disaffected mentally ill from the early '80s until it sputtered out in 2008.

"The primary goals that Darwin championed were the development of self-reliance and a community that, by example, would counteract stigma, prejudice and discrimination," Larson wrote.

Michael Nulty, longtime neighborhood organizer and a resident of the Alexander, recalled knowing Dias for 15 or 16 years. "He had a lifetime of contributing," Nulty said. "He was very much into disability rights as an advocate." Nulty cited Dias' work for the Alexander Tenants Association as treasurer, utilizing his skills from his days of working at a bank, and as a charter member of the Central City Democrats and the North of Market Planning Coalition.

> **"Watching him die was like watching my own life pass before me."**

Nulty called him a "poster child for hoarding and cluttering — he got into the paper, started advocating, and finally services (for hoarding) were created."

Susan Owsley stood up to say that she had known Dias "longer than anyone except my kids" — for 41 years. "We were horror addicts." She said she used to rent movies two at a time for them to watch. She said, though, that "King of Hearts" most made her think of Darwin.

Last to reminisce was Cruz-DeCastro, Dias' longtime partner.

"We went through many hard times in our lives," he said, and spoke of their resentments toward the Catholic Church, in which they were both raised, over its positions on gay rights and women's reproductive rights.

Cruz-DeCastro recalled the day Dias entered the hospice.

"He didn't want to go, I didn't want him to go. It was hard for me to see him leave the Alexander," Cruz-DeCastro said. "But on that day he was in so much pain. The pain was enormous, I wanted to tell him, 'Let go, let go, it's time to move on, there's only so much we can do!'

"Of all the people I've met, he was the one I was closest to. Watching him die was like watching my own life pass before me. I made him promise me to come back and give me a signal. Whether he ever will, I don't know."

After the crowd sang the final verse of "Amazing Grace," Sister Turbak ended the service "to celebrate a great man among us. We fight for justice, inclusion, dignity and respect. In the end, what do we have? Our relationships." ●

— MARK HEDIN

The Gentle Giant
CHRISTOPHER MARCUS HEVEY

CHRISTOPHER MARCUS HEVEY stirred plenty of curiosity when he moved into the Empress Hotel three years ago. Two beds had to be cobbled together to accommodate his 6-foot-8, 300-pound body. For the longest time, the young man hardly spoke to anyone. He buried himself in his computer programs.

Eventually, the residents connected. They found him to be "truly a nice person," "a gentle giant who never complained about things" and, as one mourner said at Hevey's memorial, "the most tolerant person I've ever known."

On a table near a spread of apples and pound cake were framed pictures of Hevey that his mother had sent, a half dozen lighted candles and his emblazoned blue T-shirt that was found in his closet and nicely summed up his personality: "Just shy not anti-social (you can talk to me!)."

Hevey died of unknown causes in a Palm Springs hotel on Christmas Day. He was 39. He had been visiting his mother, a nurse. She had gotten him a hotel room, according to Roberta Goodman, Empress manager. Hevey hadn't responded to knocking on his hotel door. When staff went inside, at his mother's request, they found his body.

"It's not clear what he died of," Goodman said. "And it takes weeks to find out causes."

Hevey, who used a cane, told his nurse that he had chronic pain, but she said she didn't know the cause of his "orthopedic issues."

Hevey was bright. His mother said he once worked for Time Warner as a computer expert. Born in Australia, he moved to the United States when he was 9. He attended a Quaker school in the East and a military school in South Carolina. Though he had college scholarship offers, he turned them down because he wanted to go to flight school. But the family couldn't afford that.

Christopher Marcus Hevey died Dec. 25, 2008

The residents, though, knew him as a science fiction movie buff with oodles of state-of-the-art computer programs — yet he preferred wearing beat-up earphones. He was a Trekkie and had all the episodes of the television show "The Prisoner," too, plus other collections that cluttered his sixth-floor room.

Hevey loved shopping for bargains, then telling the residents what he got. Seldom were they interested.

"He was painfully shy, but not impolite," said Robert Abate, who lived across the hall. "I miss him."

Dorothy Streutker of Network Ministries conducted the memorial, and at the end sang "Soft as the Voice of an Angel." ●

— TOM CARTER

He Didn't Die on the Street

GARRISON SMITH JR.

IT WAS THE BEST of times when Garrison Smith Jr., formerly homeless, lived in his clean, well-lighted SRO. People liked and admired him. He was honest, quiet, supportive and a smart chess player.

But even his dying too young was not the worst of times, his friends knew.

"It's an awkward moment," said Joe Jackson, one of 13 mourners who gathered in the Coast Hotel at Smith's memorial. A variety of white flowers on a forest green-clothed table made a handsome bouquet with three lighted candles to each side.

Garrison Smith Jr. died Jan. 19, 2009

"I don't remember what he died of," continued Jackson, the hotel's tenant representative. "But he died with a roof over his head among friends. He didn't die on the street. We can thank a lot of people for that and the mayor."

The Coast is a Care Not Cash hotel for formerly homeless welfare clients. Its 124 rooms house 150 people through the city program that reportedly has furnished 1,300 rooms to the homeless.

Smith collapsed while walking in the neighborhood and was taken to St. Francis Memorial Hospital where he died at age 54. His friends said he suffered from diabetes.

The mourners described him as a guy who always said hello, never lied, was "good people in a very difficult neighborhood," and a valued friend.

"All I can say is rest in peace, Garrison," said one man, sobbing. "Thanks for letting me know you."

Darwin Golden said he was in a St. Boniface shelter with Smith three years ago before they got housing at the Coast. He lightened the mood with an anecdote.

"He couldn't pronounce my name," Golden said, "He'd introduce me as darlin' and then tell people we used to sleep together. I had to correct him and say, 'at a shelter.'"

Another mourner said Smith's death was bad timing. He had worked at least 10 years as an elevator mechanic — once solving a problem when the Coast's elevator broke down — and "soon" was to come into some retirement money.

Smith surely would have liked his tribute.

"We're community," said Jackson, a 20-year resident. "The counselors do a good job here. It all gives people a little dignity. We even honor our dead pets." ●

— TOM CARTER

Celebrating the Survivors
UPBEAT MEMORIAL FOR 8

"I'M IN THE MOOD for Love" didn't seem exactly the right song to memorialize eight Alexander Residence tenants who died over a 4½-month period. But the idea was to provide entertainment to turn the survivors on to life.

The eight died in the summer of 2009

The names of the deceased and their death dates were posted in the community room, Their passing has taken an emotional toll on the mostly elderly residents of the TNDC-owned SRO. As 40 of them streamed into the room while the song played, Marvis Phillips explained that he had dreamed up this way for his fellow residents to handle grief.

"I was in bed one morning thinking about this and thought of New Orleans and what they do in Louisiana at funerals," Phillips said. "Five of ours died in 14 days. I wanted to do something besides sit around and be mopey."

Phillips said that the week before he had pitched his lively "celebration of life" idea to honor the deceased to TNDC Executive Director Don Falk. Falk liked it. The Alexander staff took it from there, lining up entertainment and food that TNDC furnished — a chicken and macaroni soup prepared by the building's volunteer, 83-year-old cook Carol Moratillo.

Greeting the celebrants were the Canon Kip Senior Center Singers — a female vocalist accompanied by keyboard and maracas. It was a leap from toe-tapping New Orleans street bands, but a mood elevator just the same. And the singers from SoMa offered dozens of songs during the 90-minute morning celebration and brunch that the crowd enjoyed.

"Death is a part of life."

The residents commemorated Edward King, who died at age 80; Ronald Urrutia, 55; Leonardo Dizon, 89; Teofilo Medlad, 84; William Maye, 57; Mark Gouguen, 52; Yan Chen, 77; and Mark Reynolds, 54.

The group's average age was 68½; the average length of residency was 10 years. Only one cause of death was known: Ronald Urrutia had cancer.

"There is a lot of sadness," Alexander Property Manager Nicole Grays said to the group. "It's hard. I think of you all as family. Now they're gone. But death is a part of life. I encourage you to remember what these people brought to us."

The Alexander has a diverse population of 200 residents in 179 units. In a recent TNDC survey, 130 responded and declared their ethnicity: 57 Chinese, 42 white, 18 black, 5 Native American, 2 Pacific Islanders, 1 Hispanic; 1 mixed and 4 "other" ethnicities.

Yue Mei addressed the crowd in Chinese. Her remarks were interpreted by a man who had been interpreting for a group of Chinese women sitting in the middle of the room.

"Even though we don't speak the same language, we live together as family and care about each other and love each other," Yue said.

"The outpouring here shows our love for the people in the building," Phillips said as staff begin delivering bowls of soup to the tables. Copies of a four-page fact sheet on Grief and Loss from the Family Caregiving Alliance were available on a table along with a list of counseling contacts at the Institute on Aging. ●

— TOM CARTER

A Merry Prankster
JASON BISHOP

THE LIBRARY and Listening Post is a cozy room just off the roof garden at the Ambassador Hotel on Mason Street. It was barely large enough to hold two staff members, four residents and Buddy, a small, well-behaved dog belonging to resident Kellie Noss. All were assembled there to remember Jason Bishop, who had died several weeks earlier at age 40.

"Jason made people laugh," Noss said. "And Buddy loved him."

Gerry Kirby, an Ambassador resident since 1999, said he and Bishop had a lot in common — "people we knew and bad habits. But we had our clear moments. What a full life he had! He was an AIDS advocate, starting when he was 14 or 15, but he also had a wild sense of humor."

Kirby praised Bishop for his work "to make the world better." And then, as if summarizing a recipe for breaking the cycle of dependency, Kirk said: "It's really hard to hold onto this, but it's important not to give up 'cause you can live better, feel better, and you don't need to get stuck in a routine."

Bishop's mother, who lives in Penn Valley in the Sierra foothills, said her son's advocacy was a source of pride for her. He was active in Reach Out, a mental health resource group, Act Up for AIDS advocacy, the Tenderloin AIDS Resource Center (now Tenderloin Health), and was a senior outreach counselor for Hospitality House. "He watched every one of his friends die of AIDS," she said. "There was no one left for him."

Bishop, who grew up in San Mateo, moved into the Ambassador two years ago, but kept close with his mother. Social worker Rachael Throm said she could always tell when he'd been with his family because he just looked better. Bishop went home at Christmas and died there the first week in February.

Jason Bishop died in February 2010

"I was comforted to know he was with his mother when he passed," Throm said.

Another friend at the Ambassador was Minyon Harlin, who recalled how she and Bishop would visit in each other's rooms and play pranks on other people. "We also did recycling together," Harlin said. "I'd go speak at schools and he always encouraged me to keep it up."

While Bishop urged others to stay the course, he wasn't good at taking care of himself, said Jim Johnson, a money manager for Conard House, who said he knew Bishop for five years. "I've learned that people don't do what they need to do for themselves, and I've learned to accept people as they are. Jason, he had a gift — he was upbeat despite his problems."

Without knowing it, Bishop may have left a cheerful legacy. Another resident admitted, shyly, "I find myself doing little pranks, like he did, making people laugh." ●

— MARJORIE BEGGS

On Oxygen, Smoked Anyway
WILLIAM HAMILTON

WILLIAM HAMILTON was a familiar sight around the Jefferson Hotel on Eddy Street. Everywhere he went he pulled along his 2-foot oxygen cylinder on wheels, its plastic tubes thrust into his nose. And all the while he smoked cigarettes.

"He smoked until the day he died," said hotel Manager Brian Samuel.

A dozen friends and acquaintances gathered at the SRO to pay their respects. "John A" wrote a poem and drew an abstract with colored pencils. It was placed alongside a page bearing the signatures of 50 Jefferson residents that was lying on a table near a colorful bouquet.

William Hamilton died July 24, 2004

No one in the room had known Hamilton well, though he called the Jefferson home for at least five years. They guessed he was 75, maybe 78. He was polite, they said, but kept to himself. He frequented Lafayette Coffee Shop around the corner, a Hyde Street landmark. Samuel said not everyone knew how generous he was. Hamilton had a retirement income, Samuel said, not simply Social Security or SSI, like most. Sometimes he'd help a neighbor pay their rent when they came up short.

Medical Examiner Charles Cecil said Hamilton died from emphysema at age 56. ●

— TOM CARTER

Thumbed His Nose at Pain
JOHN MacKENZIE

JOHN MacKENZIE, a Boston mechanic who lived in the Tenderloin for 10 years, was remembered by his friends for his "happy dance," smiling through the unrelenting pain of diabetes.

Tammy "Star" Sarmento said the medical examiner told her MacKenzie died at the hospital of "a stroke and a heart attack" at age 52. But at Network Ministries on Eddy Street, in a pastel-green room with a 20-foot-high ceiling and white flowers by his photograph, the half-dozen friends commemorating him knew the real killer was diabetes.

John MacKenzie died Oct. 15, 2004

For two years, the disease had weakened MacKenzie and nerve disease had rendered his legs nearly useless. Even so, he was elated around friends. He would stand, shake his hips, move his torso, smile and wave his forefingers in the air, bringing a laugh from everyone.

"He had such a great heart," said Sarmento, his girlfriend, who took care of him for more than two years. "And then diabetes started attacking his organs. His blood sugar counts went wild."

Close neighbors June Ruggles and daughter Tamara, 19, tearfully recalled last summer when MacKenzie made the laborious trip all the way out to Ocean Beach to celebrate June's birthday by watching the sunset.

"And he liked to tinker with things like watches and stereos," Tamara said. "It was to fix them or find what made them tick."

"He was a mellow guy and very determined to walk, especially at the end," said Dennis McFarland. "He took me under his wing a few years ago when I lost my partner, and he made sure I had food. He tried to not let his physical issues get in the way." ●

— TOM CARTER

Desk Clerk Was Brutalized

ROWENA CLARK

THE DAILY PAIN from a brutal act of anger five years ago that put Rowena Clark in a wheelchair ended when the lively American Indian desk clerk who grew up on an Arizona reservation died alone in her room at the Iroquois hotel.

The senseless incident occurred at a nearby Tenderloin hotel where Clark was a desk clerk. A domestic squabble broke out in the lobby, said her caregiver, Isabel Rodriguez, who saw Clark three times a week for the past four years.

"The man involved went around the desk and took a telephone receiver and hit her hard in the back of the neck," Rodriguez said after Clark's memorial at the Iroquois. "It severed a cord and she spent a year in Laguna Honda (Hospital)."

Rodriguez said Clark had been unable to feed or bathe herself for months. When she moved into the Iroquois four years ago, she was operating an electric wheelchair, sometimes at breakneck speeds. Rodriguez said that when she struggled to keep up with her, Clark would gleefully yell, "Take a bus!" But a year ago the chair was damaged. The manual replacement stymied her exuberant travel.

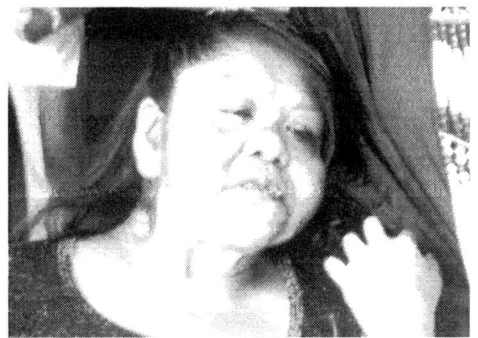
Rowena Clark died Jan. 6, 2005

Friends and staff recalled Clark as vivacious, a lady who loved life, smart, humorous and sensitive to the woes of her friends. An expert seamstress, she also meticulously crafted jewelry. But when she was drunk, she'd get feisty and swear like a sailor.

Clark was under heavy morphine medication, said Rodriguez, who sometimes went to fill her prescriptions. Her boyfriend, who lives in the Mission District and did not attend the memorial, found Clark's body. The medical examiner's office listed the official cause of death as "complications from chronic alcoholism." Clark was 54. "I loved my friend so much," Colleen Marie Diserina said through sobs, "I miss her so much."

Casey Carr said he met Clark a year ago. He was in stocking feet in the elevator, having locked himself out of his room. "I gave her some cherry blossoms and we became best friends," Carr told the small gathering. "She was a good person and had a good spirit and was intelligent and loved life. But I think lately life had become too much for her."

They talked daily, Carr said. When she called him, he always answered with "Thomas' Mortuary," then offered her a choice of opulent plans that he made up.

"She always said she wanted the $25,000 crypt with the embossed picture," Carr said behind a quickly fading smile. "I didn't know this would happen. Every time the phone rings now, I think it's her. She'll always be with me."

Her friends thought she had Apache blood, maybe Navajo, too. But Rodriguez said no, it was neither. "It was a tribe she said no one would recognize. But she spoke the language and used it sometimes when she talked to her daughter."

Clark told Rodriguez she ran away from the reservation to get married at 14. But her parents had it annulled. Friends confirmed that she said she had eight children, all in Arizona. One daughter, Laveda, had come to collect her personal effects and took her ashes back to the reservation.

"They'll put the ashes in a teepee," said Carr, "and a medicine man will chant for her for 24 hours."

It was a plan Carr never thought to offer her. ●

— TOM CARTER

Handled Intense Pain Well
JAMES 'PETE' LANE

James "Pete" Lane was a courteous, cultured man who lived with great pain, and took great pains to show his appreciation for the help he sometimes needed. This was the collective memory of those who attended his memorial at the Hamlin Hotel.

"He wouldn't let us know that he was in pain, just that he was struggling," said resident and caregiver Cassidy Blonsky, who knew Lane for the last six months of his life. "He didn't want to burden anybody because it was burden enough to him."

Lane, who moved into the Hamlin almost 20 years ago, was 56 when he died. He was born in Alabama and studied political science at Emory University in Atlanta. He planned to become a lawyer. Ultimately, however, he worked in menswear at San Francisco department stores, helping fit clothes.

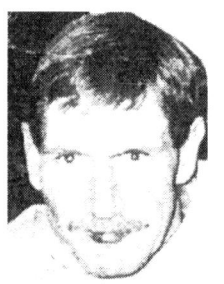

Pete Lane died Feb. 19, 2011

"He loved that," his friend, Richie Carlson, recalled. "He always talked about that — and history. He was a very smart man, liked to tell jokes. He had a lot of conditions that made it hard for him to do much, but he handled it with a lot of grace. Lane struggled with cancer that had reached his bones and was mostly bedridden in his final years. Pearl Durmas, who knew him for more than a decade in her work as a desk clerk and case manager at the Hamlin, said that Lane would get out into the neighborhood using his walker and wheelchair, taking cabs to where he needed to get, spend time lounging in the hotel's community room, or receive guests and fellow hotel residents in his second-floor room after he broke his shoulder for a second time. He was hospitalized at California Pacific Medical Center and died there two days later.

John Franklin of Community Housing Partnership, which runs the Hamlin, said Lane was an Alabama University fan and that, as an Auburn Tiger fan himself, they enjoyed friendly banter over college football.

Others who knew him recalled a man who displayed plenty of spark. One hotel resident, Mary Mathews, said Lane was "always sending me to get Miller Genuine Draft."

He'd made a lot of friends at a Larkin Street bar. One of them, John, was in daily contact, either by phone or through frequent faxes. "Every morning on his fax machine, John would have sent a poem or something," Carlson said.

"He was a great guy," Durmas recalled. "He would have his moments and he would call, saying, 'Pearl, I need this done today. T-O-D-A-Y, today!' I still get laughter, joy from that. But he would always make that extra effort to let you know he was thankful and appreciative. He was a wonderful tenant."

Lane is survived by a brother-in-law. He lost his sister about three years ago, Carlson said.

"He had a painful life," Blonsky said. "He could handle pain and he was really tough and he went through a lot of stuff. He's probably feeling the most peace he's felt most of his life."

—MARK HEDIN

Owned Top Mom-and-Pop
ABED 'ABE' EID

FAMILY, FRIENDS and the Tenderloin mourn the unexpected passing of Abed "Abe" Eid, owner of G&H Liquors & Grocery at 201 Jones St. Three days before New Year's he had a heart attack and died. He was 55.

For almost 30 years Eid ran his corner store in the heart of the gritty neighborhood. Most days he could be found sitting on a stool or standing behind the counter, for 16 hours some days. Eid was a respected neighborhood fixture and his store was a safe haven from the chaos on the streets. He ran his business with the community in mind.

"Abe loved this store. He was here all the time, and there were never any problems," says Mamum Siddi, who'd worked for him for three years. "He always treated me like a brother, never like I was just an employee."

Eid received many awards over the years, including a Certificate of Honor from the mayor's office for being a good neighbor. In 1989, he helped spearhead a campaign to remove fortified wines from Tenderloin shelves, starting with his own store, though that cost him $40,000 a year in sales.

"It's my principles, my dignity, more than money," Eid told the New York Times in a 1989 interview about why he stopped selling fortified wines.

For his loyal customers, Eid stocked the shelves according to their wishes. He made sure there were plenty of WIC products. He respected mothers and cared for children, often giving kids candy and ice cream. If a customer asked for an item not in stock, he would go immediately, sometimes leaving the store unattended, and have the product stocked within hours. He treated all his customers with respect — some as friends.

Abed Eid died Dec. 28, 2011

"Abe went above and beyond what was required of a store owner in the TL," says Linda Rochelle, an eight-year resident and assistant manager of the Marlton Manor across the street from G&H market. When Rochelle moved there, she was going through a personal tragedy. Eid, she said, was her rock, always there to lend a hand and tell her things would be okay. When she didn't stop in at the store for a few days, Eid would call her or go by her apartment to make sure she was all right.

"He was my friend, my mentor, a shoulder to cry on. He was admired by all," she adds.

Rochelle wasn't the only such customer. Eid demonstrated similar kindness to many and went out of his way to meet the needs of all.

"He had a big heart," says John Connolly, who lives down the street, a G&H customer for 11 years. "He was one of the most caring individuals I've ever met."

Connolly, a coordinator for Episcopal Community Services, says G&H is the best mom-and-pop in the neighborhood, because Eid was loyal to his customers and he never judged them.

His death was unexpected and the cause, a heart attack, caught many by surprise. Those who knew him well said he was a strong man without a history of heart problems. After his death, neighbors and community leaders brought flowers and condolences. A large shrine sprang up on the corner of Jones and Turk streets.

"I believe in angels," says Rochelle, misty-eyed. But she smiles and looks upward. "Abe is up in them clouds, with his wings on, flying over the TL, looking down and watching over us."

Eid, a Muslim, was a Palestinian. He died on a Wednesday night, and by Friday family and friends were in the mosque dedicating prayers to him. Afterward, well over 500 people met at Woodland Memorial Park in Colma and laid Eid to rest.

In the days after his death, hundreds of guests visited the Eid family home in San Bruno to pay their respects to his wife, Sylvia, their four daughters and son, Frankie.

Frankie Eid has stepped up, ending his career as a locksmith to run his father's store. "There is no way I'm going to let this go to waste," says Frankie. "My father dedicated his whole life to this store."

Customers continue to come in and offer their sympathy, bringing so many flowers that Frankie says there isn't enough room for them all.

— BRIAN RINKER

Popular Cook at Iroquois
PRESTON HOROWITZ

"WE HAVE a saying in Hebrew, 'May his memory be a blessing,' " said Rabbi Natan Fenner, who conducted a memorial for Preston Horowitz, a retired cook who made life a little brighter for his friends in the Iroquois Hotel, his home.

The cheerful Horowitz insisted on sharing the fruits of his talents, an offering that one social worker said made him a community builder.

PHOTO COURTESY OF IROQUOIS HOTEL

Preston Horowitz died March 18, 2005

"He'd maybe have to scrounge around for change to buy a pepper, but then he'd invite everyone to enjoy what he made," said Bruce Kucejko, a resident who knew him nearly three years. "And he had a humorous way of looking at things. We'll all miss him."

"Yes, I know some people gained weight because of him," said another man among the dozen friends who attended the memorial. "For a while he was charging $5, but he had to stop that."

When Horowitz died of a heart attack in his sleep he was 63. His companion of 12 years, Beverly Galaz, said he had worked as a chef in New York, Los Angeles and San Francisco. They lived at the Iroquois on O'Farrell nearly eight years.

Rabbi Fenner, from the Bay Area Jewish Healing Center, read the charming poem, "The Summer Day" by Mary Oliver, and sang two prayers in Hebrew. ●

— TOM CARTER

Got His Wish
LEE HARMONY

WHEN PEOPLE saw him, Lee Harmony was either sitting in his wheelchair in the Alexander Residence lobby, or coming or going to UCSF for cancer treatments. The rest of the time he was in his room watching cowboy movies. His caregiver visited six days a week and prepared his meals.

Lee Harmony died Sept. 19, 2006

"If he came to any social event he didn't stay," social worker Winnie Kwong said. "He'd take his food upstairs to his room. When he came back from the hospital the last time I asked him why he didn't go to a hospice or a nursing home? He said, 'What are you talking about? I want to die here, at home.'"

Harmony got his wish, succumbing in his 11th-floor room. He was 66.

"I'd see him in the lobby," said Beatrice Duran, an Alexander resident for a year. "He was quiet but always responded if you greeted him. And he is a member of this big family. I feel the loss. I pray for his eternal peace."

As Rev. Glenda Hope read Scriptures and prayed, Kwong interpreted for the dozen Chinese and Filipino women and men who attended the memorial. More than half of the Alexander's 200 residents are elderly Asians.

Harmony had once lived in Michigan, been married, and has a brother and sister in Idaho, his friends said. He worked as a carpenter and handyman, also as a waiter in New York and at a Powell Street restaurant.

Kwong said Harmony wanted to leave her everything in his will, but she said no, a social worker can't do that. She did accept his movies, about 100, including the TV series, "Gunsmoke," all of which she donated to the hotel's library. The remainder of his estate he left to Edgar Sanchez, his caregiver of 18 months. ●

— TOM CARTER

Someone Else in a Previous Life
JOHN TAYLOR

WHEN PARAMEDICS carried John Taylor into the Senator Hotel on a gurney shortly after 7 p.m., he was screaming and crying in pain. The shocked manager told them they couldn't leave him there.

"I didn't want him unattended," recalled Isabella Marshall. "I thought he wouldn't make it through the night. But he told me he'd be okay and that he didn't want to go back to the hospital."

Taylor got help that night and, with round-the-clock caregivers, recovered in a month from an excruciating foot amputation brought on by diabetes. Though never pain-free, Taylor soon ventured into the world from his seventh-floor room, driving the motorized wheelchair he was given. Friends say the 5-foot-8, 230-pound man helped as a volunteer at Alcoholics Anonymous meetings and for three more years was a congenial tenant who never complained, despite his suffering.

> **He kept his door open all the time with his wheelchair. Even in pain he was willing to try to help people if they needed it.**

But Taylor's medical complications twice sent him to St. Francis Memorial Hospital, each occasion for more than three days. The second stay was the last. He died there at age 50.

Eleven friends attended his memorial at the Senator.

"He kept his door open all the time with his wheelchair," said one man. "Even in pain he was willing to try to help people if they needed it."

"I knew him 30 years," said Angel Ichord. "I got clean first, then he followed. But he helped people out even when he was on drugs. I'm sorry he's gone, but I'm glad he doesn't have to suffer anymore."

John Taylor died Dec. 5, 2009

Ichord said she first met Taylor in the New Orleans French Quarter in the mid-1970s when he was Tina, a cocktail waitress in a drag bar. They met up frequently afterward in cities and towns across the nation as they followed "the same circuit."

"He was clean four years and then diabetes took his foot three years ago," Ichord said. "But he refused to get depressed. I'll miss him." ●

— TOM CARTER

Faced Adversity With Strength
BYRON LEE

LIKE MANY Tenderloin residents, Byron Lee finished his life surrounded by people who didn't really know him.

He died at 63 of chronic kidney failure at 990 Polk St., residential housing for low-income and formerly homeless seniors. Lee spent his final 18 months there. Staff and residents gathered in the building's community room for a service in his memory led by Rev. Glenda Hope.

No one knew where he grew up or who he had loved, whether he had gone to college, been in the service or fathered children, although a hotel staff member mentioned that Lee, who used a wheelchair, once had been a desk clerk at a Tenderloin hotel.

Byron Lee died March 18, 2010

But, according to mourners, Lee's cheerfulness and quiet strength spoke volumes about the man. They mentioned his easy smile and ready laugh, and his ability to elicit the same from others. "He had a wonderful sense of humor," said Adrianne Wynacht, a registered nurse at the hotel. "He loved puns, made plays on words. He always brightened my day."

Resident Mary Ann Humphrey said Lee's smile caught her eye long before she knew who he was. They were both patients at Laguna Honda and often passed in the halls before finally meeting while signing up to move to Polk and Geary a couple of years ago.

"He always had a smile for me — there was an unspoken bond between us," said Humphrey. "But he was a very private man. No one knew much about him."

His next-door neighbor, who ruefully observed that Lee wasn't the quietest of neighbors, said Lee enjoyed music. "I didn't talk to him much, but he was very nice — once he just sat there and listened to me while I sang."

Humphrey agreed that music appeared to be among Lee's pleasures. "He didn't attend many functions, but he did come to the ones where there was music."

Lee had lost both legs, staff and residents noted. Whether due to injury or disease, no one could say, but they agreed that he handled his condition with quiet courage. "Whatever he was facing in his life, even if it was adversity, he faced it with strength," said staffer Steve Ball.

Lee's forbearance also made an impression on staff member Kristi Lambert, who recalled passing him on the street one day. He was stopped in his electric wheelchair, they exchanged greetings, and she continued on her way. Later, she learned that his wheelchair battery had run out of juice, leaving him stranded.

"He'd been stuck outside all night and slept in his chair," she said. Mortified by what had happened, she apologized for passing him by. But Lee didn't appear to be angry or hurt. "He said he'd slept outside before," she said. "His approach to life was very easygoing."

"We won't forget him," said one resident. "He kept to himself, but he made everyone laugh."

"That's a big gift," said Rev. Hope, then led the group in a final prayer for Lee. ●

— HEIDI SWILLINGER

> **"Whatever he was facing in his life, even if it was adversity, he faced it with strength"**

A Very Caring Nurse
KATHLEEN FITZPATRICK

THE ARANDA RESIDENCE lost its welcoming angel when Kathleen Fitzpatrick, a nurse who thought more of helping others than herself, died in San Francisco General Hospital of meningitis, pneumonia and hepatitis. She was 53.

A dozen friends who gathered at Fitzpatrick's memorial remembered her as the first to greet newcomers. Five-foot-three and 90 pounds, she offered a sweet smile, a card and a gift basket of food that she prepared. She told them to stop by anytime at her room on the fifth floor where she invariably offered them food. The friends also didn't hesitate to say how stubborn Fitzpatrick was, too, a characteristic that no doubt worked against her in the end. As a nurse, she could give pills but wouldn't take them.

"She was one of the sweetest, most loving and stubborn people I ever knew," her common-law husband of 15 years, John Wells, told the group. "She was always giving and caring – she'd almost rather look out for someone else than herself."

In the newly remodeled six-story Aranda, a master lease hotel run by Tenderloin AIDS Resource Center, Wells said he first met Fitzpatrick at a bar: Murio's Trophy Room on Haight Street, a neighborhood institution named for a legendary local tennis player.

"She was a live-in caretaker nurse five days a week," he said. "She had weekends off and shopped at the Cala across the street."

Kathleen Fitzpatrick died March 24, 2006

Their budding romance flourished with hikes and picnics in Golden Gate Park. Wells, a graduate of the Marine Cooks and Stewards School in Calistoga, fried their picnic chicken. "She liked to shop for antique plates, too," he said.

They moved into the Aranda 10 years ago, shortly after she surprised him by quitting her job.

After contracting HIV and hepatitis C, she steadfastly ignored her medications despite her failing health, Wells said. Even case workers couldn't get her to take the meds. When Fitzpatrick went into the hospital in February, she was unable to speak and had to write notes to Wells when he visited. She died six weeks later. •

— TOM CARTER

Bicycle Maker Who Gave Them Away
LAWRENCE MILLER

LAWRENCE MILLER made bicycles from scavenged parts, then gave them away. A quiet man, he hadn't been a resident of the Ambassador Hotel long enough to gift many of his fellow tenants, but he made a real impression anyway.

Lawrence, tall and lean, moved quietly into a fourth-floor room and pretty much kept to himself.

"He was a good tenant and didn't seem to need us," said hotel social worker Rachel Throm at Miller's memorial at the Ambassador. Rev. Glenda Hope conducted the memorial that was held in the Listening Post room on the second floor. "He was a good guy, sweet," said another social worker.

"If you went by his room he always said hello," said Larry Edmond. "I had a vinyl record album but no record player. He sold me his for $12. It was worth a lot more than that."

Lawrence Miller died Oct. 31, 2007

When Lawrence wasn't out searching for used bicycle parts in the neighborhood, he was in his room assembling a bike. He kept his room neat and clean, his friends said. The parts were organized in one place and he worked on just one bicycle at a time.

"He gave me three bicycles," said Richard Zinser. "And he always asked me if I needed any help."

Lawrence worked until the day he died at age 49, likely of AIDS, his friends said, because of the way he deteriorated. He was found in his room.

"He was very sick at the end and worked until he couldn't get up to answer the door," said his neighbor Gerry Kirby. "Other people were affected by his death. There were more arguments, people jumping to anger. I think they were acting out their hurt, their emotions."

Kirby couldn't say for sure Miller died of AIDS, only that he had exhibited symptoms of the disease. "His hair had straightened out and his eyes were large," he said.

The Listening Post originated in 1984 during the AIDS epidemic as a place where residents could come and talk with someone from Network Ministries. It was a project of Glenda Hope, executive director. At the time, the city hadn't extended any AIDS help to the Tenderloin, though studies showed the neighborhood had the highest incidence, Hope said. And the Ambassador, then a crummy, privately owned SRO, had a number of PWAs. Many were African American men. No one showed up for the first four months or so, until the listening program gained credibility, Hope said.

Now, doubling as a library, the Listening Post is open three or four times a week from 3 to 4:30 p.m. Volunteers, including Hope, show up to listen and talk. No one knew whether Miller had ever dropped in.

Despite his limited time at the Ambassador, Hope said, "he had quite an impact." •

—TOM CARTER

Clift Hotel Cook Loved the Tenderloin
SAMUEL PINEDA

SAMUEL PINEDA loved many places in San Francisco but no place like the Tenderloin, where he returned at age 74 to live out his days.

After a long career as a cook, Pineda moved into the Ritz Hotel two years ago. A quiet respectful man, he kept to himself, staff said. When his sister called him several times recently and he didn't pick up the phone on the first ring, the family felt something was wrong. It was.

Pineda had died in his room of a heart attack. He was 76.

Samuel Pineda died in October 2004

Pineda cooked for 20 years at the fancy Clift Hotel on Geary Street. Once, he had his own small restaurant in the Mission District and, in the 1980s, one on Eddy Street. And though he had lived in other neighborhoods, the Tenderloin was irresistible to the 5-foot-5 Nicaraguan who seldom spoke English.

"He loved the Tenderloin," niece Marisol Guevara said at her uncle's memorial in the Ritz. With her was her sister, Ethel, and their mother, also Ethel, one of Pineda's three sisters. "He always came down here, even when he lived in the Excelsior and in the Mission. We offered to have him live with us, but he preferred his small room here."

Guevare recalled how her uncle inevitably was there to comfort her mother through "bad times," for which the family would always be grateful.

Pineda enjoyed having coffee and conversing with his Spanish-speaking pals, often at Carl's Jr. on Market and Charles J. Brenham Place. He never mastered English in his 40 years in the city, his nieces said. He brought them his mail to read during his twice-weekly visits to the family on Shotwell Street. He never failed to bring a toy for Jacqueline, Ethel's 2-year-old, prompting the toddler to steal his cane and try to run away with it. And how they would laugh.

"He was quite a barber, too," Guevara recalled for the small gathering of family, staff and two residents. "But he was very independent. He would cut hair in his apartment. Word got around how good he was."

The family had brought Pineda's ashes in a black plastic box. They placed them on a table next to flowers and his picture. Sisters Luz and Argentina were flying in on the weekend to take the ashes back to Masaya, Nicaragua. ●

— TOM CARTER

A Man of Lightning Wit
CHRISTOPHER CLANTON

WHEN CONNIE CLANTON visited her brother, Christopher Clanton, at St. Francis Memorial Hospital, she asked if she could get anything for him.

"Chris was intubated for pneumonia at the time and he could barely speak and couldn't eat," she recalls, "but he let me know he wanted Reese's Peanut Butter Cups."

Her brother had been in and out of St. Francis Hospital several times before he died at age 47, and she recalled his last days for mourners gathered at the Elm Hotel. Those days were precious to her, she said, because until she heard about his failing health in May, she hadn't seen him for many years.

"Sam — that was Chris' nickname — always loved to eat," she said. "Our mother, who couldn't travel here today, wrote this poem and sent it with me to read." The poem was about Christopher Clanton the child, who loved all foods except broccoli, which he said looked like little trees.

Across-the-hall neighbor C.J. Flanagan remembers Clanton fondly. He ate popcorn all the time and was very quiet, she said, "but every now and then, he'd play music really loud on his radio for three minutes, then shut it off."

Clanton grew up in Bakersfield, a middle child of six siblings, and lived lots of places, including Napa, where he worked in wineries. He moved into the Elm three years ago. No one knew how long he'd lived in San Francisco, but Connie Clanton believes it was 10 years or more.

"He was the smartest of all of us," she said. "He was a man of lightning-fast wit and infinite jest. At St. Francis he was almost a celebrity because of his cheerfulness."

Matloub Rahmey, a physical therapist at St. Francis Hospital, recalls Clanton as a "sweet and appreciative man. I taught him some breathing techniques that seemed to help him. It was a gift to have known him."

Clanton's appreciation spilled over into much of his life. Before he died, he told his sister about the things that had made him happy in recent years: moving into the Elm after being homeless, and working with the gardeners at Golden Gate Park through the city's PAES (Personal Assisted Employment Services) program, which gives employable adults a cash stipend and work-related education and training.

Christopher Clanton died July 7, 2008

Nanette Clanton, another sister who lives in Texas and who also came to San Francisco to see her brother in his last days, said the family had lost track of him almost 20 years ago in "a conflict over lifestyle." Still, to her, he was the brother who was "so good-looking, we always wondered why he didn't go to Hollywood. And he loved to laugh and didn't like any fuss — he sure wouldn't want to see us bawling over him," she said, trying not to cry.

As the memorial ended, Connie Clanton opened a shopping bag filled with Reese's Peanut Butter Cups, which she piled near a picture of her brother. ●

— MARJORIE BEGGS

Sam

Sam liked nearly every kind of food.
Oranges, apples, nuts and cheese
And when his mother gave him carrots,
he'd day, "I want more of these."

Brussels sprouts and cabbage,
Celery and green beans.
How to get enough,
He'd plot and plan and scheme.

"Give me lots of vegetables,
meat and potatoes too.
I will eat them one by one,
Or even in a stew."

"Cereal and crackers,
muffins, bread and jam,
milk and eggs and plenty of juice,
I can eat them, yes I can."

Only one food,
Sam strongly resisted.
Broccoli he would not eat,
He stubbornly insisted.

"Don't give me broccoli,
Mother if you please.
I don't want to eat them.
They look like little trees."

"You're right," his mother said,
trying her very best,
trying not to laugh
while Sam ate all the rest.

❝ If you listen with your heart, you'll hear all my love around you soft and dear. ❞

Glide Memorial Methodist Church at Taylor and Ellis streets. Photo by Mark Ellinger

PART 3: The Closer

PHOTO BY HEIDI SWILLINGER

Rev. Glenda Hope has for 35 years officiated memorials for hundreds of central city residents.

Rev. Hope Gives a Caring Sendoff

WHEN SOMEONE DIES among the Tenderloin's poor there's a crying need for a dignified closure for the life that has passed, regardless of how it was lived. One person, more than anyone, has answered the call to perform this final task.

BY TOM CARTER

She's 5 feet and rail-thin and at 74 has grandmotherly gray hair. Sometimes she's mistaken for a nun because of her clerical collar. She has fearlessly traversed the seedy hood's unforgiving streets for more than three decades on her way to honor the dead in ceremonies in low-rent hotels.

Rev. Glenda Hope, the closer, is a fixture among the residents who may one day unknowingly receive her services. In a low voice tinged with a Southern drawl, her ice-blue eyes soft and compassionate, she bestows on prostitutes, drug addicts and dealers, robbers, alcoholics and the mentally troubled the identical reverence she gives to the disabled, low-income workers, immigrant families and pensioners who dominate the central city's demographics.

Her surname — like a beacon to the city's sketchiest neighborhood — is from her late husband, Scott Hope, a San Francisco State University education professor, who died in 1997.

"The memorials are a final dignity to those who couldn't have them," Hope says. "They offer a place of comfort and the beginning of healing for mourners."

Most memorials take place in SRO lobbies or community rooms, which vary from threadbare and musty to clean and cheery. Sometimes only a couple of people show up and a few who do may not even have known the deceased. Memorials with 40 to 50 mourners are exceptional. A bouquet or two is always on a table in front, sometimes photos, cards and mementos. Mourners are anxious for closure, yes, but a side attraction to the event is free food, often ethnic — from Filipino fare to soul food — and always with sugary baked goods. The largesse is donated by the hotel, or social workers, less often by family and friends.

THE MEMORIAL RITUAL

After acknowledging the deceased and quoting the Bible, Hope asks for reflections from the mourners. Life is hard in the Tenderloin and the remarks are often revealing.

One widow, a little tipsy at the 11 a.m. rite, regretted she hadn't seen more of her late husband. The reason, she said, was that he had spent so much time in jail. Asked later what he had excelled at, she said without blinking: "Selling heroin."

Another time, a dolled-up woman said what a wonderful guy the deceased had been, but she had known him "years ago in New Orleans when he was a waitress." One man confessed his friend was a real "son of a bitch."

"Sometimes I get surprised," Hope says. "I've had to handle some sticky wickets. Sometimes people don't know when to stop."

> **The memorials are a final dignity to those who couldn't have them.**

In June 2004, Hope contacted Central City Extra and asked if we would cover the memorials. Thus began a working relationship that has produced more than 200 obituaries, most for people whose names had never been in print before.

Hope has given upward of a thousand of her simple, yet elegant, Judeo-Christian memorials. Other faiths and nonbelievers, she invariably says as the service begins, are welcome. This approach, she says others tell her, is what keeps requests coming for her. On a rare occasion, another minister, priest or rabbi will do a memorial in the Tenderloin.

Hope does two to five memorials a month, more in winter. People shut down in the cold weather, she says. The season's dark and things die. She has seen it time and again. She conducted eight memorials in November 2010.

Hope believes that when homeless people, who often are in poor health, move off the street into permanent housing they may give in to what ails them and die not long after. "Nobody wants to die alone, so outside they fight to hang on," she says. "Then, when they move in, they find peace, safety and comfort, and they can let go."

Hope, who lives in the Crocker Amazon neighborhood, is executive director of San Francisco Network Ministries, the nonprofit she helped start in 1972. It ministers to the poor, especially women, in the Tenderloin and is a team ministry — everyone earns the same salary. "The world loves a star, but that is not, and should never be, the standard of a real ministry," she says.

HOW IT STARTED

Network Ministries runs the Ambassador Hotel Ministry, SafeHouse, Tenderloin Community Church, the 366 Eddy St. Center and, with St. Anthony Foundation, a computer training center at 150 Golden Gate Ave. But the memorials keep Hope in touch with the community in a way nothing else did.

"The memorials started in '77 or '78," she says. "We had a Catholic sister on staff and she was visiting elderly people in the Dalt Hotel. In those days, the Dalt was for-profit, rundown and awful."

Sister Clare Ronzani regularly visited Ruth, a diabetic woman who was chronically depressed. One day, Ruth jumped out of a fifth-floor window.

"We wanted to do something and we didn't know what," Hope says. "Sister Clare and I called Dan O'Connor, who was a priest at St. Anthony's then, and the three of us got the word out and went to the Dalt Hotel lobby for a memorial. We didn't know if anybody would show up. We didn't know what we were going to do, either. We just made it up as we went along."

But the men turned up in suits and ties, the women in dresses. Sister Clare played the guitar and sang. The room was filled.

"Afterward, the cookies weren't very good and something like Kool Aid was served," Hope continued. "But everyone had had a chance to remember Ruth."

Word of the memorial spread.

"Hotel managers began calling us and city agencies who served the poor," she says. "Oh, it wasn't as many as we have now. But gradually the nonprofits, like TNDC, got involved."

PHOTO BY HEIDI SWILLINGER

Rev. Glenda Hope has served the TL for 40 years.

Hope's journey to the Tenderloin seems serendipitous. She came West to attend San Francisco Theological Seminary and received her master's of divinity in 1969. She was 33 when ordained that May 17 at historic Old First Presbyterian Church where she was assistant pastor 1969-72, working with young adults.

Hope hadn't a clue she'd end up devoting her career to the Tenderloin. But she does what needs to be done, and that led her to the poorest, most crime-ridden neighborhood in San Francisco.

THE AIDS HOTEL CRIES OUT

When Hope left Old First in November 1972 she found a space on Bush Street between Jones and Leavenworth and opened a nighttime drop-in coffeehouse for poor folks under her newly formed San Francisco Network Ministries. It became popular with Tenderloin people who went up the hill to Bush. Once, a man who had overdosed, stumbled in, saying, "I just knew if I got to the coffeehouse I'd be safe." He was taken to a hospital and survived. To Hope it was a sign to move down to the Tenderloin.

"We started with zero money and no connections, eight people and two dogs, making it up as we went along," Hope says. "There are a lot of stories in the Bible like that."

In the 1990s, prostitutes were being mauled and murdered. Hope went into the streets to talk and listen to the working women. More than anything, they told her, they needed safe housing. She took that on as a project.

In 1997, the Catholic Sisters of the Presentation, hearing of the plan, joined Hope. SafeHouse, 14 units at a Mission neighborhood address that's kept secret, opened in 2001 for prostitutes wanting a new life.

Still, Tenderloin memorials are the constant in Hope's life that reaches out to her.

A new chapter began for her in the 1980s, soon to be a horror that numbed the world.

"Hank Wilson was running the for-profit Ambassador Hotel (at the corner of Mason and Eddy, now a TNDC SRO), another depressingly scuzzy rathole," she says. "It had a lot of mentally ill and depressed people in it, and Hank asked if we could come for visits — he knew we weren't judgmental about gays and lesbians.

"One day, Father John Hardin (now St. Anthony's Board of Trustees chair) called and wanted to do something. He was then in the East Bay. We thought we might have an open-door room at the Ambassador for drop-in chaplainizing, you know, come in and talk.

"Hank gave us a room for it. We didn't know if anyone would come. After four months, though, they did — they saw that we weren't going away and that we were trustworthy."

That was the origin of the Listening Post, a spot at the Ambassador where residents find a willing ear.

Penny Sarvis, an S.F. Theological Seminary student, came to Hope in the early 1980s through a hands-on, for-credit class credit and stayed 10 years.

"Dennis Conklin came to me and said so many with AIDS are dying and there's no service for them. So he and I recruited to make the Tenderloin AIDS Network in 1987. Leroy Looper (Cadillac Hotel) and Hank Wilson and Les Pappas and a doctor from the Haight Ashbury Free Clinics — can't remember his name — and Jerry DeYoung who helped direct services, until he, too, became an AIDS victim and died."

Hope and Sarvis did most of the memorials then.

"People would die within three to six months. In one 20-day period we did 21 memorials — not counting the homeless ones."

> **When they move in, they find peace, safety and comfort, and they can let go.**

Ultimately the city got moving to fund a center where people could come for advice on safe sex and other help, but Hope had to pull out all the stops to swing the deal.

"We did a sit-in to get the money for it. The city had stalled so long that when they got the money, they only had three months left in the fiscal year to spend it."

Then it was arduous to cut through the city's red tape in meetings involving the rehab of the chosen building at the corner of Golden Gate and Leavenworth until the project got dangerously close to running out of time.

"We are trying to save lives here!" Hope pleaded with the building inspector at one meeting. "I cried," she said. "And I do not cry easily. The place got real quiet. Most thought I was a nun. Then he threw up his hands and said, 'I think I see a way.' "

She paused.

"A clerical collar, a Southern accent and a woman's tears," she summarized, then added with a faint smile, "I was younger and cuter then."

The resulting service, Tenderloin AIDS Network, which changed its name to TARC around 1990, was Network Ministries' program for its first five years.

WINTER RITE FOR HOMELESS DEAD

Hope's largest memorial by far is her annual celebration for the homeless who die anonymously on the streets throughout the year. It began during a bitter winter in 1990, when 16 people died of hyperthermia in the Tenderloin. Hope and 15 others gathered at City Hall, then went as a group to each spot that had been reported as an address where someone died, and paused.

"We were silent and someone slowly beat a drum. No one had a name. Then we moved on to the next place. At the end I said a prayer, and that was it."

Now the service happens every Dec. 21 at 5:30 p.m. in front of City Hall, rain or shine. Hope organizes the service and gets the names of the dead from the Department of Public Health, the Tom Waddell Health Center and the Coalition on Homelessness. Often other names are offered in the rite by representatives attending from other Bay Area cities. Clerics from a half-dozen religions speak briefly as the ceremony opens, then preselected volunteers take turns reading a handful of names. After each name is read, a bell is struck, the sound lingering eerily in the night air. At the end, Hope, wearing the familiar white silk stole her mother made for her, burns the list of names and the 40 to 100 mourners hug, then disappear into the night. In 2009, 95 names were read. In 2010, the number rose to 110.

Hope is as much a part of the Tenderloin fabric as St. Anthony's Dining Room, Glide or Boeddeker Park. Sidewalks that would intimidate a housewife from across town are her comfort zone, her paths toward passion.

A PRAYER ON THE STREET

One day a disheveled man stopped her a block from Boeddeker Park, dropped to one knee and begged her to bless him. She did, with simple dignity — the tiny, silver-haired woman in black, her hand on a kneeling man's bowed head, on an overcast day in the middle of the towering concrete jungle as cars rolled by and passing street people made mental notes. "It happens all the time," she says. "Usually they want me to say a prayer for them."

A memorial at the Ambassador for Michael Aylwin, attended by two staff social workers and resident Bill McLean, was a recent closure that gave everyone comfort. And it incidentally added weight to Hope's intimate understanding of death in the Tenderloin that often the homeless come in from the cold, get comfortable enough to let go and die peacefully.

Aylwin, who used a cane, had been homeless for five years before he came to the Ambassador. His social worker, Jackie Mollitor, said he was so happy to be there. He died less than four months later at age 63.

Part of his happiness was finding a drinking buddy.

"We hit it off from the top," McLean said with a smile. "He liked wine, I liked beer."

Sometimes Alywin stayed overnight in McLean's room to sleep it off after a long night boozing and talking about his problems and hopes for the future. The chipper redhead had mental issues, hepatitis C and was on lifetime parole status, having been in "many" prisons, McLean said.

Then, in January, Aylwin hadn't been seen for several days. He was found dead in his room, cause unknown.

"He had plans," said McLean. "He wanted to clean up and get straight. He wanted to go to Joe Healy Detox (on Page Street) — he had been there before — and wanted me to go with him. But I didn't want to. He needed to get clean so he could work on the hep C — he had to take meds every day and not be drinking."

"This reminds us to get it done in whatever time we have," said Hope.

To end this and other memorials, Hope reads from the 1970 version of the Presbyterian Worship Book about when "the shadows lengthen and the evening comes, and the busy world is hushed, and the fever of life is over and our work is done … grant us peace at last."

She asks the mourners to stand and hold hands.

"Let not your hearts be troubled, neither let them be afraid. Peace I leave with you, and my peace I give to you."

"Now," she says in finality, "turn and give your neighbor the sign of peace."

That's a hug. ●

Linked In: Born in June, Died in April
LOUIS WILLIAMS and TED CARSON

DISPLAYED at the front of the Empress Hotel's community room were tangible remembrances of two residents who died in April — Louis Williams' cane and Ted Carson's plaid bathrobe, black watch cap, glasses and cane. The stereo was playing "Everything I Have Is Yours," a cut from the album of the same name by Billy Eckstein, one of Carson's favorites.

Williams and Carson had known each other when they were homeless and living in a shelter, said Empress Property Manager Roberta Goodman, and both had lived at the Empress for a year before they died in their rooms, Carson at age 79 and Williams at 41. Their birthdays were within a day of each other — June 5 and 6, respectively.

Goodman said the men were more acquaintances than pals, but their recent history on the streets and at the Empress, and various physical ailments, including diabetes, gave them common ground.

Fifteen hotel residents and staff, and medical and social services providers who'd worked with the two men shared stories about them at a memorial.

"I remember being on the elevator with Louis and one of his sons, a College of San Mateo student," said Martha Stein, support services staff member for the hotel. "You could see how proud Louis was of him. The boy had a really strong handshake, and when I commented on it, he said, 'I learned it from my dad.' Louis just beamed," she said.

"I'm going to miss Louis so much," said Pan Fisher, a friend and neighbor. "He's always going to be here with me, but I won't have him to talk to or argue with."

Goodman described how Williams' East Bay relatives — two sons, a twin sister, another sister, a brother and his mother — visited him often at the Empress to take care of him, and, after he died, came for his personal effects.

"They went through his things and kept saying, 'I gave him that,' and 'I gave that to him — and he still had it!' It was touching," she said.

Williams was a sweet man who didn't need much to be content, said a staff member. He'd asked her to help him set up a Netflix account. "He just wanted to sit in his room and enjoy a movie all the way through," she said.

Carson was a demanding resident, but in a delightful, intelligent way. When Public Health nurse Liane Angus brought him Eckstein and Sinatra CDs, he knew every word to every song, she said. "And we'd dance around the office — when he got excited, he just had to move."

His careful enunciation and gift for words were legend in the hotel. Angus did an imitation of him that had all the mourners laughing: "I am most, most gratified, and you look quite wonderful today. Would you like to go to Paris or to Rome with me?"

Several people used less-than-complimentary words to describe Carson — ornery, grumpy, a hoarder who was kicked out of a hotel for that.

"He just made me crazy," said Mike McGinley, Curry Senior Center case management supervisor.

But mostly they recalled his wittiness and generosity. Years on the street had given him the taste for free food and the resourcefulness to

Louis Williams died April 23, 2009

Both brothers
Black men gone
dust
not to be here
found silent
in the Rooms
of God
calling
them
out
in the preparation
of the times they
must Now
spend
in His arms
at Home.

get whatever he could find. He'd "do all the routes," an Empress resident said, and come back with lots of extra food, which he'd pass out to anyone who was hungry.

"I'm just so grateful that he didn't have to die on the street," said case manager Jackie Wilson. "He was here, among people who cared so much for him."

Aaron Jones II, an Empress desk clerk, read a poem that he wrote, "The Memorial to Two, to Ted and Louis," excerpted on previous page. ●

— MARJORIE BEGGS

Ted Carson died April 6, 2009

Open to the Truth
ROSE RIDOLFI

ROSE RIDOLFI generated strong emotions in everyone who knew her, and she had acquaintances throughout the Tenderloin.

"I knew her for two decades," said Rev. Glenda Hope, who officiated at Ridolfi's memorial at the Franciscan Hotel. "I have to say, I wasn't surprised at her passing, but I thought she'd always be around. She was like the little girl who had a curl — when she was good she was very, very good, but when she was bad she was horrid.

"We can talk about Rose like that here," Hope added. "People tell the truth at Tenderloin memorials, that we're all a mix of good and bad."

The rest of the memorial was one story after another about the woman who a year and a half ago had moved from the West Hotel to the Franciscan. Previously, she had lived at TNDC's Ambassador Hotel, the former AIDS SRO at Eddy and Mason streets.

"Oh, she liked to talk, but she always apologized for talking so much," recalled Victoria Barros, Franciscan assistant manager. "You have to think that she was very lonely."

"I respected her courage and how she lived with AIDS," said a neighbor.

Rose Ridolfi died March 8, 2005

"When I first met her, I couldn't stand her," said Leo Chosa, an Ambassador resident. "She was so high-maintenance. She always spoke to me and I may have growled, but she always came back. I came to accept her. She was like an era unto herself. Things won't be the same without her."

Dan O'Connor, St. Anthony's community liaison, said he would always remember Ridolfi as a "wise woman" he respected because she'd listen to the truth and not let it hurt her feelings, even if he told her something brutally honest.

Hope agreed: "She'd come into the chaplaincy at the Ambassador talking in a stream, and I'd just shudder. Once she looked at me and said, 'You don't like me.' It gave me the chance to tell her the truth. I said, 'We just don't know what to expect from you.'"

Ridolfi was severely disabled toward the end of her life. Sunny Lovel, her former visiting nurse, noted that going from being active to a wheelchair can shut a person in and create anger directed at everyone. "A couple of days with her was all I could take," Lovel said.

Mary Ann Finch recalled Ridolfi wanted to go visit her daughter, but delayed because she felt she looked so bad. Finch, who operates the Care Through Touch Institute, which gives fully clothed and seated massages to the homeless and others living on the margins, was approached to give Ridolfi an "extreme makeover," with shower, manicure, haircut.

"I kept putting it off," Finch said ruefully.

Ridolfi's age was unknown. She is survived by a daughter and grandchildren who live near Sacramento and two sisters in Southern California. ●

— MARJORIE BEGGS

Survived Wild '90s at the Ambassador

TERRY DILLARD

IN ITS WILDEST days, the Ambassador Hotel was an important way station in the troubled life of Terry Dillard. Whatever his shortcomings, Dillard made lifelong friends there.

Eight of them gathered at his memorial at the Ambassador, remembering him as a "kind, caring person" who had survived the ravages of the hotel's sex and drug era of the 1990s. The 1911 structure was rundown and reeling from an AIDS epidemic when TNDC bought it in 1999, and remade it.

Terry Dillard died July 4, 2008

"I remember the great card he made for me," said Mary Monihan, a nurse who worked with the hotel's residents. "The colors were like a kaleidoscope, very beautiful. I've thought of it ever since I heard of his passing."

"He worked on it all night," said his good friend Cecil Baker.

Dillard died at St. Francis Hospital, where he was being treated for kidney problems. He was 45. "All his organs shut down," said Baker who had seen Dillard through a battle with AIDS-killer pneumocystis in the 1990s.

Dillard came from an Arkansas family with 14 kids. He never learned to read or write well and left home at 14. He worked a spell in a chicken processing plant before his wanderings took him through New Orleans and eventually into California. The thin, 6-foot-2 man with black hair landed in the Tenderloin. He lived off and on at the Ambassador with friends, and other friends elsewhere, but was basically homeless.

"I knew him here since 1990," Baker said. "He was nice-looking — of course he was god to me. It was the first time I felt love, and I couldn't handle it. I ran away (to Fresno)."

But longtime residents say Ambassador tenants never stay away very long.

"Everybody comes back to their master, the Ambassador," Baker said. "It wasn't just the drugs and sex, it was family."

Baker brought a tray of brownies to share. "Terry once said, 'I don't want you to ever say I can't live without you.' And I said, 'I'll never say that. I'll say I don't know *how* to live without you.'" •

— TOM CARTER

Touched People Deeply

LEO BRADSHAW

REV. GLENDA HOPE has officiated at countless memorials for central city residents, always mixing her keen perception and professional, no-nonsense attitude with kindness that comforts mourners.

So it was disconcerting to see her pause for long stretches and stumble for words at Leo Bradshaw's memorial.

Leo Bradshaw died Dec. 14, 2009

Bradshaw lived at the Senator Hotel on Ellis Street for 14 years. He died in a hospital at age 64.

"At these gatherings, usually you know the person who's died, and I don't," Hope told the 10 SRO residents and staff. "This time, I knew him well — 20 years ago, when he was an electrician. It was before he got into drugs and lost his license, and he did a lot of work at my house and in my yard. I stayed in touch with him for a long time afterward, and Leo's work is still all over my house.

"Leo was really a constant and always a sweet presence among us."

"I knew him a long, long time," said Senator resident Jesse Brown, recapping, with emotion, his relationship with Bradshaw. "Him and me and Jennifer and Pat and old Joe

— we were the old-timers, here from the git-go, close, supergood friends. I ran errands for him, to the post office and the store, and I listened to him. I have a good listening ear."

Brown said he knew Bradshaw's health was failing fast. "When he was taken to the hospital, I wasn't sure he'd be back, but I was still shocked when I heard he was gone."

Case Manager Anne Dudley said Bradshaw had family members who also cared deeply for him, especially his daughter, Tonya. And Tanisha Hughes, tenant services supervisor, remembered his positive attitude, despite his physical ups and downs, and his strong feelings for his Senator community.

"At the end, he talked a lot about his extended family here at the hotel," Hughes said.

At the end of the memorial, Hope added some emotion-tinged levity: "Here's the last thing I want to say about Leo: All my dogs loved him — they knew they could trust him."

Later that day, Hope emailed The Extra: "I barely made it back to the office before I went to pieces. Thankfully, I have loving people here. Grief, as I often say to others, is just the price we pay for love. A more than acceptable tradeoff." ●

— MARJORIE BEGGS

Beautiful Spirit, She Only Wanted Love
LINDA SLINKARD PARSONS

THE CLIENTS at Tenderloin Health were enamored of Linda Parsons' joy, smile and her youth. But in the end, the 13 mourners who attended her memorial knew she had gone to a better place, wherever that may be.

"She was my friend," said a young man in a front seat in the center's lobby, "and she always had a kind word for everyone and a smile on her face. I heard she was in the hospital. And then I heard she had passed."

He turned and sobbed in the arms of a friend.

Linda Slinkard Parsons died of liver failure after suffering in St. Francis Hospital for a month, her friends said. She was 37. Four pictures on a table in front, beside a bouquet and two lighted candles, showed her smiling; two photos showed her steady companion of three years, James Sellars, who didn't show up for the memorial.

"I know she's in a better place," said case worker Sandra Torres. "She had HIV and hepatitis C, and she was in a lot of pain."

"She had a beautiful spirit," said another, "and I just know she's up there looking down, hoping we're doing the right thing."

Five years ago, the blonde Parsons left her parents and her children — sons Jacob, Joey and Alex and daughter Amanda — in Sacramento. The case worker said the estranged young woman came to the city to party and at the time was HIV-negative. She was living in a Leavenworth Street hotel.

Linda Parsons died May 8, 2008

"She was sociable and caring and all she wanted was a stable, loving relationship," Torres said.

Parsons' therapist and Torres said that in her final days Parsons made up with her mother and oldest son, Jacob, 18. A service was held for her in Sacramento. ●

— TOM CARTER

The Man on the Cover
ERNIE MERCHANT

ERNIE MERCHANT, the face of the moment of TNDC, but for 15 years the heart of the Ritz Hotel, died in June after battling illnesses for several months.

A black and white photo of Merchant, wearing a hat and jacket in front of the Ambassador Hotel, graces the cover of the nonprofit TNDC's just published "Strategic Plan, 2008-2012," along with a color photo of the renovated hotel.

The former nurse's aide and maintenance man greeted each day with a smile, was generous and got along with everybody, said the three friends who attended his memorial.

"He was a beautiful human being," said one man. "He shared with everybody and he loved doing it."

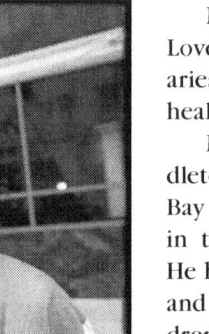

Ernie Merchant died May 20, 2008
PHOTO COURTESY TNDC

Merchant died in Pacifica at Gift of Love AIDS hospice, run by the Missionaries of Charity, after fighting failing health for months. He was 69.

Merchant left his hometown of Middletown, Ohio, to make his life in the Bay Area, the friends said. He served in the Army but didn't go overseas. He had a brother who he lost track of, and was once married but had no children. Merchant had been a nurse's aide at UCSF Medical Center and San Francisco General Hospital, and a maintenance man at the nearby Ambassador and other hotels.

Tyrone Perry, a 12-year friend, said that in January he didn't see Merchant for a week. Staff said he went to the hospital and never returned.

"He was an energetic man and took pride in himself," Perry said. "He helped people individually, and shared his food and his room."

Three bouquets in cellophane lay on a table, awaiting a vase in the hotel's community kitchen where the memorial was held. ●

— TOM CARTER

Sports Talk Show Regular
CARLOS NUNEZ

BOXING FANS lost a colorful sports commentator when Carlos Nunez, a regular contributor on Tony Bruno's "Into the Night" radio show and Gary Radnich's broadcasts during the day on KNBR, died after collapsing in front of Boeddeker Park, a block from his Ritz Hotel room.

At Nunez's memorial at the Ritz, Craig Martinez said his friend had been in apparent good health but had collapsed the other morning at Eddy and Jones at the park gate. Paramedics arrived, but after 45 minutes still couldn't revive the 74-year-old Cuban American.

Nunez frequently called the three-hour, weeknight Bruno show and Radnich's KNBR 680 weekday morning show twice weekly. The talk show hosts always welcomed

Nunez's comments with a hearty, "Buenos dias, Carlos!" before Nunez launched into the fine points of some fighter's skills or explained what made another great. Radnich frequently saw Nunez at sports events.

"Whenever you talked to Carlos," Radnich said from his studio, "he always had a twinkle in his eye and a smile on his face. He could poke fun at himself and he could come back and poke fun at you with a back-and-forth. He was a great, great guy."

Nunez commented on other sports, too, and promoted American sports to Latino youth. But his specialty was boxing.

"He was on (radio) at least once a week," said William Leary, a social worker who formerly worked at the Ritz where Nunez lived for 13 years. "They dedicated a program to him, talked about him, remembered him. Bruno's show-previews used his voice, too. I heard him hundreds of times."

Nunez was born in Cuba. His father was a doctor. Linda Barr, a neighbor, said Nunez was in the Bay of Pigs battle and was taken prisoner. "The United States traded a tractor for him and he came to Florida," she said. "But he didn't want to talk much about his past." His friends thought he came to California in the 1970s, but were unsure when he arrived in San Francisco.

A half dozen friends drew a colorful personality profile of Nunez who looked younger than his age. He loved adults and children, Latin music and dancing salsa, singing karaoke, and all sports, even sailing. His press connections got him into Giants' home games. He also wrote movie reviews for newspapers. Someone said he once interviewed Cher in Las Vegas as part of his sports and entertainment contribution on a sports channel.

PHOTO COURTESY LINDA BARR

Carlos Nunez died Feb. 2, 2011

He was very neat and insisted his clothes be dry-cleaned. But sometimes he was broke and hit up his friend Martinez for a loan, using a big trophy he had won as collateral. Nunez won the 20-inch-high, gold-colored trophy topped with a boxing figurine in 2000 for being "Spanish Boxing Broadcaster of the Year," the inscription on the base reads. But the organization giving the prize isn't mentioned. Barr said she thought it came from the American Broadcasting Association.

"He'd leave it as collateral and I'd give him 50 bucks," said Martinez, holding the piece he brought along to show everyone. "We did this over the years, maybe five or six times. He'd always pay me when he got his monthly check."

Nunez got his check on the third day of each month, Martinez said. But when he died Martinez was still holding the trophy.

Martinez eyed it with admiration. "It must be worth something," he said but was unsure what to do with it.

"I just don't want it to go into mothballs," he said. ●

— TOM CARTER

Gone With the Wind
JENS LARSEN

JENS LARSEN lived a life that was quiet, self-sufficient, private. When he died at age 84, no one at the Franciscan Towers, where he'd lived for 23 years, knew the cause. His records listed no family, and the several hotel residents who attended his memorial said he'd never talked about his past.

"But he was my neighbor and friend, the kindest old man, and I loved him," said Tom Edward Heintz Jr., who has lived at Franciscan Towers for 23 years. "We'd pass in the hall, say 'hi.' I might ask if he'd seen anything good on TV, or if he'd read any good books. The last book he mentioned was Gone With the Wind — I can't read, but I sure wouldn't mind reading that."

Jens Larsen died Oct. 4, 2005

Through Larsen's open door, Heintz said, he could see a clean, almost bare room, nothing much more than a bed, a chair and a TV. "And he never cooked," Heintz said. "I'd see him bringing in his food — all TV dinners."

Hotel social worker Liz Delgadillo said she remembered Larsen as independent, someone who never asked for any special assistance. He was still mobile when he took ill, and was hospitalized a month before he died.

"I'd see him walking with his cane and he looked so fragile," Delgadillo said, "but if I asked how he was doing, he always said, 'Fine.' "

Midway through the memorial service, officiated by Rev. Glenda Hope, three more neighbors stopped by: Penny and Phillip Abraham and their 15-month-old daughter, Jasmine. They'd lived across the hall from Larsen for seven months.

"I'd stop him and tell him if he needed anything to let me know," Penny Abraham said.

Phillip told the small gathering that the Abrahams knew that Larsen had died in the hospital. "We could smell death, we could sense death."

From her stroller, Jasmine cooed and made sweet baby noises. When her mother tried to hush her, Hope intervened. "No, don't stop her," Hope said. "She reminds us of all the good things in the world." ●

— MARJORIE BEGGS

Constant Advocate for Alcoholics, Addicts
'SELFLESS' SAM VARNADO

THE IMPACT Sam Varnado had on the lives of many alcoholics and addicts in the city was in great evidence at his memorial service in a community room of a low-cost family apartment building at 555 Ellis St. One by one they stood, gave their first name, declared their addiction, got greeted noisily by the others, then told of their experience with the charismatic man they said never stopped giving of himself. Some said he saved their life.

Varnado's fervent message that they counted for something — even when they were soiled and in a gutter someplace — gave them strength and hope to carry on, they said. Indeed, they agreed Varnado would drop everything in a second to come to the aid of an alcoholic in trouble.

Some sentiments were delivered through tears as more than 40 mourners told how special Varnado was to them.

A Vietnam War veteran, Varnado died at Veterans Administration Hospital after battling liver cancer for five weeks. He was 59. From his Facebook page it was known he attended college in Arkansas in 1972 and came to California a year or two later.

"He was an amazing man," said Rev. Glenda Hope, who conducted the memorial. She had known Varnado since 1996. She let him run AA meetings at her Network Ministries' office.

"They called it Sober Across the Board," Hope said. "And it was held in our former 366 Eddy St. space until we moved in our computer center and then it went to the William Penn Hotel at 160 Eddy."

Varnado, once a homeless alcoholic, led the sessions for more than 10 years at 8 a.m. six days a week, convinced that the same time, same place were essential for anyone in need. His invitation to "keep coming back" became his mantra. And on Sundays, he volunteered all day at Laguna Honda Hospital across town.

"Sam was an extremely selfless person and gave all his time and energy to others," said his friend, Abdi Habad, who had visited him in the hospital. "Sam related to other addicts and alcoholics in a special way because he knew the suffering of addiction."

Varnado was an imposing figure — well over 6 feet, handsome, with a bass voice and a warm smile that had wondrous melting powers.

Sam Varnado died March 30, 2010

"He'd stop me on the street and say, 'Come to a meeting,'" said one woman. "He helped me save my life. He was there no matter what shape you were in, even in the gutter."

"He was there 24 hours for everybody," said a man. "He was a patriarch and mentor, a friend to everyone," said another, as more alcoholics stood and tried to find fitting phrases equal to the love that welled up:

"He never met a stranger."

"He was a stalwart, the JFK of recovery."

"He was smart as a whip — he helped me with my English composition when I was in school."

"I never saw him alone — he was always with someone."

"He made me feel peaceful and hopeful, and I kept coming to meetings because of Sam."

"He taught me it's never too late to be of service."

"We had wonderful conversations."

An example of Varnado's enterprise came in 1990 when he walked into Daniel Bacon's law office wanting to sue Catholic Charities. He and Bacon shared the same primary care doctor, who encouraged patients to network.

"When he was in my office," Bacon said, "Sam saw a stack of outgoing mail that was to be served on people. He said, 'Hey, I can do that.' And he became a process server for me. He worked at a credenza in my office and took other lawyers as clients, too, and formed his own company, Quick Serve.

"He worked part-time. But when he was there, and anyone called and needed help, he'd leave right away."

To conclude, a man stood and sang a cappella, "Let There Be Peace on Earth" in a flawless and dynamic baritone.

Hope assured everyone then that Varnado "wasn't perfect" — and there may be "unresolved anger and sorrow and grief in the room." But that the things Varnado stood for — "reaching out, befriending and standing with people in recovery and being there for anyone" — are beacons to follow.

Varnado was to be cremated and his ashes buried at the Sacramento Valley National Cemetery in Dixon. And a memorial was to be held for him at Laguna Honda Hospital. ●

— TOM CARTER

Janitor, Union Man
JOSEPH JACKSON

WHEN SOMEONE commented on Joe Jackson's faithful attendance at Coast Hotel memorials — as Rev. Glenda Hope once did — he'd quip:

"If you don't go to your friends' funerals, they won't come to yours." It amused Jackson to quote the Yogi Berra paradox, tongue-in-cheek.

Memorials were close to Jackson's heart. He had been the first to encourage memorials at the Coast. A few months ago, before a memorial began, he distributed copies of two Central City Extra obituaries featuring residents. He said he believed in the dignity the obits bestowed on the have-nots. He had sought, and received, the newspaper's permission to reproduce the stories.

Such was the sensitivity of a man who was something of a paradox himself. As a promising English graduate student, articulate and mannerly, he later chose a janitorial career and became a lifelong activist fighting to improve conditions for workers and the poor.

Joe Jackson died of heart problems at S.F. General, where he had been hospitalized 3½ months. He was 70.

Jackson had lived at the Coast for 24 years, longest of any resident. He assumed the guardianship of the SRO and its formerly homeless tenants, while he took on other community issues, attended neighborhood meetings and advocated at City Hall hearings.

Joe Jackson died Dec. 9, 2009

"I know if he were here today — and I feel he is — he'd want to quote Joe Hill — 'Don't mourn, organize,' " said Joan Jackson, Joe's former wife.

She was among 20 mourners, including the Jacksons' 40-year-old son Neil, seated in a semicircle in the Coast community room. The former Mrs. Jackson recalled how passionate her husband was, but when she said how she always worried about Joe's eating habits, a woman assured her that she made sure he ate a good meal every day. Another woman said Jackson was crazy about her meatloaf.

"Oh, I'm thankful," Joan Jackson said. "But he didn't take care of himself, and that's why he's not with us now."

Joe Jackson was born and raised in Pasadena. He met his future wife when he came to school in San Francisco. "I knew him 50 years," Joan Jackson said, "we discovered the city together. Oh, it was so much fun. And he was an incredibly smart guy."

FAMILY PHOTO
Joseph Jackson at age 21

She passed around a photo of him taken in his parents' backyard in Pasadena when he was 21, just before he arrived in San Francisco. The mourners marveled at his good looks.

In the mid- and late-1960s, Jackson attended San Francisco City College — growing his activist beard in 1964 — went on to San Francisco State where he earned a B.A. in history. In grad school, his professors encouraged him to pursue creative writing, which he did, as a teaching assistant. By then he was immersed in political issues.

He was in Chicago's Grant Park on Aug. 28, 1968, with 10,000 other demonstrators during the Democratic National Convention. Police charged in, clubbing, gassing and arresting Yippies. Joan Jackson recalls watching the television news fearfully. But her young husband wasn't bashed or carted off to jail, and the experience, she said, became "a high point in his life." She was glued to the radio during the 1968 S.F. State student strike over the need for diversity. But Jackson, then a graduate student and strike leader, eluded jail again. His labor friends said later the experience turned him into a lifelong activist.

Jackson soon dropped out of school and took a job as a janitor. He became an activist in SEIU Local 87. Joan Jackson became a librarian in Mill Valley. Her husband was an indefatigable speaker and champion of leafletting. Unhappy with the leadership, his enthusiasms led him to form a dissident rank-and-file group called Workers for a Strong Union. It got him temporarily kicked out of the union.

A memorial for Jackson had been held in Golden Gate Avenue SEIU union hall a week earlier, and his old cronies had assembled to remember the fiery labor leader. Tenderloin Housing Clinic, too, planned a memorial. Jackson had gone to Sacramento with the nonprofit group to protest rising Lifeline telephone costs, his ex-wife said.

At the Coast, Jackson became known for keeping abreast of political topics affecting the residents. He could scarcely wait to launch into the issues in conversation with anyone who would listen. Several residents said they learned from him. "Yes," said one man, "we gotta stick together. He kept saying that. He was a pleasant soul and politically motivated. He could light up and spark a dialogue."

Support Services Manager Scott Ecker said Jackson was suspicious of him when Episcopal Community Services began its staffing at the Care Not Cash hotel, "until he realized we were all on the same page. Then we were fine."

In a final paradox, Jackson became a new man in the hospital.

"They shaved off his beard and cut his hair," his ex-wife said. "His son had never seen him without a beard — and I fell in love with him all over again."

Joan Jackson remained afterward talking with residents, fitting faces to the names her husband had mentioned during her hospital visits. ●

— TOM CARTER

Hospitality House Icon
KAREN WASHINGTON

MORE THAN 60 mourners jammed the Central City Hospitality House reception room to bid an emotional farewell to a charismatic woman who transformed herself — and many of them — becoming a beloved peer counselor to countless clients at the landmark Turk Street service. For six years, Karen Washington, who insisted on being called "Ms. Washington," was a popular figure at the self-help center that serves 6,000 homeless and poverty-stricken clients a year. A strong person who could handle a barrage of details at a time, the 5-foot-8, 180-pound transgender woman started as a client, then became a volunteer and soon a full-time staff member. She left her peer advocate job when she was diagnosed with cancer. She died at 61.

"Everybody here makes their mark in their way," said Jackie Jenks, longtime executive director of Hospitality House. "Her mark was her caring personality. She challenged people to grow in their individual lives. She created a space here for transgenders and facilitated the support group. She'd talk about her 'girls' and how we needed to provide for them.

Karen Washington died April 10, 2007

"She was a larger-than-life presence in the drop-in center, especially during the evening shift. And she started the outings. The folks here were her family."

Washington used to say that people needed to get out of the neighborhood to see how they could enjoy themselves elsewhere. She organized picnics, trips to the zoo and parks, even a trek to see the Blue Angels soar and roar, Jenks recalled.

But Washington wasn't always so confident. Rev. Glenda Hope, who conducted the memorial, said she first met Washington 15 years ago at Network Ministries, which Hope founded, when Washington came looking for human contact. One reason Washington was reclusive then was because she was ashamed of her bad teeth.

To motivate herself to get her teeth fixed, Washington said she needed someone else to care. She asked Hope: "Will you be my friend?" Hope said yes. And the next time the two met on the street, Washington flashed the beaming smile of gleaming teeth that would later enhance her popularity.

"She had incredible courage and will to transform her depressed and isolated state to become the Ms. Washington we all know and love," Hope said. "She gave away so much love to so many."

Several mourners recalled her personal advice to them and how they had cherished her counsel. One man said she was a shining example of the self-help that the center holds dear. "I loved the woman," he said. Four people sang songs to her in tribute. "She never looked down on anybody," said Karen. "I saw her give away her lunch to someone who was hungry. She had a lot of capacity, something that's lacking in the world." ●

— TOM CARTER

A Tireless Force for Seniors
JOHN MELONE

FOR A MAN who publicly pushed as hard as he could for others, especially seniors, John Melone kept an exceptionally low personal profile. When he died at a hospice in Richmond, the Contra Costa County coroner's office could find no relatives. Neither could staff at Canon Kip in San Francisco, where, for many years, Melone had been first a client, then a volunteer.

At his memorial at Universal Unitarian Church, speaker after speaker praised Melone's tenacity and feistiness in advocating for senior housing and health care, but personal anecdotes were spare.

John Melone died Oct. 8, 2009

"John just didn't talk about himself," said Hene Kelly, board member of Senior Action Network and the California Alliance for Retired Americans. "But he did the job of many. You can be sure, John will not rest in peace. He's an organizer, so you can enjoy yourself when you get there. He fought for all of us."

Melone, a Vietnam War veteran, was 74 when he died from complications of liver cancer and brain cancer.

More than 50 people gathered in the modern, airy church community room for the memorial, which opened with music from the Canon Kip Senior Band and introductions by Rev. Glenda Hope of S.F. Network Ministries and Zen Buddhist priest Jana Drakha, who co-officiated.

"John was a friend of mine, a political ally, one of the first volunteers for our computer center 15 years ago," Hope said. "It was John who had the idea that we should have seniors-only time at the center, and he helped people fix their computers."

Melone had come through "some tough stuff — homelessness and painful illnesses," Hope said later. "He could be a curmudgeon sometimes, clashing with clients, but he was someone you could always talk to. He was a voice for the voiceless."

Melone also spent hours at the computer at Senior Action Network, where he was an activist for 10 years and a board member for five. He tracked senior-related legislation rigorously, sending copious email messages with complicated legislative attachments to fellow activists.

"We fought a lot," said Jodi Reid, executive director of Northern California Alliance for Retired Americans. "This man was stubborn and that's what made him so committed. He forced me to figure out his legislative summaries and Excel spreadsheets." And, she said, for that she thanked him.

Barbara Blong, Senior Action Network executive director, called Melone "a force to be reckoned with. It was John who put us on the map."

Remembrances were filled with pugilistic motifs.

"John was a fighter — I'd see him every day at SAN, checking his computer to see what was going on in Sacramento," said James Chionsini, Planning for Elders health care action team member. "He was one of those people who came out swinging and never stopped. He's probably up there organizing right now."

As a Senior Action Network board member, Melone represented SAN at the South of Market Project Area Committee, which advises the Redevelopment Agency.

SOMPAC Parliamentarian Raymon Smith called Melone "a true warrior, a sincere man who walked the walk and brought invaluable insights." Smith sang a few bars from "Kansas City," which reminded him of how Melone tackled issues: " 'I might take a train, I might take a plane, but if I have to walk, I'm goin' just the same.' John got to meetings however he could," Smith added. "He never accepted that something couldn't be done."

Others besides seniors benefited from Melone's hard work at SOMPAC. Alex Torres, executive director of Bindlestiff Studio, was here to honor Melone. Torres credits him with helping Bindlestiff, the performance company of emerging Filipino American artists, get a permanent home in the Plaza Apartments at Sixth and Howard streets.

"John was fair when considering Bindlestiff," Torres said. "He didn't just give us a pass — he asked good questions, and when he understood us, he supported us."

Another part of Melone's life came to light through Michael Lyon, who said they met at S.F. General Hospital when Lyon was a medical equipment repairman. "John was a social worker in the AIDS clinic and other places in the hospital — he seemed to be everywhere and always active," Lyon said. "I'll miss his sense of urgency."

San Francisco was just one base for Melone's activism. A Richmond resident for many years, he earned kudos for his Contra Costa County work on behalf of seniors and, after he died, a commendation from the county Board of Supervisors, which Arnie Kasendorf, chairman of the Richmond Commission on Aging and president of the Richmond AARP, read aloud at the memorial. San Francisco and state officials weighed in, too.

"He was a gift to our city, especially to those who are struggling and those who have the least," Supervisor Chris Daly stepped up and told the mourners. "He was a real hero of those without anything."

Hene Kelly read a California Assembly tribute, signed by Tom Ammiano, and a state Senate certificate of recognition signed by Mark Leno. Both were Melone's representatives and beneficiaries of his activism. "John loved tracking their legislation — for health, housing, benefits —and they appreciated him," Kelly said.

Kelly also introduced David Phillips, whom Melone met 28 years ago in San Francisco: "When David was struggling with drugs and was homeless, John invited David to come live with him and found him a job at the Chronicle," she said. "Later, when Mr. Melone was homeless himself, David invited him to live with him in Richmond."

She described a tiny computer flash drive that she carries in her purse, a gift from Phillips to her after Melone's death. He wore the drive, which holds a huge collection of legislation files, on a lanyard around his neck so he'd have access to the information as he moved from computer to computer.

"I also have some of John's ashes," Kelly said. "I think I'll place some of them where John always tried, but never managed, to get in — in Sen. Feinstein's and Gov. Schwarzenegger's offices."

— MARJORIE BEGGS

Lives on as a Garden
LINDA CHIKERE

A BRIGHT LIGHT burned out at the San Cristina Residence when Linda "SuSu" Chikere died in her room of complications from AIDS.

Known for her tenant organizing since 1992 and driving personality, Chikere had recently returned from the hospital, rejecting doctors' advice to stay under care. She wanted to go "home," she said. When her condition worsened, she refused an ambulance back to the hospital. She was 49.

Chikere helped organize the hotel's first tenant board in 1993, soon after Community Housing Partnership renovated it. Alternately cantankerous and loving, she became the board's first president, served nine years and inspired a host of tenants to join the board and speak up for their rights.

More than 50 friends celebrated her life, packing a small room off the hotel lobby. A dozen lined the walls.

"I look at this gathering and know this was quite a woman with a legacy of love of life and drawing people into the larger community," said Rev. Glenda Hope.

Marcelee Watkins and Earl Gadsen sang solos a cappella and their voices filled the room. Clapping and humming, the crowd got down with Gadsen's rendition of "Take My Hand Precious Lord."

"In honor of people who give help, we honor SuSu," Gadsen said. The nickname, her sister Lucille Daymon said, she gave herself.

Linda Chikere died Feb. 18, 2007

Chikere was well-known for being tough and "cussing people out," yet she won people's hearts. She was a "beautiful, strong woman" who advised people wisely.

"Very sweet, very feisty," said former San Cristina Manager Brian Quinn.

"She got me out of my shell," said a friend of 10 years. "She said get out and talk to people. I became a photographer. She's up there now wanting a bigger house — and saying she deserves it."

"She was unofficially known as 'the warden,'" another man recalled.

A resident told of the time he was making french fries in the community kitchen not long after he moved in, but somebody ruined the batch and he was so furious he wanted to lash out. But Chikere calmed him down. "'Don't worry about it, baby,' she told me, 'your housing is more important.'"

She had battled AIDS for years and at 5-feet-4 weighed 75 pounds when she died, said Laurie Rudner, her friend of a dozen years. "She came back," said Rudner, "and we were lucky enough to say goodbye."

Chikere's spirit filled the room, her friends said repeatedly. They said they needed to remember that the gathering was an inspiration to come together more frequently as a supportive family.

Tenant board President Benjamin Wynn said the board wanted to name the hotel lobby's garden with its tropical wall mural painted by residents and fountain "SuSu Garden." ●

— TOM CARTER

Activist With a Radio Voice
ROBERT SMITH

ROBERT SMITH was as at ease in City Hall as on the street when expounding in his resonant voice on his favorite topic: affordable housing for the poor.

He was a familiar sight alongside fellow activists, a tall, thin, Southern gentleman dressed typically in T-shirt and baseball cap and carrying a rumpled paperback mystery novel held together with a rubber band.

Robert Smith died March 7, 20100

"He had a knack for simplifying gobbledygook and making things understandable," said James Tracy of Community Housing Partnership, among more than a dozen mourners at Smith's memorial at the CHP-owned and -operated Senator Hotel. "He was always very excited about housing and knew how to use his voice for public speaking."

Smith died in the Senator Hotel where he'd lived for 11 years. He was 52. The medical examiner has not determined the cause of death..

Smith's friends said he was from Alabama, where he'd been a radio announcer. He came to San Francisco in the 1980s. Smith was seeking a more tolerant environment, Tracy said, but came to realize that real change to eliminate racism would "have to come up from the South" — because San Franciscans "were too polite" to confront racism.

Smith testified at city hearings on affordable housing for the poor, was active with the Coalition on Homelessness and promoted Safe Havens, shops that offer safety and a phone call to anyone fleeing street violence. He served on the neighborhood committee of activists that adopted the Safe Haven concept four years ago.

"He had a Southern accent and was always pleasant and thoughtful," said one mourner.

"He was very grateful for the services at the hotel and often expressed that," said another. "He was glad to be here. But outside of his activism, he kept to himself."

Tracy will remember Smith as a "Southern gentleman" always ready to help causes that aid the poor.

"I could put him on a phone bank — and with that voice — he was fantastic," Tracy said. ●

— TOM CARTER

4 Who Died Days Apart
FELICIANO DIAZ, KATHLEEN GANNON, MARK STROFACE, LINDA RAE LEE

DEATH CAST ITS PALL over the Alexander Residence when four neighbors died within days of each other, two at S.F. General and two in their rooms in the 179-unit Eddy Street SRO. The unusual coincidence gave residents a righteous pause, if not mortality jitters, and grief set in like a low fever.

"It really hit us, tenants and staff," said manager Theresa Flores. "It is really, really hard for people. Basically, seniors are here and some have lived here more than a decade." About a third of the residents are Filipino, a quarter Chinese, the remainder pretty evenly mixed.

Flores said a dozen sorrowing tenants came to the office to update their emergency contact sheet. The staff suggested having a grief and loss seminar and doing more frequent "well checks." Mark Stroface was dead for four days before he was discovered.

But, to bring a measure of peace and assurance to the hotel, one immediate line of action was apparent: Call Rev. Glenda Hope to conduct a memorial service.

Rev. Hope is a legend in the Tenderloin for giving a spiritual closure to a life. And every life, to her, is worth celebrating. Requests average two or more a month. The Alexander's request for a memorial for four is rare.

Hope introduced herself to the gathering of 24 residents and staff seated on the mezzanine. "Every one of us is a child of God," she said. The memorial honored Feliciano Diaz, Kathleen Gannon, Mark Stroface and Linda Rae Lee, four lives that reflected an intriguing Tenderloin diversity.

"It is important that we remember who has been born," Hope said, then read Scriptures followed by a prayer.

Behind her a table held candles, statues of Mary and two angels, and cards signed by the residents. Above the table, flyers proclaimed the names of the deceased with their birth and death years. Across the mezzanine, fruit, croissant sandwiches and sodas were ready for after the service. As always, Hope invited participants to speak about the departed.

Feliciano Diaz died Aug. 23, 2004

Maria Diaz, a tiny lady of 73, rose to speak quietly in a quavering voice about her late husband, Feliciano, a Muni driver for five years who died of diabetes. Diaz was handsome and he loved late nights of mah-jong and dancing. He squired her nine years, taking her to church but never attending.

Then his disease got real bad. They married last February. Just weeks later his leg was amputated. But the wounds wouldn't heal. They moved to the Alexander. She changed his dressings three times daily before he went to the hospital for the last time.

His last night, she said, over and over he asked God to take him. She lay down beside him and held his hand. The nurse came in an hour later and he was dead. Feliciano was 60.

"His last night," Mrs. Diaz whispered, "my husband, a good man, say, 'I will wait for you in heaven.'"

Kathleen Gannon died Aug. 13, 2004

Kathleen Gannon had lived at the Alexander since 1999. She was 52 when she died in her room of a pulmonary disorder, "natural causes," the medical examiner called it. Few people knew the short, wide woman because she had kept so to herself. Even her next-door neighbor couldn't say what Gannon was really like other than she was mannerly, quiet and alone.

Mark Stroface died Aug. 18, 2004

"Mark was a good friend of mine," James Willis announced in a booming voice from the back. "He never had anything bad to say about people. And he was upset by evil. I'm sorry he's gone. We'll be poorer without him.

"We're here for you, Debra," Willis concluded, glancing over at Mark Stroface's girlfriend of 20 years, Debra Worchesger.

She met Stroface in Healdsburg 23 years ago. He was a plumber then. After taking classes, he became a computer wizard, but didn't own a PC. He was a licensed minister, too, and wrote religious poems. His favorite movie, she said, was "Michael," starring John Travolta as an angel.

But heroin ruined him, she said. A narcon shot from paramedics two years ago was a life reprieve from an overdose.

She had knocked on his door for four days with no reply. An assistant manager found him, dead at 54, with his arm tied off and a needle stuck in his shirt.

"He was spiritual and that's what attracted me to him," Worchesger said. "I could have helped this time. But he had to do something for himself and didn't. Maybe it was a hot shot. Maybe he just said, 'Enough, let me out of it.'"

Linda Rae Lee died Aug. 20, 2004

It is unlikely that anyone at the memorial knew the life story of Linda Rae Lee, who died in the hospital of bone cancer at 62. Her next-door neighbor said only that she had once befriended her during a power blackout. Lee was painfully bedridden then and sharing a two-room space on the 11th floor with her husband, George Ray Lee, 79, also bedridden.

George Ray said his quick-witted wife had had a career as stripper and fan dancer Honey West. She had married into the Kansas City mob, he said, but her husband got rubbed out in a garage door explosion. Lee said she also went to City College and S.F. State and in her 50s nearly got her law degree from UC Hastings. They were married 25 years ago in San Quentin when he was in prison. Their relationship, Lee said, was platonic.

Rev. Hope slipped over her shoulders a white stole that her mother had made for her shortly before she died. "All of us have a lot of grief in the Tenderloin," Hope said. She read Scripture about souls finding "peace at last."

The memorial ended, as do all with Rev. Hope as officiant, with the mourners holding hands in a circle. She offered a short prayer and asked them to turn to the next person and give the "sign of peace." Most were confused by this until they saw a few people hugging and they followed suit.

It felt like both a conclusion and a beginning. ●

— TOM CARTER

A Man of Many Parts, All Good
JOSEPH SOLDIVELA

JOYFUL JOSEPH "Doctor Joe" Soldivela was a poet, songwriter and singer who gladly shared his gifts, thereby becoming the life, if not the patriarch, of the Hamlin Hotel where he lived 10 years.

The retired dentist was in his third-floor room watching John Wayne in "True Grit" with his visiting son, Greg, when he said he should have taken his heart medicine an hour ago. He walked to the medicine cabinet, dropped to one knee, fell over and died. He was 78.

"I went to him and a neighbor came," the son said after Soldivela's memorial. "But I couldn't do anything for him. He hadn't been sick but he had heart problems. The paramedics were there immediately."

Greg, a frequent visitor, said his dad had auditioned for the annual Hamlin talent show the day before. Soldivela played ukulele and four-string guitar and sang songs he composed. He won the contest twice and once came in third.

Joseph Soldivela died Jan. 28, 2011

"He wrote songs and poetry about things he thought about ever since I was a child," Greg told the 14 mourners. "I liked the way he thought. He was a good father and a good friend. He taught me don't hit women, spoil 'em. And he spoiled me and my mother. But I'm at a loss here. He was one of my favorites."

The Hamlin desk clerk said Joe Soldivela liked making people laugh and always had something nice to say. One day he called her and said if he won the talent show he'd take her to dinner. And he did.

"A charming ladies man," someone called him.

"He was more than a loving person," another said. "He was an awesome person."

When I Am Gone

When I am gone, release me,
and let me go
I have so many things to see
and do
you mustn't tie yourself to me
with too many tears
but be thankful we had so
many good years.
Though you can't see or touch
me, I will be near
and if you listen with your
heart,
you'll hear all my love around
you soft and dear.

"Yes, a great man, my family man," said another. "He liked Joe Louis, I liked Ali."

"He was the patriarch of the Hamlin," his neighbor from the third floor piped up. "He leaves a big hole. And who's going to fill it?"

Soldivela was born in Los Angeles, earned a degree from UC Berkeley, but his son didn't know which dental school he went to. And he didn't know how long his father had a dental practice at Portola and Evelyn streets in a far out San Francisco neighborhood. But Greg did recall that his stepmother had died in 1997.

After the memorial, a short, wiry black woman burst into the community room carrying a guitar case and a large piece of cardboard. She couldn't stop crying. Through her tears she said she was Joni Perkins, Soldivela's wife, then corrected that: "girlfriend."

"He proposed to me but we weren't married," Perkins said. She first met Soldivela in a shelter in 1998 and they hit it off.

She lives on the fourth floor, but they were together a lot. They loved going out to the Olive Garden in Stonestown to eat. "He wrote a song about me and sang it in the talent show," she said. It was the year Dr. Joe won third place.

The room was practically deserted now and Perkins cried softly as she methodically taped the cardboard to the wall close to a piece of butcher paper where residents had written farewells to "Doctor Joe."

The cardboard had information about the day's memorial on it, separate pictures of the smiling Dr. Joe and Perkins, and a poem he had written about his own death, "When I Am Gone." ●

— TOM CARTER

Security Guard With Good Friends
LACY GRIFFIN

LACY GRIFFIN, a lanky and youthful-looking security guard who liked wearing button-down collar shirts in his off hours, died peacefully in his sleep at the Ambassador Hotel where he had lived more than 14 years.

"I didn't know him well, but he was quiet and polite," said social worker Ivet Lemus. "He was very neat. I thought he was in his 30s."

Lacy Griffin died Oct. 17, 2006

Griffin was 52.

After his friend Jerry Kirby missed seeing him around the hotel for two days he asked management to check his room. Assistant Manager Barry Stevens found Griffin lying on his bed, his head resting on a stuffed alligator that Kirby had given him.

"It's very emotional to discover someone like that," said Stevens. "Everything in the room was neat and tidy and he looked asleep. I clapped loudly. But I could see he wasn't breathing. Then I closed the door and went downstairs and called the police."

The social workers at his memorial said Griffin had lost weight recently but appeared healthy. The medical examiner's office didn't yet have a cause of death.

Griffin was an unusual SRO denizen. The 6-foot-2 former Air Force airman was employed full time as a security guard and seemed to have no problems or character blemishes. He had no drug or alcohol addictions, but was a cigarette smoker. His friends said he never caused trouble. He liked movies, they said, especially science fiction.

Kirby brought Griffin's favorite shirt to the memorial for the four people in the room to see. He hung it on the window latch above a table with a small vase on it that contained three white lilies. Kirby lit a candle. The handsome, short-sleeve garment featured deep red masks and red candles with yellow flames figured on a rich tan background showing Africa with its longitude and latitude lines.

They knew each other nine years. Kirby played a rousing gospel song they were fond of on a cassette player. "There's a leak in this old building," it began.

"I gave him a pedicure the day before he died," Kirby said. "I am so glad I did. I kept some things of mine in his room. I cried when he died. I thought it was a dirty trick. We do feel it. We do hurt. And then I thought, oh, I am so glad someone cared about me." ●

— TOM CARTER

Gospel Singer Has Caring Neighbors
LEE JENKINS

SAN FRANCISCO-BORN Lee "Pop" Jenkins, a gospel singer and former amateur boxer, was remembered as a kind man who was easy to talk to, with friends eager to help him as his health deteriorated.

Jenkins was 58 when he died at St. Francis Hospital from respiratory complications, two weeks before his first grandchild was born, an event he longed to live for, said his friends at his Dalt Hotel memorial. A family service had already been held.

Jenkins was HIV-positive, but asthma and emphyzema had him in and out of the hospital for the 2 ½ years he lived at the Dalt. In recent months he was in a wheelchair.

"My husband was a friend of his and asked me to take care of him," said Irma Crandle. "So I did for many months, like he was my own. We all called him Pop." Jenkins lived in Room 448 and the Crandles in Room 445. "I was raised up to try to help people. I was glad I could do that. It helped me out of my own depression."

Crandle said Jenkins told her she looks strikingly like his mother. Crandle got him walking a little but his legs were badly ulcerated. She finally said he should go back to the hospital.

Lee Jenkins died Jan. 26, 2007

"He was very depressed over the holidays," she said. "And he was afraid if he went he wouldn't come back."

He didn't.

Jenkins' brother, James, who lives in the hotel, didn't attend the memorial but said afterward that Lee liked singing and had boxed in Golden Gloves competition. But he wouldn't elaborate.

"Oh, we used to sing together," said Crandle, who had gone upstairs to get her photo of him. "In our rooms, in the car, on the sidewalk. I hadn't done that since my choir days. He made me get up and go."

Jenkins leaves his mother, brother James, a second brother, children who live across town, and a grandchild.

In bestowing Jenkins' "final dignity," Rev. Glenda Hope remembered that the first TL memorial she conducted more than 25 years ago was at the Dalt. Then, it was a dirty fleabag occupied mostly by old winos, she said. A woman had recently jumped out a fifth-story window. And it became notorious for killings there.

But a major TNDC rehabilitation through the Mayor's Office of Housing and counseling services have made the hotel clean, pleasant and caring.

"I'm grateful for the changes," Hope said, "and for the people who have made it a place of safety and refreshment." ●

— TOM CARTER

Loner Who Didn't Die Alone
JAMES JUVE

JAMES JUVE spent most of his time watching movies in his fifth-floor Camelot Hotel room, and when he did come out he displayed the enviable sensibilities of a gentleman. He was polite and generous and knew how to talk to people. And he brought the ladies flowers.

"He was a gentleman," Camelot Manager Shannon Hugon said at Juve's memorial. "If he knew you liked something, he'd talk about it to you. He loved beauty and the outdoors. And every Friday he brought all the ladies on the staff flowers. He picked them up at the Rescue Mission."

Juve brought other gifts. Hugon adorns her office walls with pictures of butterflies and a dozen mounted specimens, and near the ceiling is a 6-foot by 8-inch plastic strip depicting 10 different kinds of butterflies.

"It came from a shower curtain someone was throwing away," Hugon said. "He cut off the top and brought it to me."

Juve died of heart failure the day before he would have turned 54. He had been a fisherman in Maine and had worked as a lapidary somewhere and fashioned jewelry as a hobby. Nobody knew when he came to California and none of his friends had seen his work. He had lived in the Camelot two years.

James Juve died Aug. 9, 2006

On a table with 18 votive candles was a vase of irises and purple hydrangeas, another of red carnations, and two pictures of Juve with his handlebar mustache and wearing his trademark hat.

Alan Garceau, using a cane, shuffled in late and eased into a chair.

"Nobody really knew him because he was a loner," Garceau said, haltingly. "But I did because I lived next door and would talk to him. I found another friend. A nice guy. It's sad he passed on. May he rest in peace."

Garceau went slowly to the table and lit a candle.

Thomas Wells told how Juve had visited Wells' girlfriend Angela the morning he died. While sitting on a chair, he lost consciousness.

"We first thought he was asleep," Wells said. "I gave him mouth-to-mouth for 15 minutes. Then the paramedics came. They said there wasn't enough rhythm in his heart to bring him back. I spent 15 minutes breathing for him. You'd think they could give him a shot or something.

"But he didn't die alone." ●

— TOM CARTER

Candle and a Prayer
ANTHONY SHELTON

A SHORT LIFE, much of it lived on the streets, ended for Anthony Shelton when he died of complications from AIDS. He was 40.

Anthony Shelton died May 24, 2005

Shelton had lived at the Franciscan Towers for six months in the Shelter Plus Care program. His memorial, marked by a small vase of roses and a candle on a table off the lobby, was attended only by the hotel's social worker and Rev. Glenda Hope, who offered a short prayer.

Shelton died at St. Mary's Hospital. He is survived by his mother in San Diego. ●

— MARJORIE BEGGS

Teresa of the Tenderloin
HANK WILSON

THERE'S A JOB that can't wait, Hank Wilson told the volunteer from Network Ministries. Upstairs, in the Ambassador Hotel that Wilson managed, George was in bad shape, deathly sick, incontinent. He needed a bath. They went upstairs. George had gotten out of his filthy room and was crawling down the hallway naked, covered in his excrement.

They got him into the bathroom. Wilson drew the bath and with effort pulled George into the tub and started cleaning the tenant who always gives him a hard time.

"That's who Hank was at the core," Rev. Glenda Hope said. She recalled the story in her Network Ministries office, sniffling and dabbing her eyes, not long after Wilson's death. The incident was more than 20 years ago, and the volunteer was one of hers.

"That's what we saw in him. This guy who had so ripped him off — and was screaming obscenities and cursing him — and Hank was tenderly washing the shit out of his hair like a mother with a baby, and then drying him off with fluffy towels. And meanwhile, someone was changing his sheets."

Hope paused as memories from 28 years of knowing Wilson, often working side by side with him in the Tenderloin's deepest trenches, flooded her mind. As Network Ministries' guiding light, she has ministered to the hood's poor and dispossessed since 1972.

"He was a giant in my life," Hope said. "More than any other person I've known, he showed me the meaning — taught me — forgiveness and unconditional love. What an odd couple we were."

Henry "Hank" Wilson, gay activist, innovator and humble servant of the Tenderloin's sick, poor and homeless, died at Davies Medical Center. A nonsmoker who had survived the ravages of AIDS, he was 61 when he died of lung cancer.

Wilson's achievements are so epic some friends have called him the Mother Teresa of the Tenderloin. Others said he created so many organizations here and in the Castro that he was the Johnny Appleseed of gay and AIDS causes.

He clearly had no equal.

Henry Wilson died Nov. 9, 2008

PHOTO BY DON FUSCO

BORN IN SACRAMENTO, Wilson came to San Francisco in the 1970s after getting a B.A. in education from the University of Wisconsin. Soon the handsome, energetic young kindergarten teacher was fighting for gay equality in the city's schools and against a national anti-gay movement led by religious right wingers.

Wilson and fellow teacher Tom Ammiano, who went on to become a San Francisco supervisor and state assemblyman, helped defeat the statewide Briggs initiative that would have banned gay teachers in public schools. Wilson started the Gay Teachers Association and, with Ammiano, created a Gay Speakers bureau to educate public school students grades seven through 12 about gay and lesbian issues. That's how it began.

"The number of organizations that Hank was involved in founding that are now the pillar organizations of the gay and lesbian community both in San Francisco and nationally is staggering," his close friend, UC Davis Professor Bob Ostertag, wrote on the Huffington Post Website.

Others include: Bay Area Gay Liberation, Lavender Youth Recreation and Information Center (LYRIC), Butterfly Brigade, ACT UP San Francisco, Survive AIDS, AIDS Candlelight Vigil, San Francisco Gay and Lesbian Film Festival and Tenderloin AIDS Resource Center. He also served on the San Francisco Human Rights Commission's Youth and Education Committee.

But his unique work in the Tenderloin, first with the very poor and homeless, then with the poor who were dying of AIDS, made him a neighborhood hero. On Dec. 1, AIDS Day, a memorial for Wilson was held at Tenderloin Health, the nonprofit he co-founded that originally addressed the AIDS scourge and now serves an average of 350 homeless people each day.

The crowd picked up whistles, blowing them along a half-block march down Golden Gate Avenue to St. Anthony Foundation's community room. The crowd grew to 75. (As co-founder of Coalition United Against Violence, Wilson helped start a Blow the Whistle Against Violence campaign to combat gay-bashing in the Castro.)

Speakers, including Hope, told how Wilson's work with suffering people had profoundly impressed them.

"His memory won't end here," said Blackberri, a large black man who sang a song he composed 30 years ago when Harvey Milk was assassinated. "Hank taught San Francisco how to stand tall."

A FEW DAYS LATER, the AIDS organizations Wilson started and others held a "Thanks to Hank" commemoration in the Eureka Valley Recreation Center gym, sponsored by the GLBT Historical Society and attended by 350. It culminated in a spirited march led by Extra-Action Marching Band through the Castro as more celebrants spilled out of bars, restaurants and shops to join the throng.

Wilson, a stout 5-11, handsome, bespectacled, sporting a mustache, lived a Spartan life totally dedicated to his work.

Indifferent to making money, Wilson lived in a small room in a Market Street apartment building. He slept on an air mattress on the floor. When the daily sea of troubles deluged him, he recharged by swimming laps at the Tenderloin YMCA.

His personality suited him well. Through 35 years of the endless challenges he sought as an activist, he maintained a droll, sometimes dark, sense of humor. He disarmingly spoke the straightforward truth and was relentlessly critical of wrong-headed policies. He never asked anybody to do anything he wouldn't do himself, including getting arrested at protests and going off to jail. He became an inspiration to all around him, and a mentor to hundreds.

His friends say he had no interest in politics, although he ran for District 6 supervisor in 2000, finishing seventh in a field of 18 with 508 votes. The irresistible flame that drew him, however, was people in greatest need of help. His focus after he left teaching in 1977 fell on the Tenderloin.

He and friend Ron Lanza saw a want ad for an SRO hotel manager. They applied and got the job. The next year, Wilson leased the 150-room Ambassador Hotel, a milestone in his legendary impact on the neighborhood, at a time that AIDS was not yet a word.

The Ambassador soon became a haven for the poor and afflicted. Wilson seldom said no to anyone.

Tom Calvanese, a freelance marine biologist now, worked seven years with Wilson during the Ambassador's wildest days. His interview to be Wilson's assistant, he told the memorial crowd, consisted mostly of Wilson recapping dire episodes at the hotel, "giving me reasons not to work there." But Calvanese, too, couldn't resist the challenges at the barrel's bottom. He took the aide's job and soon was marveling at Wilson in action.

"HE HAD a selfless compassion, incredible grace and demeanor to continue in this madness," Calvanese said. "He was this combination of qualities — I've never seen anyone embody more — and he lived for the work, and he got people to help in it."

He often astonished friends with innovative ideas that he acted on quickly, as they scrambled to support him. "He was brilliant," Calvanese said. "He had these ideas, and never spent much time thinking. He just did them and left the rest to others. Those were just details, he said. It was the big idea that counted, like, 'People with AIDS can have a decent life.'"

In 1980, Hope ran a roving "house church" project. She, staff and volunteers went into SROs just to talk to and listen to the people. Sometimes there would be prayer or Bible study, but the idea was to be present to support people. She knew what sort of people Wilson was bringing into the Ambassador.

Wilson said to her one day that people were dying on the street at an alarming rate. Nobody knew what was happening — there wasn't a name for it yet — but he wanted those people at the Ambassador.

"HANK SAID he was going to take into the hotel all the homeless people with AIDS and would I help," Hope said. "I told him yes. Nobody was doing anything. And we didn't know what it would be.

"You just didn't say no to Hank, even if you didn't know where it led. He saw that where people lived they needed these services. And he was the first, honest to God.

"Hank was hesitant at first to let us come in. I guess he had had some bad experiences with religious people beating people over the head with the Bible. But little by little he came to trust us, and then he started giving us names of people to visit."

Hope remembers the first death in the winter of 1987 officially linked to the nascent AIDS epidemic. Mel Wald was a member of the hotel's active group despite his plummeting health. They found him sweating with a high fever in bed, nearly unconscious, and took him to a hospice where he soon died.

Network Ministries had an Urban Ministries training program then. Out of it came Penny Sarvis, a Brown University graduate, divorcee and lesbian, "perfect" for the Ambassador.

"She really picked up the work for us. Hank would leave her a note for who to visit. And everybody loved Penny. She was one who cared, a good listener with a big heart.

"People died pretty fast, maybe one a week. Hank was taking in really sick people and there was no medication."

"Hank was running the hotel with an all-queer staff: drag queens, pre-op and post-op transsexuals, dykes and fags, queers of all colors," Ostertag wrote. "As AIDS began to fill the hotel, somehow Hank connected with a nurse who, during his off hours from his full-time nursing job, would come to the Ambassador and provide nursing to scores of dying people, working out of the trunk of his car."

Besides the nurse and the clergy, Wilson got Project Open Hand, the Visiting Nurses Association, Lutheran Social Services and others involved.

Calvanese said people were attracted by this emerging model of care. "But mostly we were attracted by this force in the middle of it all named Hank Wilson."

WILSON had no nonprofit organization. If the Ambassador's landlord wouldn't fix something, he'd dig into his own pocket. He had a knack for knowing what touched people, too. Calvanese recalled at the memorial that Wilson bought flats of seedling plants to give to tenants so they could nurture life, a subtle image of optimism for their individual and collective struggles.

"Tenants trashed the place a lot and didn't pay rent," Hope said. "These weren't appealing people. But it didn't matter to Hank as long as he could do something for them. He'd evict some, then let them come back. Once I saw a woman on the stairs he had kicked out the week before, and I asked why she's here. Hank said, 'Well, she didn't have a place to stay.' "

At the memorial, Hope acknowledged a remark Calvanese made years ago, saying, "Tom said it best — 'Hank not only forgave, he forgot.' "

Wilson was aware some people thought he was nuts.

"'I know people laugh at me and what I do,'" Hope said he once confided to her. "'But I like that about myself.'"

Wilson launched harm reduction 10 years before the approach was labeled. Harm reduction recognizes that a person can do drugs, be an addict even, but shouldn't harm himself or anyone.

"Hank and company were providing homeless services beyond what the city agencies were providing, without a penny of public money, paid for by the meager resources of the clients themselves," Ostertag wrote. "This was not supposed to be possible."

It was evident to Hope and Wilson and their support team that the Tenderloin desperately needed the city's help, especially for prevention and harm reduction measures. But the city thought the AIDS problem lay mainly with the Castro's better-groomed citizens.

"The city wouldn't listen," Hope said. "We had different people dying here, the poor and destitute."

But then a $2,500 grant from Columbia Foundation came to the activists' group led by Wilson, Hope and Dennis Conkin. They coalesced in 1985 as Tenderloin AIDS Network, and hired an analyst to do a neighborhood needs assessment. The resulting recommendations were to get a storefront out of which to dispense condoms, bleach and disinfectant for needles, make referrals to city programs and send out "CHOWs," low-paid community health outreach workers, to spread the word.

Until the late 1980s, Hope said, the city claimed it had no money for this sort of thing. "But then the heavens opened up."

A PARTICULARLY RAINY season brought the city an excess of hydroelectric energy to sell, and the windfall revenue made new programs possible. So the 3-year-old AIDS Network, with no office, successfully answered the Department of Health's request for proposals and became the Tenderloin AIDS Resource Center with $100,000 city funding. Wilson, a TARC co-founder, wanted to be close to clients and not be the boss. So he managed the drop-in center so he could personally provide support to the homeless and people with AIDS. He had been diagnosed as HIV-positive the year before.

TARC moved into a battered, abandoned storefront on Golden Gate Avenue in 1990, as AIDS raged on.

"Hank had AIDS himself," Ostertag wrote. "Bad AIDS. Terrible Kaposi Sarcoma. Lesions all over his body and eventually on his face. Tuberculosis. And finally AIDS-related dementia. Protease inhibitors came along just in the nick of time to pull his one foot out of the grave and give him back his health."

Still, Wilson managed the Ambassador. When Father John Hardin of St. Anthony Foundation wanted to join in, Wilson gave him, Hope and the nurse a bigger room — "one he could have rented," Hope recalled — so a chaplain was present every day.

Even now under TNDC ownership, the concept lives on in an Ambassador mezzanine room called the Listening Post, where Network Ministries volunteers still go, and where lives are celebrated.

"Meanwhile, Hank is involved all the way," Hope said. "He started ACT UP because he thought all this was taking too long. He was like that. He wanted things done at once. He kept pushing us. And that was good."

IN THE EARLY 1990s the Metropolitan Community Church gave annual awards to "living saints" for their neighborhood work and wanted to name him. Wilson never wanted recognition or praise, but Hope convinced him to accept, arguing that the award "recognized the value of the work."

Wilson's sanctification ceremony took place in the basement of St. Mary's Cathedral. "When his name was mentioned, the place erupted in cheers," Hope said. "They'd never had a chance to cheer him before." Later, Wilson told Hope he was "happy" he'd accepted.

> **The master has left this world.**

In 1996, after 18 years at the Ambassador, Wilson left to care for his dying parents. When he returned, he picked up his work at TARC and set an example for scores of TARC volunteers and staff.

"He was a true advocate and mentor on every level of life for so many who were so desperately ill and in need of help — in a time when few paid attention to this neighborhood and its residents," said Colm Hegarty, spokesman for Tenderloin Health, the organization TARC became.

Wilson quit TARC in 2006 when it merged with Continuum HIV Day Services to form Tenderloin Health. That year Wilson went to work on an unusual homeless program at St. Boniface Catholic Church that offered its sanctuary pews during the day for sleeping. He finally stopped when his medical treatments became too much of a drain.

"There's no telling how many thousands he helped," Hope said.

ONE WAS Norman Hampton, 56, a Tenderloin Health staffer who led the AIDS Day memorial for Wilson. Hampton returned to San Francisco from Ohio in 2005 after shaking a drug habit. He landed at TARC, and Wilson called around and got him a shelter bed. Two days later, Hampton came back to volunteer.

"I didn't know any of the clients, but they all said this was a good place. And Hank treated me like a person. I was motivated. My passion is helping people, I told him."

After a few months, Wilson asked the rangy black man to join the staff.

"I'm a slow learner," Hampton said one afternoon in a Tenderloin coffee shop. "I'm living with AIDS and it was real motivation to have Hank there. He was easygoing, nothing bothered him. He was dedicated, loving, understanding — in a word, a real human being."

Wilson turned over two of his group sessions to Hampton. One emphasized positive movement in life, the other encouraged purging stultifying thoughts that block personal growth. And Wilson gave Hampton other responsibilities that showed his trust in him.

"It was the jump-start I needed," Hampton said. "I don't have a high school education, but I've been trained in life. Hank could talk and train people on many levels, and his humor always kept me going. I never saw him in an altercation.

"The master has left this world," Hampton said. ●

— TOM CARTER

❝ We could smell death ... we could sense death. ❞

Police officers reach out to a man atop a Tenderloin building, threatening to jump. Photo by Tom Carter.

PART 4: Murder in the Tenderloin

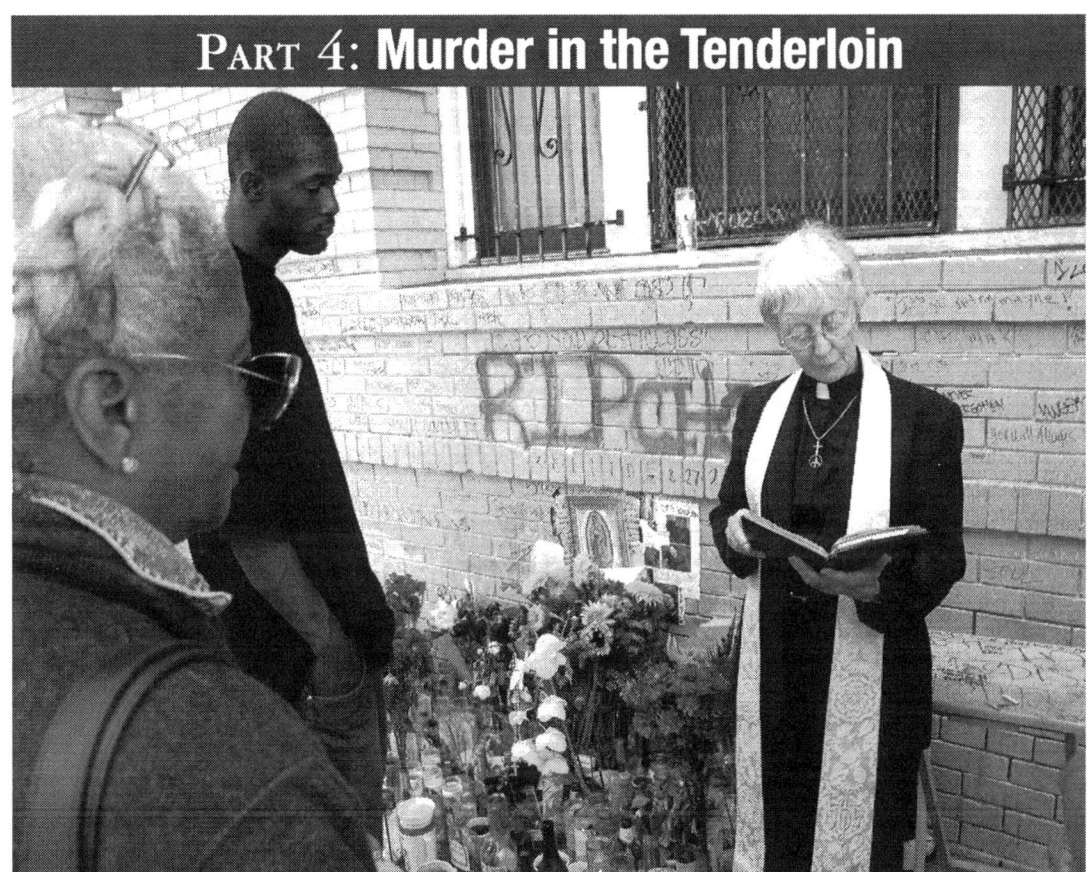

PHOTO BY TOM CARTER
Rev. Glenda Hope reads Scripture on a Leavenworth sidewalk for a 20-year-old man who had been fatally shot in North Beach. He grew up in the Tenderloin, and was the new father of a son.

Commuter Criminals Do Most of the Killing

BY TOM CARTER

ON THE first day of 2011 at 3:20 p.m., 20-year-old Larry Lacy was in the wrong place at the wrong time. He was sitting with another man on the sidewalk at the corner of Turk and Taylor streets in front of the 21 Club when somebody gunned him down. Lacy lived in East Palo Alto and generally hung out in the Bayview across town. He was under a stay-away order from the court for selling dope, banning him from that part of the Tenderloin.

The shooter fled and, as with 86% of homicides in San Francisco in 2010, no one was arrested.

"It should be noted that the victim ... was from the Hunters Point-SF area," Tenderloin police Capt. Joe Garrity wrote in his community newsletter, "and the suspect was from Oakland. We continue to recognize that both the victims and suspects do not live or work in the Tenderloin area."

"That seems to be what's taking place and the trend in street crime," Garrity said later. Outsiders bring their bad business here, act out their deadly animosities, and so the Tenderloin's bad rap grows. Normally, the TL has its crimes of passion on the street and its domestic violence inside homes, "which is unpredictable," Garrity said.

The previous killing in the Tenderloin had been more than four months earlier, Friday, Aug. 19, 2010, just after midnight at O'Farrell and Jones streets, four blocks from where Lacy became 2011's first statistic.

A 10-year police report shows the Tenderloin averages 5.1 homicides per year, not even close to the city's leading district. The numbers here may seem higher, however, as media reports often place nearby slayings inside the Tenderloin because neighborhood boundaries do not coincide with police district borders. Two homicides this year ascribed to the TL in media reports — one on Geary, one on Larkin — were out of bounds, though Tenderloin cops often respond first to such scenes.

Tenderloin murders are no match for the number in Bayview, which last year had 14 homicides but arrests for only one. Five other police districts in San Francisco had more homicides than the Tenderloin district in 2010.

"But my biggest fear," Garrity said, "is that somebody going to a store, or to a nonprofit, or a kid walking on the street, will catch a bullet."

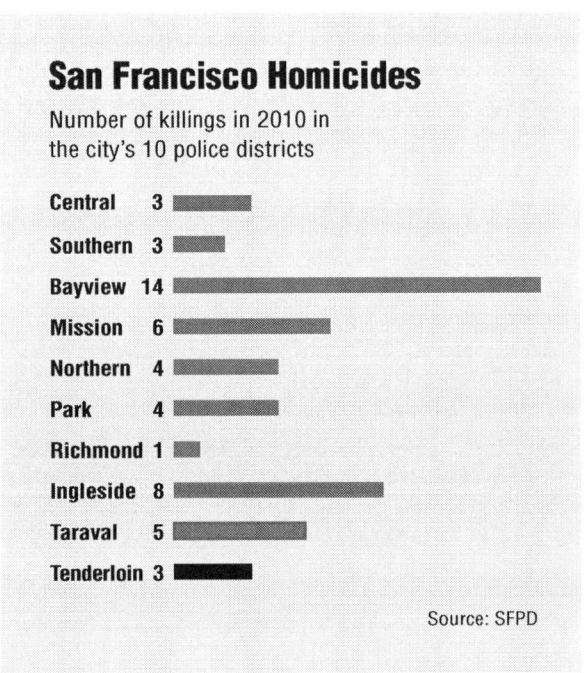

THERE HAS BEEN BLOOD

ERIC LINDSAY, 52, was being pushed in a wheelchair by his fiancee on his way to buy a pizza at 7:45 p.m. Aug. 3, 2006, when he was suddenly in the middle of a botched drug transaction that turned violent on the 400 block of O'Farrell Street. He caught a bullet in the chest and died.

April 18, 2007, after midnight on the lawless 300 block of Ellis Street, Lena Allen, 54, recent Sixth Street hotel resident, became another innocent victim of a gun battle. Police said Walter Simon, 32, of Richmond was on the block returning gunfire when his rounds killed Allen. Simon, who police said had a rap sheet for drug dealing and weapons possession in the Tenderloin, was in a wheelchair, himself a victim of a shooting.

There have been other wild situations that could have easily meant curtains for a bystander. The afternoon before Allen's death, at 4:20, seven blocks away in what police called a gang execution, 16-year-old Kelvin Mencia of Oakland was chased into a donut shop at Golden Gate Avenue and Hyde Street, where he was gunned down. Police arrested five suspects, four of them juveniles.

Drive-bys, because of their recklessness, are another source of fear, though the Tenderloin is nothing like the Bayview scene. So Tenderloin residents are still talking about the shooting two years ago near Grand Liquor where small idling crowds gathered out front day and night.

At 10:20 p.m. a silver Mercedes-Benz SUV with temporary license plates was traveling west on Turk. As it approached Taylor Street, gunshots poured out of the vehicle, wounding five men and killing Leticia Hunter, 33, from Sacramento, who police believed to be part of a drug deal. The Mercedes sped off chased by San Francisco police who said the SUV hit 110 mph going over the Bay Bridge. Police lost the vehicle in Oakland where it was discovered three hours later, abandoned and aflame.

REALITY BEHIND THE REPUTATION

THE TENDERLOIN'S historic bad reputation is its albatross. But, despite the substantial number of Chinese and Southeast Asian families and the numerous longtime residents who live out their lives quietly and unassumingly, the reality behind TL's notoriety is unmistakable.

The Tenderloin is where poor people and addicts hang out and where criminals and misfits gravitate for drug transactions. It's a Jekyll and Hyde neighborhood, the city's poorest, with scores of historic, well-kept hotels and other buildings. Hardworking Latino and Asian families co-exist with a grungy, poverty-stricken underclass seeking soup kitchens and detox centers. Mental health patients find help from a plethora of nonprofits; a relatively high percentage of parolees and ex-cons tries to rejoin the law-abiding, and tempers flare. Anything can happen, cops say, in the neighborhood that "never sleeps."

One man, accused of killing another at U.N. Plaza in front of Carl's Jr. by clobbering him over the head with a boom box, was sent to Napa State Hospital. A judge in May 2010 found Edward Holloway, 55, incapable of helping in his own defense. The year before, Holloway had been arrested for stabbing his girlfriend at Turk and Taylor in an argument over $30.

That spontaneous violence on the streets is as unnerving as the sometimes homicidal terror of gangs.

It would seem that the Tenderloin drew Joevon Bowen of Oakland. He was convicted of first-degree murder in February 2010, eight years after his involvement in the slaying of a 26-year-old man walking near Polk and Willow streets at the westernmost edge of the Tenderloin. Police believe the deed was a rite in Oakland's notorious Nut Case gang to gain prestige. Another man who had driven across the Bay Bridge with Bowen had been convicted three years earlier of the killing, but gang members ratted out Bowen as an accomplice.

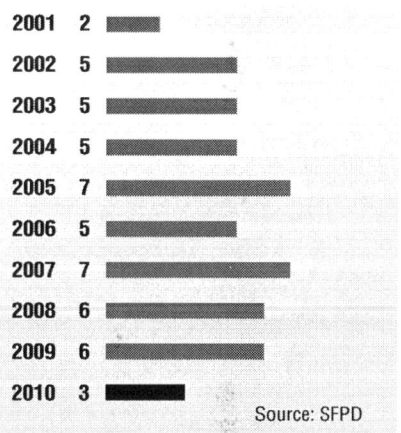

Tenderloin Homicides
Number of killings per year from 2001-10 in the police district

Year	Killings
2001	2
2002	5
2003	5
2004	5
2005	7
2006	5
2007	7
2008	6
2009	6
2010	3

Source: SFPD

All of this begs the question, jilted by the trend, who's getting killed in the Tenderloin? The Extra asked the Police Department to find which homicide victims over the past five years lived in the Tenderloin police district. The Extra's total for that period, 29, came from an analysis of department statistics.

Sgt. Michael Andrechak, in SFPD public relations, said his total for this search might be different. It was: 27. Further analysis showed that missing from the SFPD statistics was one of the three homicides of 2010 and one from 2008. Thus, consistent crime stats can be hard to come by.

The search results showed 12 victims were from the Tenderloin, four were homeless but tied to the TL, and nine were out of the district, the majority from towns from Vacaville to Santa Cruz. Two of the victims police said were Tenderloin residents — and had been so identified in newspaper accounts — were from Sacramento and Oakland. In 2007, five of the nine victims were from out of town.

It's clear that people are coming to the neighborhood to kill and some get killed.

Out-of-towners waging war-bent crime in the Tenderloin is a wicked problem that looks unstoppable. It rankled and frustrated Capt. Gary Jimenez no end. He was Tenderloin police captain from 2006 to 2009, the longest stretch any captain has served in the neighborhood.

"It has long, long been a trend," Jimenez told The Extra. "The best place in California to commit a crime is in San Francisco. The system is less likely to prosecute you. It's almost against sending you to jail, especially if it involves drugs. It's the revolving door here."

Jimenez got into hot water three years ago for announcing at his monthly community police meetings that commuter criminals were causing the vast majority of crime in the neighborhood and then naming their home communities. It was like he was "pointing a finger" at other cities, he was told; he wouldn't name the superior who told him to shut up.

85% COMMUTER CRIMINALS

EVEN SO, two Tenderloin CBD staffers, acting as volunteers — Dina Hilliard and Elaine Zamora — examined the station's April 2009 arrest logs to see if Jimenez's claim could be substantiated. The results, Hilliard said, showed that 83% of the arrests that month were people from out of the district, and 17% were Tenderloin residents. Half of those from out of town were from Oakland, she said.

More often than not, Jimenez said, dealers are armed and on parole.

"Search the car," he said, "and you'll find a weapon, or someone is carrying it for him. They carry arms because of the threat to them — violence is a reality in that business. And some of the gangs in the 300 block of Ellis are vicious."

On Jimenez's watch, the Pink Diamonds strip club at 220 Jones St. was "an ugly battle" that eventually led to a homicide that police connected to it. There were unruly crowds outside late at night, fighting and gunshots. The enraged neighborhood held community meetings to pressure the manager to control the long lines of customers. Police shut the club briefly at times after inspections found permit violations. But the club persisted. One man police tied to the club crowd was shot and paralyzed. Another, on June 27, 2009, was shot and killed.

"It was the city that had refused to act on it," Jimenez recalled, "not the police."

But in September 2009, finally the city attorney moved to shutter the club and a Superior Court judge in October ordered Pink Diamonds closed, citing its 230 police service calls in the previous six months.

"It could very easily happen again with that kind of venue, if it's not well-managed," Jimenez said. "In the old days it wouldn't happen because a captain could close it. But City Hall is fickle."

Solutions to stem future violence are hard to come by. Capt. Garrity is working with his police community advisory board on a plan to post signs in order to expand the use of stay-away orders for loitering drug dealers.

But Jimenez says a bigger swipe at the problem, and maybe the ultimate solution, is a long way off.

"Legalize drugs," he said. "It's going to have to happen — maybe not for 100 years — but it's the only way to change it." ●

Sidewalk Memorial
LOGAN 'CITO' KAUSMAN

A DOZEN BROTHERS mourned the mysterious death of a fallen Tenderloin neighborhood son at a memorial conducted on a Leavenworth sidewalk, a hangout spot in front of an apartment building where some of the young mourners live.

Grim and silent, most wore the uniform of street youth — oversize white T-shirt, baggy pants and baseball cap askew. Next to the building, they had created a shrine of candles, bottles, bouquets and small paper images from cell phone photos of the dead man, Logan "Cito" Kausman. He was 20. A few photos showed him holding his year-old son, Jeremiah Cito Kausman. "Cito" had been scrawled on the wall in several places.

Kausman died of a gunshot wound, his friends said. But details were hard to glean.

"He didn't die in the Tenderloin," said Capt. Joe Garrity the next day. "It was in the Northern (police) district, in a side alley, and we don't know if it was a homicide or suicide."

Sgt. Troy Dangerfield, SFPD spokesman, said there was no police report of Kausman's death.

FAMILY PHOTO

Logan Kausman, who died Aug. 27, 2010, and son

"We have nothing in the system, which leads me to believe it's a coroner's case," Dangerfield said. "They can investigate their own cases."

The medical examiner's office acknowledged it is investigating the cause of death.

Rev. Glenda Hope said she conducted the memorial at the behest of a neighborhood woman. Traffic and other street noises practically drowned out her words as she faced the crowd, her back to the brick wall. She had been told erroneously that the young man had grown up there at 245 Leavenworth St. and had died at that spot on the sidewalk. But Kausman had actually grown up around the corner near Eddy and Hyde, his friends said later, and as an adult had acquired his own apartment in the same building.

Hope asked the mourners to share memories. A black woman said she didn't know the deceased as well as the young men had but concluded he was "a passionate young man" and thanked them for letting her "celebrate" with them.

No one else spoke, and it was over. The black woman hurried away. The young men lingered, looking lost, some leaning on cars. When asked, some did share information about their pal.

Michael Viera, 21, said he was Kausman's best friend; he'd known him all his life. In 2006, Kausman had moved to Los Angeles where he earned a welding certificate and a high school diploma, Viera said.

"He said it changed his life. He didn't want to go, but he later realized it was a good thing."

Kausman got hired by the Department of Public Works under federal stimulus money and worked in Glen Park, another said. He had been employed since his son was born. His girlfriend, the mother, took care of the child during the day.

"Yeah," said one young man, "he had his own apartment, a car, a job, a kid — he was cutting it pretty good, doing better than the rest of us."

Kausman was an ideal friend, they said, always smiling, had good vibes, never argued, always wanted to do things for people — "about the best person you could ever meet, a brother," said Ty, a tall, thin black man who kept lighting votive candles even after the memorial was over.

Kausman was buried at Holy Cross cemetery in Daly City. The next day his friends were back at the patch hanging out. The shrine, which had become a mess, had been removed by the police. •

— TOM CARTER

Shocking Death of a Young Grandmother
BRUNETTE 'NELLY' HUNTER

BRUNETTE "NELLY" HUNTER'S fatal accident in front of her Ambassador Hotel home denied her dream of celebrating the birth of a grandchild who would visit her often and make her proud. Her daughter was to give birth soon.

"She was so excited about the birth and had requested a larger room," Rachel Throm, a social worker at the Ambassador, said at Hunter's memorial. "We were looking for one, but then her terrible accident happened."

Nelly Hunter died June 22, 2010

Hunter was out in front of the hotel talking to someone in a car. Suddenly, the car lurched forward and took off with Hunter holding on. J.L. Marrible, an Ambassador neighbor, was outside and saw her fatal fall. Hunter hung on for a few yards, then lost her grip, her body and head violently smashing the pavement as the car sped away.

"Two white dudes held her down because she was really bleeding and trying to get up," Marrible said after the memorial. "I think they got a license number."

Hunter was taken to San Francisco General Hospital's intensive care unit and never woke up. She remained in a coma for a month before she died of her many injuries. She was 50.

Her pregnant daughter, Monica Hunter, visited her several times in the hospital but Hunter never knew that her granddaughter, Lauryn Brunette, had been born six days before she died.

News of the accident and its particulars sent a shock wave through the SRO.

At the memorial, the mourners sat in a circle in the Ambassador's Listening Post room where a colorful and fragrant floral spray had been placed on a ledge in Hunter's honor. Several of the eight mourners who had visited Hunter in the hospital lamented the tragedy and the coma that had cheated her.

"But you never know what a person in a coma can realize," said Rev. Glenda Hope, who conducted the memorial. "And she didn't die alone."

Hunter was born in Conroe, Texas, came to the city at 18, had four children, Monica, Jasmine and Dominque, all born in San Francisco, and a son, Toussainte Hunter, born in Conroe. Toussainte flew here twice after the tragedy. Hunter had three grandchildren from her son: all live in Texas. A memorial service was held in Bayview and 100 people attended.

Her friends said Hunter was "sweet," "good people," "a nice lady who never complained."

"She taught me how long to boil eggs," one man said.

Monica Hunter, who didn't attend the memorial, said her mother was "outspoken" and a "people person" with a good sense of humor who loved to read books and work the Chronicle's crossword puzzles. She had lived at the Ambassador nearly four years.

Police found the driver, Monica Hunter said, but he wasn't held. She asks that any eyewitness to the incident that killed her mother, email her at garlingtonmonica@yahoo.com. •

— TOM CARTER

A Good Boy Who Got Gunned Down
JASON MOSLEY

JASON MOSLEY was a friendly young desk clerk who, everyone could see, was blooming like a spring flower. At 29, he had turned his life around. He loved his job at the San Cristina hotel on Market Street. The residents appreciated his smiling face and that he was always eager to help. He was going to get married soon, and he was excited about becoming a father.

But his life ended one day in April at 6 p.m. when he was shot in the Western Addition neighborhood he grew up in near Fulton and Octavia streets. He was pronounced dead at the scene. Police have no suspects.

An Examiner story reporting that weekend's shootings described the incident without naming the victim, Mosely. But the numbing truth spread quickly among San Cristina's residents, news no one wanted to hear.

"He was always smiling, courteous and considerate — the kind of people we need," said San Cristina desk clerk Paula Elliott as people filed into the community room for Mosley's memorial. "There was nothing about him to suggest" he'd be shot to death.

The tragedy gripped all 30 mourners. Some had to stand for lack of seating.

"My name is Rita and I lost my son in West Oakland in December," said a woman who came to the front of the room. "He was shot in the head."

Jason Mosley died April 27, 2008

Then she burst into her strong Mahalia Jackson rendition of "How Great Thou Art." The swell of applause that followed seemed to momentarily relieve the intensity of grief.

Another mourner said he had recently lost his mother, and it was only with considerable courage that he could come to this memorial to pay his respects when it brought him so much sadness. "But my uncle said. 'It's a good old world, if your knees don't weaken.'"

Amen to that, people said.

Selina Arceneaux, Mosley's mother, seated in the second row, was overwrought. Mourner after mourner came to hug her. She repeatedly thanked them for their kindness and support. It was her only child, she said, her baby, and suddenly he was gone. The inescapable thought nearly made her delirious.

"He would come home and fix meals for his grandmother and take care of her and walk the dog," she said. "He was a good boy."

Yes, the audience chorused.

"I tried so hard," she continued, speaking with difficulty, clutching a handkerchief. "I made him come here and take this job — and be became interested in it. And he came home and fixed dinner for me and his grandmother and went out to his car and it was the last I saw him. My baby, my baby, my baby."

Mosley was the only man left in her family and his manner of death scared his mother until she feared for her own life.

In others' descriptions, the stocky Mosley grew in dimensions he never heard while alive. They loved his smile, his desire to learn, his gentleness, they said. He never bothered anyone, knew his job well and when to be calm. One man called Mosley's love of his job and delight at becoming a father inspiring. Another said he came across a homeless man who told him Mosley would give him a dollar every time he saw him.

Roger said he wanted people to know that Mosley wasn't in a gang, but "was a victim of where he was staying." The tall, husky young man choked back tears when he said he had been Mosley's mentor and one night had sat with him in the street discussing life crises, and crying, holding hands and praying.

"I want you to know," he said to the mother, "that he had Christ in his life."

Aceneaux could not linger afterward with the mourners as they delved into three large trays of sandwiches and drinks. The funeral for her son was the next Tuesday across town, she said, and she had to finalize arrangements and deliver the clothes he'd need for his final viewing.

— TOM CARTER

Former Probation Officer
CHARLES MOBLEY

CHARLES MOBLEY packed a lot of living into his 72 years, made many friends along the way and had a fruitful career. He had lived at the Pacific Bay Inn only five months when he died.

"He was my next-door neighbor," said Jerome Peters. "I like to play music in my room, and after he moved in, I asked if it was too loud. He said, 'Play it as loud as you want.' We forged a bond, even in that short time. He was a very good man. I know he's going to be in good shape in the other world."

The memorial honored both Mobley and fellow resident Timothy Poulos, who died the same day in March. As the memorial began, Charles Jones, a longtime friend of Mobley's, arrived bearing huge foil-covered platters of food to feed the 15 mourners.

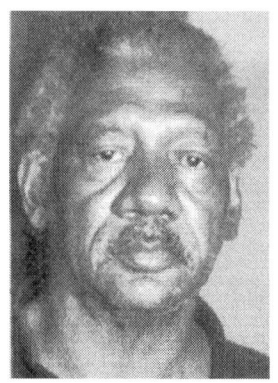

Charles Mobley died March 5, 2005

"He was my good friend for 35 years, and many people thought I was Chuck's probation officer," said Jones, who was wearing a hat with an S.F. Probation Office insignia and a badge. "Actually, he was my supervisor when we worked together at the California State Youth Authority in San Francisco and Sacramento."

Mobley grew up in Miami, the youngest of four kids. He was a National Honor Society member, got honorably discharged from the Air Force, and received bachelor's and master's degrees from Sacramento State University. He was a state parole agent in San Francisco until he retired in 1983.

Jones said that last year Mobley was inducted into his Miami high school's Hall of Fame.

"He was a special person," Jones said, "the kind of friend who took me in for eight months after my wife and I separated. I think the system made him bitter, but that was later. I know he's looking around here and asking, 'Why'd you bring all this food?'"

The spread included roast chicken, rice, green beans, green salad and lemon bars for dessert. Also special was a smaller dish, prepared by one of Mobley's fellow tenants, who said his name is Missionary Yem. He'd sauteed the red, fragrant onions in wine in a rice cooker in his room, he said proudly.

"Charles was such a quiet person, but look at his picture," Yem said, pointing to a photo of Mobley. "He looks so youthful and shows such energy."

Mobley is survived by a sister in Miami and a brother who lives at the Veterans Hospital nursing home in San Francisco. •

— MARJORIE BEGGS

Such a Spirit

HERBERT IVAN SCHWARZ

REMEMBERED for keeping people laughing as well as driving them nuts, Herbert Ivan Schwarz was a friend and fellow resident of the 20 mourners who gathered at the Coast Hotel for his memorial.

"Ivan — we knew him as Ivan — came by to see me every day," said Coast resident Sabrina Pickford. "He did my dishes and emptied my garbage and insisted on coming with me when I went outside."

Pickford, crying throughout her remembrance of Schwarz, said that now when she hears someone coming down the stairs, she "keeps hoping it's him, my friendly neighbor." She tries to keep the good times uppermost in her memory. "He could be a real nuisance, but he always cheered me up."

Schwarz was more than a friend to Pickford. "Sometimes it was like he was my sister from another mother," she said. "Our families pushed us away because of our sexuality. He told me he was always trying to make his family happy, but couldn't."

Herbert Ivan Schwarz and Sabrina Pickford — he was found dead March 23, 2010

Schwarz died in his room at the Coast Hotel, on O'Farrell Street, where he had lived for two years. A resident said his body was discovered during a routine pest control inspection; he'd been dead at least a week. Schwarz was not yet 40.

"I saw him the week before last — we were supposed to go to a pizza party, but I didn't want to take his friends, so I didn't take him," said another friend. "I don't feel guilty, but I am angry with myself. He invited a lot of crappy people into his life. Maybe it would have been better if I had taken him."

He said he used to tease Schwarz about his mixed parentage — his Guatemalan mother and Jewish father — and wished his friend was still here to tease. "I am glad I knew him."

Others reminisced — David Selogie, who hadn't known Schwarz long, called him "a touching, caring, sweet person who kept me feeling young." Luis Chable, a friend of 19 years, went back to the 1990s, when they had worked together at the Stinking Rose, a North Beach restaurant famous for its garlic dishes.

A.J. Fiorella was Schwarz's case manager for six months before he died. "Herbert was full of life and energy, always willing to tackle anything," Fiorella recalled. "He always helped out — but he also could be a pain in the butt. He made me earn my paycheck. Still, it's tragic to lose such a spirit — it's what makes me want to do my work well. He forced me to grow."

Schwarz's maternal aunt and a cousin, both Bay Area residents, attended the memorial and, with the mourners' permission, videotaped them as they shared memories.

The tape, they said, would be sent to Schwarz's mother in Guatemala. ●

— MARJORIE BEGGS

Night Dispatcher of the Help Van
ROBERT BRUCE BROOKS

ROBERT BRUCE BROOKS, a stern, unsmiling man, was the smart, dependable dispatcher dedicated to sending Mobile Assistance Patrol vans out in the dead of night to rescue drunks, addicts and anyone unfortunate enough to be incapacitated.

Brooks, 20 years in recovery himself, knew that helping people in need gave them another chance to recover and find a better life. The MAP vans, a program of Community Awareness and Treatment Services, scrape people off the streets and take them to where they can be helped. Eight years with MAP, Brooks worked graveyard.

Brooks died in the Western Addition home of his significant other, Martha Johnson, where he lived since moving from a Turk Street SRO. He had suffered heart problems for several years. He was 60.

A day after his funeral, a dozen friends and co-workers gathered at a memorial for him at CATS in a second-floor conference room. They remembered him as a dependable worker, self-sacrificing, but opinionated, sometimes to the point of being cantankerous.

Robert Brooks, left, with his idol Smokey Robinson. Brooks died May 20, 2007

Two women said they admired his ability to show up and do his job, but his insistent "his-way" attitude had alienated him.

Max Haptonstahl, MAP program director, called Brooks "a seminal figure in establishing our 24-hour dispatch" and in maintaining CATS' high standard for the city. Brooks handled the graveyard shift's calls — usually 6 to 15 calls of MAP's total 125 calls daily — while monitoring and transmitting radio calls to the vans. Haptonstahl later explained that though graveyard gets fewer calls than other shifts, the calls are more critical "as far as preventing homeless deaths." Early morning is when incapacitated people on the street are most vulnerable.

MAP driver Jack Harris Jr., who worked with Brooks for two years, said he thought Brooks was "odd" at first, but got used to his personality. As soon as Harris arrived for work, Brooks started talking to him, always emphasizing a professional attitude.

"He said no matter what kind of situation I got into out there to use my better judgment and deal with it — not call him — and get the result to him and he'd back me one hundred percent," Harris said. He paused. "And when I walked through that door he could tell at a glance when I wasn't feeling good, and we'd do a process on it. It's hard to accept he's not here."

Born in Philadelphia, Brooks went into the Army after high school, serving in Vietnam and Taiwan in the mid-1960s. According to obituary notes on a table holding two bouquets and a display of 10 large color photos, he bounced around Los Angeles after the service until resuming his education. He was graduated from Los Angeles Technical Trade School in 1980 then moved to San Francisco and got a job with Multi-Services Center-North. He received a bachelor's degree from San Francisco State in 1989 at age 43. Nine years later he joined MAP.

"Robert was most proud of the fact that he was clean and sober over 20 years," the notes said. "His sobriety allowed friends to see the real Robert."

He was known as an avid reader and a computer buff and was considered quite knowledgeable. He impressed people with his "encyclopedic" recall of old films and popular music — admiring Smokey Robinson above all singers — and appreciating people who contributed to African American culture.

One of two framed pictures showed Smokey Robinson with his arm around Brooks' shoulders.

"Robinson was in a grocery store somewhere in town," said Haptonstahl, "and someone pointed at Robert and said: 'That's your biggest fan.' So Smokey walked over to Robert and somebody took their picture."

But Haptonstahl said there was a side of Brooks that few knew. He was surprised, after eight years of knowing him, to see among the several pictures of Brooks with his companion and her two daughters that he was smiling. "I just learned, too, that he taught the daughters how to swim," Haptonstahl said.

Brooks was buried in the 500-acre National Veterans Cemetery in Sacramento. •

— TOM CARTER

Soul and Sunlight
MICHELLE VAN RIJN

A ROOMFUL of distraught mourners gathered to remember Michelle Van Rijn, who was 49 when she jumped to her death from a window in the five-story Coast Hotel, where she lived.

Neighbors described her as "full of genuine soul and sunlight," warm and caring toward everyone she met.

One man said that though he'd known her only a few months, she always looked out for him. The week before she died, he recalled, Van Rijn knocked on his door early one morning, reminding him to make sure he kept his General Assistance appointment. She even gave him $2 bus money. "She was supportive of everything I've ever done."

Another man remembered how she had reached out to him during a particularly troubled personal time. "I had a dire need, and she looked after me," he said. "She always had a happy smile and a cheery attitude."

Van Rijn had spent time in Zimbabwe, another mourner said, maybe even was born there.

A couple dozen people gathered in a circle in the sun-drenched community room of the Coast Hotel for Van Rijn's memorial, conducted by Rev. Glenda Hope. Several wept openly, others comforted a man who was distraught.

"Michelle and I met in precarious places," he told the group. "But even on the worst days, we'd find some magic."

Michele Van Rijn died in February 2009

A table held a photo of Van Rijn, bouquets of flowers and candles. One tenant brought a book of drawings Van Rijn had made of his dog, which died recently. One was a good likeness she'd made from a photograph and another gave the dog wings. In lovely calligraphy she had written, "I see him skipping now, because you gave him wings of love — look how big his wings are."

The manner of her death was a particularly harsh blow for her friends at the Coast Hotel, where many residents are physically or mentally fragile. Before her memorial service began, a staff member reminded the group to reach out for help if they are troubled, and added that special grief support groups will be offered for a few weeks.

Nobody expected her suicide, said one resident after the service ended. "Everything I got from her was always positive," he said. "She had one of the straightest heads of anyone in this hotel." •

—HEIDI SWILLINGER

Loved Rock 'n' Roll and NASCAR
ERIC LUTZ

AFTER TWO YEARS at the Hotel Essex, Eric Lutz still had few friends among the residents.

"He was an avid reader who mostly kept to himself and didn't participate in our events," said Lisa Howe, the hotel social worker. Lutz died of complications from MS and seizure disorder, she said. He was 49.

Fiercely independent, Lutz seemed to have had no family relationships, Howe thought he had lived in San Francisco for many years, and she knew he'd been a sergeant in the Air Force but didn't know if he had seen action.

Most of the eight people who came to Lutz's memorial were SRO staff, with a notable exception.

"Eric was one of my best friends," said Conde J. Peoples, who lives in another Tenderloin SRO. "We met two years ago and we just clicked — it was amazing because we were opposites in so many ways."

Peoples tearfully tried to describe what his friend had meant to him. He shook his head in disbelief at the rarity of their relationship and the contradictions in Lutz's personality: "He was a gentle, loving man, and shared what he had, but he was also crazy sometimes and a stubborn son-of-a-bitch."

Rock 'n' roll was a passion. "Whitesnake, Crosby, Stills & Nash, the Rolling Stones — he especially loved those groups, and we'd go to the Gangway and listen to them on the jukebox," Peoples recalled.

Eric Lutz died May 24, 2010

Another of their favorite pastimes was to watch NASCAR races on TV. "Eric knew all the cars, what they were, who the drivers were," Peoples said. "It gave him real joy. NASCAR is so completely not me, but I enjoyed his enthusiasm."

When his health worsened, Lutz rejected Peoples' offer to help him physically — "which pissed me off so much," Peoples said. "But I respected his choice and it taught me a lot about 'going' — about dying — in one's own way."

Two weeks before he died, Lutz was quite ill and hadn't budged from his room for many days, Howe said. Suddenly, he showed up downstairs, insisted he was feeling good, went out and ate a big meal and brought flowers back for the staff.

"He really was a lover of life," Howe said. ●

— MARJORIE BEGGS

Transgender Artist
GHIA PARKS

WHEN GHIA PARKS moved into the Jefferson Hotel, she joined fellow tenants, all formerly homeless, in finally having a safe roof over her head.

"She was a regular at our coffee hour and would sit in the lobby, enjoying her coffee and doughnut," said Mary Catherine Flynn, a Jefferson case worker, at the memorial for Parks. "She'd sit quietly at the end of the first-floor hallway and enjoy the fresh air. She had a quiet, pleasant demeanor and long, well-cared-for fingernails."

Ghia Parks died Jan. 5, 2007

She also had a full beard.

"Ghia identified as a transgender," Flynn said.

Parks, who died in her hotel room from unknown causes, was 58. Assistant Manager Steve Williams found her. "She was someone who was always smiling and could always make you laugh," he said. "If anything was wrong, you wouldn't know."

Still shocked by Parks' death just six days earlier, several friends at the memorial said they'd seen her the morning of the day she was found.

"I'm going to miss her a lot," said Matthew, who didn't give his last name. "I was her neighbor for a year and a half — she was a fellow artist, an amazing painter and weaver, and she had a supreme mind and wit. Ghia was truly exceptional, but she also was sweet and never arrogant."

Many people have stopped by the hotel to ask about Parks since she died, Flynn said. "You can tell that a lot of people cared for her."

"She's done her deed here on Earth," said Williams. ●

— MARJORIE BEGGS

'Blew Hot and Cold'
MARLA COOMES

MARLA COOMES had flash. You could see it in the pictures assembled for her memorial at the Camelot Hotel, and the mourners confirmed it.

"She was always full of spunk, full of life, with lots of spark," said Shannon Hugon, the hotel's support services manager. "Happy, she was very happy; unhappy, she was very unhappy."

"She definitely was one who blew hot and cold," said John Miller, Coomes' Camelot neighbor and friend. "Once, she invited me over, offered me a cigarette and told me the doctor said she had six months to live. I told her, 'Take care of yourself and prove the doctors wrong.'

"She went from being able to explain her condition to me calmly, then breaking down in tears. At the door, she said, 'I love you, too. Now goddamn it, stay away from me.' And blam — she slammed the door on me."

Hotel staff recalled that Coomes was "joyful, her own woman," when she arrived at the Camelot 18 months ago after living on the streets, and she was delighted to finally have housing. She made many friends, inside and out, even as her health was deteriorating.

Marla Coomes died Jan. 12, 2006

Coomes was in and out of St. Francis Hospital for several months, and died there of "medical complications," said Hugon. She was 59.

Miller said Coomes talked to him about her sister and father in Pennsylvania, her days as a club dancer in San Francisco, and her husband, a veteran, who died of a heart attack three years ago. But he shared few details. ●

— MARJORIE BEGGS

A Diva's Ill-Timed Death
LORAINE MCGEE

THE LAST THING on Earth Loraine McGee wanted was to cause her 4-year-old great-grandnephew pain, but it was in fact her final unfortunate act.

At approximately 4 a.m., the boy, who was visiting overnight, as he often did, woke the West Hotel's third-floor residents with crying and screaming. He couldn't wake his aunt; she had died during the night.

"A sad trauma," Rev. Glenda Hope commiserated with four mourners at McGee's memorial in the SRO's community room.

"I was so sad to hear the boy was there," said one woman. "He'll remember that the rest of his life."

"The paramedics and child services came right away," said Vanessa Sacks, a social worker who had come to work at 8 a.m. The boy was turned over to his mother, who had been at work during the night.

"I saw her every day," said her friend Geraldine Krause. "I liked to go outside and she did, too. She wasn't like many people here who are suffering and stay in their rooms. And the boy was always running around. But she made him behave."

The mourners didn't know the boy's name and they thought he was her grandson. But the desk clerk later said emphatically he was her "great-grandnephew."

Loraine McGee died Nov. 14, 2011

McGee's friends called her "the diva of the West." A stocky woman who smoked cigarettes tooling around on a motorized wheelchair, McGee wore a nose ring and was a nonstop fashion statement — color-coordinated every day from wardrobe to wigs, which never failed to match her boots. "Even the fuzzy pink ones," her friends said. Blue and brown ensembles were other memorable statements.

"I asked her once how many pairs of boots she had," Krause said, "and she said, 30."

McGee was also a vision with her beautifully groomed beige Pomeranian at her side. Feisty one minute, the eager hotel gossip the next. "Vibrant," McGee's friends described her.

"She wanted to move to another neighborhood, and we were working on that," Sacks said. "But it was a bit difficult with Section 8 vouchers because they are for one specific place."

McGee, who was 59, was the seventh death at the West in 11 months. "All from natural causes, but she was a surprise, and it's pretty hard on all of us," Sacks said.

Eighty-five people live at TNDC's West Hotel. ●

— TOM CARTER

Badass Vietnam Vet
STEVEN PANGLE

STEVE PANGLE could scare you to death just by looking at him. He had a full beard, long hair and no teeth. In his black leather jacket, the 6-foot-1, 200-pounder looked like a glowering Hells Angel. He was gruff and irascible besides.

But his looks didn't keep a handful of his friends-at-a-distance at the Iroquois Hotel from liking the loner, or his understanding sister from her unconditional love.

Pangle, a Marine who served in Vietnam in the early 1970s, died in his room two weeks after returning from seven months in the hospital. He was 49 when he moved into the O'Farrell Street SRO. He lived there six years. At his memorial, several residents told how they had appreciated him.

"He was a character who had his ups and downs, and some attitude," one man said. "But he always said hi to me." A big lady described how much Pangle had admired her arm tattoos; it became their friendship bond.

"Oh, he was so handsome and kind," said another woman, fighting tears. She glanced at Pangle's sister seated in the front row. "I had a crush on him, by the way," she added. Everyone laughed.

"He was rough around the edges," Cory Reese said from his wheelchair. "I think we related through disability. He could be a big tough guy but he told me once how hard it was for him to parachute out of a plane the first time. He wet his pants."

Pangle's sister, Pamela Hageman, and her husband and one of their two sons had come up from Monterey for the memorial. On a bulletin board leaning against a table with two candles she had put up pictures. One showed her badass brother as a sweet little boy in a striped, dark T-shirt; in another he was a handsome, strapping high school student in coat and tie. A black-and-white snapshot showed the siblings as children sitting on a step. In a leap to 2002, a color photo showed the burly, leather-jacketed brother with his arm around his pretty blonde sister.

Pamela said Steve ODed, backsliding after his long hospital stay. She and her brother had been raised in China Lake near the Mojave Desert where they rode bikes and hunted lizards, and he was big-brother-protector.

"Nobody messed with me in high school," she said. "He could be scary. But unfortunately he didn't get the love and attention at home he needed, and at 13 or 14 he turned to drugs."

She lost track of him after high school. She later learned he had been in the Marines, worked for the Post Office, was married twice and has an estranged son, 24. A father-in-law of his once said he was "a great guy when he was clean and holding a job," she said. "But drugs were a demon he was never able to conquer."

She reconnected with her brother 17 years ago when he was diagnosed schizophrenic, went on SSI and needed a sponsor to receive his monthly checks. In his impatience for money, he'd call her at home and leave messages laced with foul language.

"I was a wife, a mother with two children and working two jobs," she said, "and I didn't need that. So I told him to forget it. But he apologized and said he loved me. I was the one solid thing he could count on."

When she had to call him and he'd answer gruffly, she cut him down with sweetness.

"I'd say, 'Hello, Sunshine,' and he'd immediately change and be nice. 'Hi, Sis,' he'd say."

They met infrequently over the years as he bounced around before landing in San Francisco. But when he got sick in February they started talking a lot more. And two days after he returned from the hospital, she came to visit.

Steven Pangle with his sister Pamela Hageman. Pangle died Oct. 5, 2006.

She learned he had given the nurses such a bad time that he was passed from one hospital to another to get rid of him.

Hageman brought him clothes, food, a microwave and two tickets to a Nov. 2 concert starring his favorite group, Arrowsmith, at Shoreline Amphitheater in Mountain View. He could walk, but painfully. His colon and three-fourths of his stomach had been removed. His room had knives and swords on the walls. They talked a lot and said they loved each other. She stayed seven hours.

"My brother liked pizza, Arrowsmith, the Raiders, motorcycles, the Roman Empire, lemon meringue pie, Butterfingers and weapons," she said standing next to the pictures. "Some people asked if he overdosed on purpose. I don't think so. He was looking forward to getting rid of the colostomy bag and going to the concert, and I was going to come back for a visit.

"But he had been in the hospital so long and then he must have resumed the same level of drugs. His body couldn't take it.

"Some say people like him weren't meant to be here. But I thought he was here for me. He was ornery and reclusive and a very big bad guy – but he really wasn't. I'll miss him."

She said she would donate his body to a college here because "I'm sure they can learn something," and thanked people for coming

Then the group broke up and ate the pizza that Hageman offered and listened to an Arrowsmith CD she brought. ●

— TOM CARTER

Vietnam Vet With an Affinity for Heroin
PHIL BRUNNER

TWO DOZEN of Phil Brunner's friends crowded into the television room in the San Cristina Residence on Market Street to bid farewell to their friend whose checkered past didn't diminish their love for him.

In front, symbolizing Brunner's veteran status, an American flag hung from a green chalkboard on which his name and final statistic, 1965-2005, was written. The picture on the memorial program cover showed him hugging his little son, Joseph. Both are smiling.

Brunner had suffered medical complications for weeks before his wife, Collynne Cook, took him off life support at St. Francis Memorial Hospital.

Ben Wynn, who knew Brunner for nine years, said they both were Vietnam War veterans, Wynn serving in the Navy. Though they talked often, he said, it wasn't about the war.

"He'd do anything for anybody," Wynn said. "He was a stand-up man, a brother. I think about him every day, and there's a place in my heart for him. I know he's in heaven and his spirit is with us."

A man who lived on the fourth floor called Brunner "a wonderful gentleman" for always acknowledging him. Several women praised Brunner as sensitive and a kind-hearted friend. Others noted his dry wit, and his fondness for his cat, Panther, and for good old rock 'n' roll. Tony Baldwin, a tenant supervisor for nine months, described Brunner as the "quiet, caring type who always asked how you were doing."

Cook said Brunner had a congenital hearing impairment. After graduating from high school in Union City, she said, he wanted to join the Marines so badly he talked a friend into taking the hearing test for him. "But he got his ass kicked by the drill sergeant because he couldn't hear," she said.

Phil Brunner and son. Brunner died Feb. 21, 2005.

Brunner was sent to Vietnam, an experience he wouldn't talk about unless she prodded. Then, she said, he'd get upset and his reluctant stories were so graphic and blood-curdling that she stopped asking to hear more.

"He did a lot of time in federal and state prison," Cook told the gathering. "We spent a lot of time together when he didn't get caught. He did heroin."

She met Brunner 22 years ago. A friend introduced them with the hope that Cook would leave the stepson of Hells Angels' leader, Sonny Barger, for Brunner. They clicked, Cook said, as Brunner "wined and dined" her. They moved from Fremont to San Francisco in 1989 and into the San Cristina in 1997. She said their son, Joseph, now 12, was born with methadone and heroin dependency, plus a hearing problem. He lives in a foster home in the East Bay.

Cook said Brunner read the Bible every day.

"Seventy-five percent of the time when I walked into his room he was reading the Bible," she said. "He is the best thing that happened to me in my life. He was such a very, very giving person. I am surprised he didn't open a center for youth."

As for the drug dealing, Cook said it was "in his blood. Phil said it was what he did best."

Refreshments were available afterward. Many people stopped by to offer Cook their condolences. •

— TOM CARTER

Budding Rock Star Takes His Own Life
JESSE MORRIS

FAMILY, FRIENDS and fans of musician Jesse Morris are mourning his early death and struggling to understand what happened. He took his own life in his Ellis Street apartment. Two days later, he would have turned 27.

"His death was a disaster," said Joe Dean, guitarist in Morris' backing band, the Man Cougars. Dean knew him six years and was a mentor to him. "I've been through suicides — my dad committed suicide — but this was tragic as could be."

Hundreds turned out for a wake where musician friends took turns singing Morris' songs while the Man Cougars backed them. A week after his death, at Oakland's Uptown nightclub, at what had been scheduled as a gig for Morris and the Man Cougars, friends and admirers raised the money to pay for his cremation.

"Everybody liked him, he had a lot of friends," said Carole Lennon, owner of Lennon Rehearsal Studios in SoMa, where the wake was held. "A very warm, wonderful person."

Morris packed a lot into his lifetime. He played music in a variety of genres, in several bands including HeP.Si, in which he used the stage name Jesse Jaundice, the U.S. Kings, the Tenderloin Two and, for the past few years, the Man Cougars. The band got its name when Morris teased them about their appeal to younger women.

PHOTO BY HEIDI ZUMBRUN

Jesse Morris, two nights before he died, Nov. 4, 2011.

He was a familiar sight at the 24th Street BART Station, singing and playing his father's Guild acoustic guitar for commuters. Many clips of him survive on YouTube to validate astonished testimonials to his uncannily faithful renditions of Johnny Cash songs — and his popularity. His Cash-sounding version of Kris Kristofferson's "Sunday Morning Coming Down," filmed at 24th Street BART, had almost a quarter-million page views two weeks after his death.

"He could mimic anybody," Dean said. He had a voice like "honey on tits. He could do me better than me, he could do Cash better than Cash."

BART featured him in a video on its Website and the SF Weekly named him "Best BART Musician" in 2008. Dean said Morris could bring in $180 in a few hours' work at BART, and that other BART buskers said Morris "showed us that we could do this — everybody in BART stations loves and thanks Jesse." Over the years Morris played at BART stations more than 1,000 times, he told online magazine Alarm Press.

At a Board of Supervisors meeting, Supervisor John Avalos paid tribute to Morris, screening a YouTube video, paraphrasing "Folsom Prison Blues," to wit: "I hear the BART train comin' ..." and remembering "a big tattooed guy singing Johnny Cash songs with an uncanny impression of his baritone. While his appearance may have been intimidating, he was a warm and friendly guy with a great sense of humor. For years, commuters enjoyed his songs echoing up the walls. He was a much-loved member of the community."

"JESSE MORRIS and the Man Cougars" was the group's only album released during his lifetime, but Dean says they recorded another, which he expects to come out in 2012. "This was a good band," said Dean, who, at 43, was its next-youngest member. For the first time in his career, he said, instead of the usual drill of calling around for gigs, he was fielding offers and picking and choosing from among them. Opening for the Dwarves, he said, "we would absolutely slay crowds of a thousand people. ... We have a record contract. In this day and age, who even has a record contract?"

Before meeting Morris, the Man Cougars had toured Europe repeatedly and been hired by the U.S. Department of Defense to play for troops in Afghanistan and Iraq.

The band produced its own album. A friend in Los Angeles played it for Jimmy White, national sales director of Cockroach Media, an independent record label distributor.

"I just flipped over it; it really is an amazing record," White told The Extra, and he got in touch with the band to talk about pushing the album.

The record is selling particularly well in Japan, Dean said, and seems to be experiencing the all-too-typical surge in sales after a musician's death. White said it's sold in at least 11 European countries, South America and Canada.

The album is available only on vinyl or as a download, not on CD. "He was an old school vinyl junkie, and saw no use for a CD version," White says. "Being involved with the release of this album was a labor of love for me."

Morris was a commanding presence, 6 feet 4 and heavily tattooed. Though at one time he weighed 390 pounds, his mother, Julie Augustine, said that the medical examiner weighed him in at 230. The weight gain was due to his prodigious appetite — and perhaps his mom's "amazing" cooking — but when he decided to lose it, he worked it off through diet and exercise over about 18 months.

Morris also worked the door at the Minibar on Divisadero Street, which is where his fiancee, Apphia Williams, a writer, met him in 2010.

Morris was bipolar and struggled with depression and had been prescribed medications for these conditions since he was a teenager. He also was known to self-medicate. He'd been hospitalized after a suicide attempt two months earlier that had been thwarted by Williams with the help of their next-door neighbor, Jesse Harper, a musician and close friend.

Morris lingered in an induced coma after that incident, and his mother said he subsequently entered a rehab center in Burbank dedicated to musicians, a visit paid for by an admirer. He was apologetic in person and online — his Facebook page linking him to hundreds of "friends."

The page also hints at his sense of humor, stating, for instance, that he "studied ADD at GED."

"He does have that quick, wicked, sorta dark sense of humor," said Dina Silver, who knew Morris since he was "about 4."

"He had a 'don't give a damn attitude' — shake 'em, and if they're still standing, then maybe they're worth talking to."

"It was fun playing with him, he was a great kid," recalled longtime friend, guitarist Jimmy Crucifix, citing as fun years the "hard-core punk thing" when Morris performed as Jesse Jaundice. But he said Morris "was uncomfortable in this world."

"I just saw him always as a great kid. He seemed a little lonely, depressed. He wasn't afraid to sit down and cry." His emotional side, Crucifix said, was in part "what made him such a good player. Playing music put him in a different world."

He said Morris eventually told his friends he had blacked out and that the suicide attempt "was a stupid thing to do," blaming it on a bad mix of chemicals. "To me," Crucifix said, "it means he was hiding something."

WILLIAMS said they'd been enjoying a romantic evening together when it happened. She went to the bathroom, came out, he went in, she heard a noise and found him hanging.

"He had a perfect moment and figured that's when he wanted to leave," Silver theorized.

"There was so much more to Jesse than his music," said Sunny McEwing, who has a son a bit older than Morris, knew him since his early teenage years, housed him at different times in his life, became "best friends" and traveled with him. "I can't tell you how many times, wherever we went, he'd just get crowds around him — people he didn't know. He'd get everybody laughing.

"He wasn't inhibited at all. That was part of the wonder of Jesse. The flip side of that was that he was incredibly sensitive, really, really sensitive and he did care," McEwing said.

"He was a very charismatic guy. I didn't mean to fall in love with the guy, but I did, and always will be," Dean said. Dean said his band was looking for a frontman when they met Morris, and that they worked with him to get him to be less derivative, and comfortable with his own identity.

When they started working together, Dean said, he could hear Morris' influences in his songs — Flipper, the Buzzcocks, Merle Haggard, Cash. "We kept pushing him to try to find his own voice," Dean said. "Fortunately, in the last year of his life he had gotten further away from the mimicking and got to where he sounded like himself."

"We had a lot of success," Dean said, citing how quickly they'd risen to headliner status at the now-dark Folsom Street Annie's Social Club, where they'd get $500 for a show.

"He was never comfortable here unless he was performing," Dean said. "I think he was scared of himself, unsure of how to be. He said that over and over again."

Although he left no suicide note, Dean said, "over and over and over, in 80% of every song that he wrote," he'd cite how he had everything to live for yet felt hopelessly despondent. "If you try to kill yourself once on dope, and once when you're sober, that's a decision that I have to respect," Dean said.

"No matter what anybody said, he would have done what he wanted to do," Silver said. "He was done; he wanted to leave." If you believe that people should be allowed to live freely, she said, "they should be able to leave in any capacity they like, as long as they don't take anybody out with them."

"The one thing Jesse failed to realize in his life," Crucifix said, "was that a lot of people loved him."

Working with him in a business mode was enervating, Dean said. "It's the completely insane people that have the talent. If I was half as talented as he was — I'm two times as skilled, but there's a difference — maybe I would've killed myself.

"He used up all his fuel."

"Suicide is about pain," said Eve Meyer, executive director of San Francisco Suicide Prevention, the city's most knowledgeable expert on the subject. Meyer didn't know Morris, but said:

"He must have been in tremendous pain, and you worry that he couldn't find his way

> **If you try to kill yourself once on dope, and once when you're sober, that's a decision that I have to respect.**

Jesse Morris' "don't give a damn attitude" and love for Johnny Cash has him mimicking an iconic photo of his idol. Photo by Troy Holden

out of that. What you really need to concentrate on is trying to nurture the part of them that wants to live. And try to remove the pain, because the pain is what gets in the way of them wanting to live."

Attempting suicide "absolutely" is a cry for attention, Meyer said, "and that's appropriate. If they're in pain and crying out for help, they need help and you try to help them get help."

MORRIS was born in San Francisco and raised largely in Pacifica. From a very young age, his love of music was evident. Augustine recalled him at 2 saying, "Mom, I gotta sing you a song," then fetching a hairbrush from the bathroom to use as a microphone, climbing on a chair and singing her the Beatles' "Love Me Do."

He was a quick study, good with words and mimicry, his mother said, articulate at an early age and always highly responsive to musical stimuli. They would sing together in the car, and "even though he didn't like doing his homework, his writing skills were pretty amazing."

Morris' father, Jim, separated from Augustine when Jesse and his older brother Jamison were toddlers. He stayed close and visited them every weekend while their mother was working. Augustine worked evenings at the Cliff House and Ritz Carlton and the boys were often in the care of "amazing babysitters" — two sisters who lived nearby in Pacifica and cared for them over the course of many years.

"I wasn't the best mother, but I wasn't the worst," Augustine said. She and others freely admitted that her youngest son "was a mama's boy" and said they were in constant contact.

Jim Morris died of a heart attack in his sleep when his sons were teens, Augustine said. Sixteen-year-old Jesse found the body. "That was devastating."

Jim Morris, a contractor, was a hobbyist musician. Augustine said that when Jesse was about 8, when the boy's love and aptitude for music began to emerge, his dad bought him a guitar.

He announced later, "I want a keyboard."

"But you don't play piano."

"I'll learn."

And he did, she said. Drums, too.

Augustine said that Jesse's father resembled Johnny Cash, and that Jim's Memphis heritage also probably had an influence. On his left biceps, Morris had tattoos of Hank Williams, Cash, Iggy Pop and others.

"Every time I saw him, he had a new tattoo," his brother said. He got his first at 18, "as soon as it was legal," and was so outgoing and friendly that he was able to get tattoo artists to work on him almost at will. He'd get new ones on a whim, sometimes "just to mock his friends."

He held a job at one point at Tower Records, where his gregariousness made him a "great salesman," Augustine said. But he couldn't hold a job. "He'd have a job for a while and be OK, then depression would hit and he couldn't get up and he'd lose his job."

FOR A WHILE, he was a resident at Catholic Charities' Guerrero House in San Francisco and also worked with the Job Corps on Treasure Island. For the past several years, after he qualified for disability benefits, he lived on Ellis Street in the subsidized apartment where he died.

Morris attempted suicide as a teenager, swallowing a full prescription bottle of Wellbutrin. Morris attended Alcoholics Anonymous and Narcotics Anonymous groups and had counselors in addition to medical interventions throughout his life.

"He was better when on his meds," Augustine said. "His lows were pretty awful. The older he got, the worse they got."

In the past, Jamison Morris said, his brother had reached out for help when he needed it — often when he was "really drunk. ... When he would become suicidal, he would check himself into hospitals. It happened more times than I can count."

Morris had a long history of addiction to prescription opiates, his brother said. "He was able to hide it from some people with the same old bullshit stories you hear from prescription addicts," for instance, that the drug use was no cause for concern because it was prescribed.

"Addiction just runs in the family," he said.

Like so many others, though, Jamison Morris said that despite all of his brother's issues, he was stunned by his death. "He had a lot of people he could've called, and had in the past," he said. When they last saw each other, at Halloween, Jesse had played him a reggae song he'd recorded and was "really happy and positive, talking about the future. People who are suicidal don't talk about the future," he said.

"Every moment that I spent with Jesse was a gift," Williams said. "He experienced love deeply, he experienced pain deeply, and unfortunately, the pain seemed to take precedence a month ago.

"We both invested in our relationship. We were rich in love. Other than that we had enough to sustain ourselves," she said. The couple had a cat, Odin, that Morris adopted after it had been abandoned. They loved dogs and spent time together in dog parks, smoking, drinking coffee and talking. "Low-cost activities," Williams said.

Morris left scads of journals, now in his brother's possession. "Eventually I'm going to go through it and try to compile it, but it's a lot," Jamison said. "He wrote on napkins and transfers and everything."

His ashes will be divided and shared among his many friends who have expressed a desire to have a part of him, his brother said, "because he pretty much shared himself when he was alive." ●

— MARK HEDIN

" He'll be a permanent part of my heart. "

"Sunset — the Cadillac." This is the hotel where supportive housing began.
Photo by Mark Ellinger

PART 5: Analysis

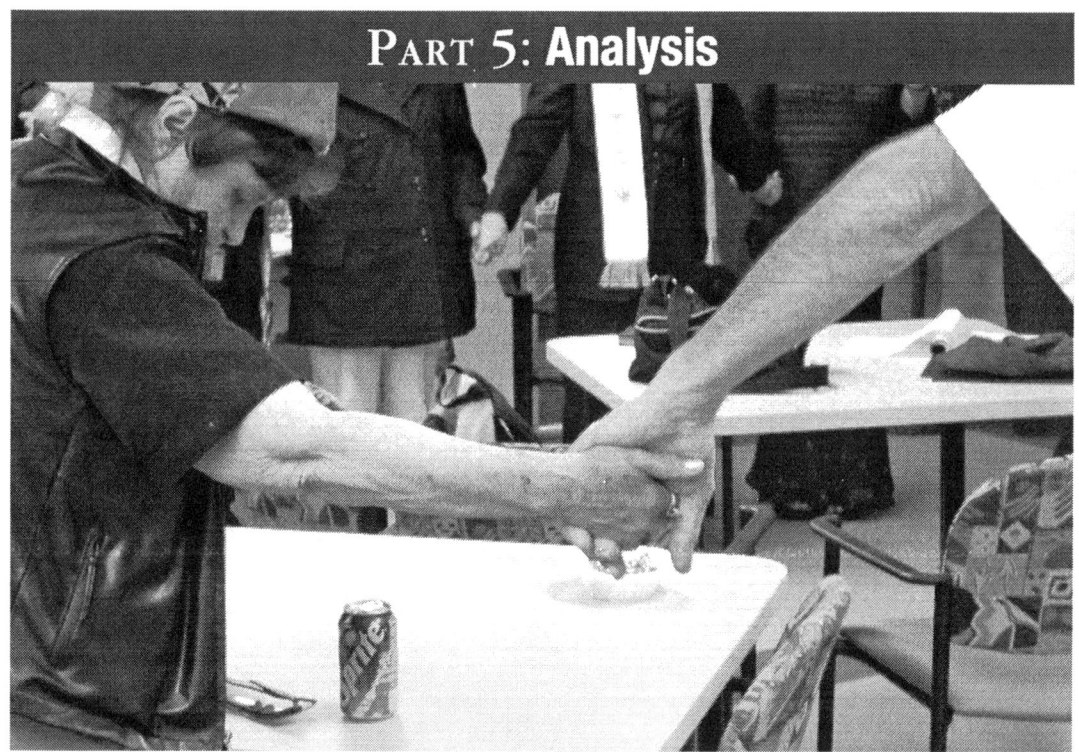

PHOTO BY LENNY LIMJOCO

Rev. Glenda Hope's memorials, including this one that she conducted at Alexander Residence, end with mourners holding hands in a circle, then giving the sign of peace.

Those Who Died

BY
MARJORIE
BEGGS

CENTRAL CITY EXTRA'S obituaries are a snapshot of who dies — and, by extension, who lives — in the Tenderloin. Since 2004, when The Extra was invited to attend memorials and obituaries became a regular part of our coverage, and the end of 2011, our reporters had written last words for 220 of our neighbors. The oldest was 101-year-old Dalt Hotel resident Willie Leach, born in Rosebud, Texas, a Pullman cook in the 1930s and a Bay Area shipyard worker during World War II.

The youngest were two 20-year-olds: Logan "Cito" Kausman, who died of a gunshot wound, leaving an infant son, apartment, job and car, and Jimmy Mai, who grew up in the neighborhood, a regular at the oasis of the Tenderloin Children's Center, who died of a rare blood disease.

Tenderloin residents die younger than their fellow San Franciscans, not surprising considering their harsher lifestyle. They're also poorer and more likely to be mentally or physically disabled, SSI their only income.

The average age of the deceased in our obituaries — 55 — wasn't even close to the city as a whole, where men are expected to live 78 years and women 84, according to Health Matters in San Francisco, a Website developed by Building a Healthier San Francisco, an 18-agency public-private coalition, and the Healthy Communities Institute, which gives cities and other locales tools to measure and analyze their health data.

ANALYSIS

Women comprise just about half of all San Franciscans. Central city is a different story. City Planning estimates that only 39% of residents living downtown and around the Civic Center are women. Among those for whom we wrote obituaries, the percentage dropped to 25%. Perhaps the discrepancy is because women generally prefer not to live in this dangerous neighborhood, or because we cover few deaths of monolingual Asian women, of which there are many living in the Tenderloin.

BEYOND AGE and sex, facts about the deceased are scanty, drawn primarily from memorials held in the SRO or apartment building where they had lived. This is a transient neighborhood with a smaller, permanent community of residents, but most of those we wrote about had lived in their building five years or less. Still, two of our subjects lived in the same place for 30 years and nine for two decades.

To write the obituaries, Extra reporters have become adept at patching together the story of a life from remembrances at memorials that begin, "I didn't know him well, but … " The last name of the person who died frequently is unknown to the mourners, yet they come to the memorial to acknowledge a neighbor's passing.

Many people here are estranged from their families. Relatives rarely attend the memorials. When they do, they help broaden our understanding of their kin, including how relationships often eroded and contact dwindled over the years. Some have never seen where their relative lived in the Tenderloin. It can be an eye-opener if they do.

When Mike McKenney's parents visited him at the San Cristina, his father told Tenant Services Coordinator Lucinda Walls that he finally understood why his son had chosen to stay there. "He saw that this was his family, too," Walls told mourners at McKenney's memorial.

Nonprofit housing developers own most of the SROs where the memorials we cover are held. Besides upgrading the deteriorating buildings that the vulnerable populations call home, the developers provide on-site social services, cultural, educational and recreational activities, laundry and cooking facilities, and other amenities — including memorials — to encourage a sense of community among residents.

"I remember a man telling me what it used to be like," recalled Rev. Glenda Hope, who has officiated, she guesses, at more than a thousand memorials. "Residents would see first the police come in, then the coroner. A body would be rolled out on a gurney, the room would be cleaned up and that would be it. Someone new moved in. No one knew what had happened."

Hope says stopping to remember the dead tells neighbors, hotel staff, family, the public that "the life of the person who died is precious, and yours is, too. It dignifies and shows respect for all life."

Regular memorials date from 1999, when the city's early master leases with nonprofit contractors brought supportive services to SRO residents. Staff include on-site social workers and others who help residents get benefits, keep appointments, handle paperwork and give other day-to-day assistance that encourages a more independent, productive life.

Acknowledging the death of each resident is an essential part of TNDC's continuum of services, says Don Falk, executive director of Tenderloin Neighborhood Development Corp., which owns and operates 26 SROs and apartment buildings that are home to low-income central city residents.

The memorials are an effort to build community, Falk says. "The housing provides a place where they can live out their last years in dignity, and the memorials bring people together at an emotional time — for residents and for staff whose sense of loss also is palpable."

Support staff at memorials occasionally add a few personal recollections about the deceased, but, as human service professionals bound by federal HIPPA privacy rules, they can't give reporters much beyond the person's age and how long they lived in the hotel. Even in death, a resident's personal information remains confidential, adding to our frustration in telling the person's story.

Another challenge is that many SRO-dwellers live in self-imposed isolation, reticent even with close neighbors about their physical or mental health. "He never complained" and "I didn't even know she was so sick" are frequent comments from mourners.

> *Jens Larsen lived a life that was quiet, self-sufficient, private. When he died at age 84, no neighbors at the Franciscan Towers, where he'd lived for 23 years, knew the cause. His records listed no family, and the several hotel residents who attended his memorial said he'd never talked about his past.*
> — Gone With the Wind, page 66

Lacking information from neighbors or staff — and with medical examiner's office reports unavailable for months — we were unable to list the cause of death in 97 of the 220 obituaries we wrote between June 2004 and December 2011. Among those for whom the cause was known, 22 were related to cancer, 17 to lung disease, 16 to heart problems, 10 to liver complications, nine to AIDS/HIV complications, seven to diabetes and six to kidney problems.

Seven people died of "natural causes," we were told, and 15 of varied but specific causes. Two were shot and three died in accidents. Six were confirmed suicides with another three possible suicides. Each year in San Francisco, 100 to 120 people commit suicide, one every third day, according to the S.F. Medical Society.

Health Matters reports that citywide, self-inflicted injuries were the eighth-ranked cause of premature death citywide in 2004-07. In the 94102 ZIP code area (Tenderloin, Hayes Valley and North of Market), however, self-inflicted injuries were the fifth-leading cause for men and the ninth for women. HIV/AIDS was the first cause for men, followed by heart disease, unintentional drug overdose and hypertension. For women, the first cause is heart disease, followed by unintentional drug overdose and HIV/AIDS.

> *The manner of her death was a particularly harsh blow for her friends at the Coast Hotel. ... Nobody expected her suicide, said one resident after the service ended. "Everything I got from her was always positive. She had one of the straightest heads of anyone in this hotel."*
> — Soul and Sunlight, page 95

OUR OBITUARY subjects were overwhelmingly single, and more than 1 in 10 had been homeless before moving into their SRO. The S.F. Department of Public Health and city Health Services Agency subsidize approximately 1,500 units for the homeless in 50 residential hotels and apartment buildings, many in the Tenderloin and South of Market. Among the 31 people we were able to identify as previously homeless, a handful had lived in their SRO but a few months; most had been there two to three years.

Work histories, a staple of traditional newspaper obituaries, are elusive in this population. Despite the deceased's relatively young age, their physical or mental disabilities probably made holding down a job difficult for years, if not decades, before they died. Only a few were still working at the time of their death. Many of the older residents got Social Security while younger people often were on SSI. Our reporters were unable to get information about past employment for 40% of our obituaries.

But, sparse as the details are, they reflect a neighborhood whose residents are noteworthy: There was a Doublemint gum twin, a strolling flower vendor, the fan dancer "Honey West," a Stanford linear accelerator engineer, rocker Eddie Money's roadie, a dentist, a fisherman, a "Hollywood Squares" writer, a musician who played with Patti LaBelle, a Time-Warner computer expert, a co-founder of the spoken-word Molotov Mouths troupe, the gay and AIDS activist Hank Wilson, noted mental health advocate Darwin Diaz and supportive housing pioneer Leroy Looper.

About 10% of the deceased were veterans, one served in World War II, others in Vietnam and the Gulf wars. The Department of Veterans Affairs says approximately 26,500 vets live in San Francisco, 3% of the city's population, but disabilities force many into poorer neighborhoods like the Tenderloin or onto the streets. Swords to Plowshares estimates that 17% of the city's 6,455 homeless people are vets.

More and more Americans today are choosing to die at home, surrounded by family and friends, away from the sterile hospital environment. Our neighbors, too, may have died "at home," but not necessarily by choice.

> *In Morgan's last weeks, Davis and others noticed that he had lost a lot of weight, yet kept drinking. "I don't know if he was afraid to go to the doctor," Davis said, "but I never saw him go." Morgan, apparently ignoring his failing health, died in bed reading his newspaper. He was 53.*
> — Batman, page 6

Among the deceased in our obits, 88 died somewhere in their SRO — one in the lobby, another in the elevator. But most died in their rooms, lonely deaths that sometimes went undiscovered for days, piteous postscripts that even the most dignified obituary can't alter.

A HANDFUL of the 220 obituaries published by Central City Extra during this period were for South of Market, not Tenderloin, residents, Market Street being the great divide separating San Francisco's inner-most city. While not part of *Death in the Tenderloin*, the western SoMa obituaries were included in this analysis.

Our published obituaries reflect but a fraction of the deaths in the central city where hundreds of families handle their own funerals and cultural farewells. ●

Profile of our obituary subjects

An unscientific look at demographics of SRO residents who passed away 2004-11.

1. Most were single.
2. 1 in 10 had previously been homeless.
3. SRO resident for 2 to 3 years or more.
4. 40% had no discoverable employment history.
5. 10% were veterans.
6. 72% died in their SRO.
7. 75% were men.
8. Average age at death, 55.

How they died

Among the 220 obituraries, we were able to discover the cause of death for 123.

1. Cancer (22)
2. Lung disease (17)
3. Heart disease (16)
4. Liver disease (10)
5. AIDS/HIV (9)
6. Diabetes (7)
7. Natural causes (7)
8. Kidney disease (6)
9. Suicide (6)
10. Possible suicide (3)
11. Accidents (3)
12. Shooting (2)
13. Varied specific causes (15)

Source: Central City Extra research

Troubadour Touched People
JOSEPH WILLIAM SHELTON

JOE SHELTON and Rene McIntyre were a hit at the reopening of the Empress Hotel in September 2005, he on guitar, she on keyboards, both of them singing. A song the amateur troubadours did with great feeling was "Angel," made popular by Sarah McLachlan, about traveling musicians facing hardships on the road.

This was one of many memories shared at Joseph William Shelton's memorial in the Empress' Community Room where Shelton had often performed. The 14 mourners said his smile, sensitivity and generous personality won him as many friends as his music.

An electrician by trade and Vietnam War veteran, Shelton was diagnosed less than a year ago with brain cancer. He died at Maitri Hospice near Church and Duboce. He was 55.

"He was the epitome of an honest man," said a man in the front row.

"He had a vision of how people should be treated," said a woman in the back, "but not always the solution."

"He faced death with dignity and courage," another man said.

Joe Shelton plays and sings during a talent show at the Empress. He died Sept. 4, 2007. Photo by Lenny Limjoco

Property Manager Roberta Goodman said Shelton was instrumental in achieving camaraderie at the hotel. When he served on the tenant council, he had big ideas for everyone's welfare. "He was full of them," she said. "He had a passion to create a food program. And he wanted people to change. The frustration (when change didn't come) would drive him batty."

Shelton's wish for more nutritious food for Empress residents came to fruition a few months before he died. Goodman created the Empress Food Market at which residents every Thursday afternoon can pick up a large canvas bag of produce and grains that she gets from the Food Bank. "It's enough to last almost a week," she said. "These are people with very limited means. And it's hardly $1.18 a person."

The hotel for formerly homeless is operated by the nonprofit DISH (Delivering Innovation in Supprotive Housing) under Department of Public Health guidelines. Shelton became a resident through the Health Care for Homeless Veterans program.

Nutrition was among Shelton's many concerns for all in the Tenderloin, said Shavi Blake, 31, a friend from the Noe Valley neighborhood who plays the guitar and met him during an open-mic music session four years ago. The two played at Bazaar in the Richmond District, Dylan's in the Fillmore and at Canvas Gallery in the Inner Sunset. They went to music festivals together and camped and hiked in Marin County and around Lake Tahoe.

"He was very talented and had written about 10 songs," Blake said. "He had lyrics for another 30. He was interested in politics, homelessness and technical things about electricity and cars."

Shelton, born in Birmingham, Ala., joined the Air Force in 1972 after two years of junior college and served till 1976. He took his discharge in Alaska and rode a motorcycle down the West Coast to Half Moon Bay, a place that enchanted him. But he went back to Birmingham and landed a job as an aircraft mechanic.

"'He was smart, well-traveled and self-taught,"' his former wife, Carol Balch, at the time a college art student, wrote in a letter to Goodman that she read aloud. " 'That was the Joe Shelton I fell in love with.'" They married and had a son, Joseph Allen Shelton.

Shelton, 29 in 1981, ran for Birmingham City Council. He wanted to "create a mass transit industry that would provide jobs and revenue for the city," he was quoted in a reprinted Birmingham News article. He lost, and his wife wrote that the city still lacks adequate transportation.

Copies of the article were on a table alongside copies of the Central City Extra's issue that featured a tenant talent show at the Empress, and on page 7 was a photo of Shelton. He had opened with a song that was about being transported back to love, family, beauty and serenity. He finished with "Get Together," a 1960s anthem that goes: "C'mon people, now smile on your brother, ev'rybody get together, try to love one another right now."

"He really helped knit people together," said Goodman. "He's someone who cared about the community. He touched people."

Blake had a half dozen of Shelton's self-produced CDs for the taking on a table near the candles and bouquet. He had been assigned to take care of Shelton's ashes, which will be scattered in San Francisco Bay and maybe Half Moon Bay, where another memorial for Shelton will be held.

At the end, before refreshments were served, Rene McIntyre went to the front and played an electric piano and, in a pretty voice that didn't waver, sang "In the Arms of an Angel," which ended:

> "… you are pulled from the wreckage of your silent reverie
> you're in the arms of the angel
> may you find some comfort here." ●

— TOM CARTER

Musician Who Almost Made It

GARY MAGUIRE

GARY MAGUIRE narrowly missed his 15 minutes of fame as a musician. The drummer once tried out for the Jefferson Starship band and had just about everyone's vote, Stephanie Olson, his wife, said after Maguire's memorial at the Coronado Hotel where they had lived for six months.

"Grace Slick liked him and the others in the band wanted him, too — he could play all the instruments but excelled at the drums — but the execs didn't," she said. "So he didn't get it. If he had, I told him he wouldn't have lived very long, leading that kind of life."

Maguire didn't have a long life, as it was. He died at the hotel, presumably of liver complications, at age 49.

A half dozen mourners recalled with affection the tall man with a raspy voice. One elderly woman called him "a beautiful person." Olson sat in the front row sobbing. She could manage only a few statements through her tears.

"As all of you know, I loved him very, very much, and his forgiveness, and most of all his love for me," Olson said of their 10 years together. "He was my dearest friend, among other things. I'd like to say a lot. There is so much I can remember."

But she couldn't continue and sat back down.

After the memorial, as the social services staff prepared plates of food in the next room for the mourners, Olson gathered herself and talked more about the 6-foot-5 Maguire who, she conceded, "died from alcohol." She started talking about him and their life together.

Several generations of his family were from South San Francisco, so he knew a lot of people. He worked in construction for a while, then was homeless with her for several years. Even so, they made the best of it. Once, when they had a little cash, they took bicycles to Woodside and rode around looking at fabulous houses.

"We walked everywhere together and did a lot of talking," she said. "Gary was the only man in my life I could be completely honest with. My best friend."

Gary Maguire died Jan. 6, 2009

The city's Homeless Outreach Team got them into the Coronado and Maguire started to change, got edgier. He was cheerful enough indoors, but not out in the hood where danger lurked. He was sensitive about cruelty and injustice.

"If he saw some guy hurting a woman he'd step in and beat the shit out of him," she said. "He was outraged at abuse. And you didn't see as much of his soft side here."

Among her fondest memories is when they were homeless in Burlingame and bought a big six-person tent — Olson, 39, is 6 feet tall herself — and pitched it by the railroad tracks. They had nothing but each other.

"We'd lie there and talk about nothing and everything. He was so happy and generous. There was nothing he wouldn't do for me. And nobody bothered us."

A pack of cigarettes went missing one morning. She said squirrels got it. He said rats, then showed her where they were in the bushes, and they laughed over it.

"We had no water or electricity," she said. "But I was so happy to be with him and wake up to the songbirds."

She paused and, growing sorrowful again, looked forlornly toward Maguire's photograph on the table in front.

"It gets worse every day," she said. ●

— TOM CARTER

One of a Kind

KATHY FIELD

PURPLE MUMS in pots, glowing candles and a copy of a poem that began, "Light a candle for those we mourn ..." graced the table at the Hamlin Hotel in memory of Kathy Field, a resident there for almost eight years after being homeless for nine.

She died in her fifth-floor room a month shy of her 60th birthday.

Eighteen people came to remember a woman they admired but who, they admitted, often drove them nuts with her honesty and abandon.

"You just had to love her, even though she shocked you," Donald Thomas, an eight-year Hamlin resident, said at her memorial. "She had an incredible passion for all creatures. There was even a rumor that she was feeding milk to the hotel mice. There was only one Kathy, and I'm going to miss her."

Kathy Field died Jan. 5, 2008

Loretta Ball lived on the sixth floor, right above Field, and they became fast friends. "We had good times and bad times, like all friends," Ball said. "Often we'd bang on our floor and ceiling to communicate — bang, bang, bang with a broom to say good night."

By the time a few more people had shared memories, many in the room were in tears.

Vanessa Brown, a former case worker, called Field "a bright light, a warm, caring soul."

A man called Dr. Joe said he was her special friend: "When I was ill, messing myself, she brought me clean clothes and took care of me 24/7."

Ma Anand Rekha remembered how Field would hang clothes to dry on the back fence. "Then she'd bring them to me, smelling of fresh air. I just wish she'd taken care of herself. I wanted her to heal, and maybe I was mean to her toward the end, but she was getting worse and worse."

Kathleen Flanagan, tenant services supervisor, said it was she who found Field dead, the latest of seven residents' bodies she's discovered since working in SROs. The cause of Field's death, she said, was "uncertain." ●

— MARJORIE BEGGS

Desk Clerk Like a Professor
JAMES WILLIAMS

JAMES WILLIAMS, a former Maritime Museum employee, was a well-read Tenderloin intellectual who charmed people with his knowledge and inspired them to read and learn.

He was a desk clerk at the Cambridge Hotel for the past 17 years, until he got too sick to work. In his friendly way he bent people's ears coming and going through the lobby, about history and music and other subjects close to his heart. Some reverently called him Mr. Williams. Alabama-born, he referred to himself simply as "a Southern gentleman."

After a long battle with cancer, Williams died at Kaiser Hospital at age 65.

Forty mourners filled the Cambridge Hotel's community room to capacity for his memorial, spilling outside where a dozen stood in the lobby. The unusually large turnout was a tribute to Williams' kindness and impact on others, said Rev. Glenda Hope, who officiated.

On a small easel next to Hope were a dozen photos showing Williams as a toddler and, in uniform, his dad, who had been killed in World War II, and boat sketches that Williams liked.

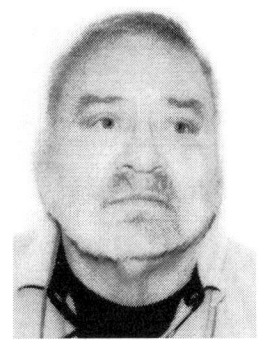

James Williams died Jan. 12, 2008

"I've been here 12½ years and I learned so much from him," said an older man.

"He was like a professor," a woman said.

"He loved IMAX 3-D movies and documentaries, but only good ones," said longtime friend Walter Lilly who now lives at the Columbia Hotel. "He felt ripped off if they were inferior and dramatized like a Hollywood movie."

"When he found out I liked to read he'd give me three or four books a week!" a woman exclaimed, raising a laugh. "But I couldn't read that much."

The mourners recalled Williams' love of Southern cuisine, his "calming ways" and many kindnesses: taking a resident out for a steak on her birthday and insisting she order the most expensive one; taking a friend during Fleet Week to see the Blue Angels and explaining aerodynamics; taking friends to Davies Symphony Hall to hear classical music, but not the modern stuff, which he hated.

Williams' former wife, Janet Cydel of Larkspur, and their son, Michael, and daughter, Chandra, attended and talked with his friends after the memorial. She had met Williams at Ohio State and they came to California in the 1960s, hoping to get into UC Berkeley, his "fourth or fifth college." She got in; he went to San Francisco State. He never got a degree, she said.

Williams came from a large Alabama family, she said, and was "the only one" without a Southern accent. They were divorced after 10 years. He had "a lot of demons," she said, mainly alcohol.

He worked for the Maritime Museum in the 1970s. Once, when on the clipper ship Balclutha's deck, he jumped into the bay and saved a stranger who had fallen over the railing.

Williams beat a brain tumor in 1996 and stopped drinking. But his cancer battles continued until a more aggressive form put him back in the hospital. He died there two weeks later. ●

— TOM CARTER

Onetime Investment Banker
HARVEY WHITLOCK

HARVEY WHITLOCK was a former Wall Street investment banker. White-haired and maybe 5-feet-8 and 100 pounds, he was polite and never swore. He was sensitive and had a sense of humor, too. And he earned respect and affection at the Ambassador Hotel where he lived for nearly five years.

But Whitlock had his demons. They led him to drink and, in the last year of his life, drugs.

He was found in his room on the sixth floor. He had been dead two days, social workers said. Cause of death was unknown. Whitlock was 60.

"He was very polite and easy to get along with, when he wasn't battling demons," said Cecil Baker at Whitlock's memorial where a half dozen mourners gathered in the hotel's Listening Post room. Baker lived across the hall from Whitlock.

Harvey Whitlock died Jan. 27, 2008

"I'd ask him about a stock — but I don't have any — and he'd say, 'Don't buy that shit, it's fantasy.' It'd make him mad."

"A gentle presence," someone said.

But sometimes Whitlock wandered out at night and got beat up on the street.

"He'd end up with the most horrible black eyes," Baker said.

Baker talked to Whitlock several times a week and learned that in the last year he had turned to speed.

"It's amazing what we remember of him is all positive," Baker said. ●

— TOM CARTER

Essex Hotel Favorites
JEFF DEATON and DAISY YEPIZ

THE NEWLY renovated Essex Hotel conducted a double memorial for two of its formerly homeless residents: one, a towering, highly literate man from Colorado affectionately known as "the gentle giant"; the other, a tall African lady whose courage and optimism had inspired those who helped her.

Jeff Deaton and Daisy Yepiz moved into the Community Housing Partnership hotel within six days of each other, among the first of Department of Human Services homeless referrals. They died in their rooms a day apart. Both had been happy in their new community where help and new friends were at their fingertips.

Yepiz was 61 when she died in her room of heart disease.

Deaton was the first of 84 residents to move into the Essex after its $23.2 million, yearlong renovation. He had postponed an operation on his trachea, a staff member said, and then had the surgery after he got situated. He was found dead in his room at age 46. Cause of death yet undetermined.

It was a testament to their popularity that more than 30 residents and others from the Bay Area attended their memorial and spoke affectionately of them. Some people had to stand for lack of seating.

Because of his operation, the 6-foot-5 Deaton could hardly speak. So the "gentle giant" became a prolific writer. He penned eloquent letters to the staff and other residents about the housing and its appurtenances, and about his love of nature, hiking and rock climbing, and how he missed them. He had come from a shelter but it wasn't known how long he had been homeless or when he originally came to the city.

Deaton reveled in his new stability and his future. In one six-page handwritten letter to the staff, he wrote in part:

Jeff Deaton died March 26, 2008

"I never dreamed a few months ago I'd ever live, or have a place to live, have dignity, comfort and a chance to attain the things that I believe I need in order to live an enjoyable life — or have the physical wellness to do so."

His Colorado relatives sent a large bouquet of purple and yellow flowers that were on a table in front next to a bouquet for Yepiz.

Little was known about Yepiz when she first moved in. "She chose her company carefully," said the social worker. Few knew she had children in Africa.

Yepiz was born in Zimbabwe and left her family to work in America and send money home. Zimbabwe, one of the world's poorest countries, has an unemployment rate of 80%.

"She was tall, maybe 6 feet, and thin, and wore colorful clothes," said one staff member. "And she had a good sense of humor. She valued people and could connect with them. She had no compunction about just walking up and talking to anyone."

Her African name was Daisy Shekede; she was named after her village.

Mr. Ibangi, from Nigeria, brought her to the Bay Area as a nanny for his two children and to help his wife, a family friend said.

"She lived with us," Ibangi said at the memorial. He was in Nigeria when she died, and had just returned. "She was a true mother at heart and a no-nonsense person."

At some point she left the Ibangi family and moved to Oakland. It wasn't known when she married a Chinese man and changed her name, but she took a job waitressing in Sukhi's Indian restaurant for several years. She became good friends with the owner, a woman who often gave her Indian clothes. Somewhere, Yepiz lost her green card.

Marni Temple of Richmond met her at Sukhi's 11 years ago and struck up a friendship. When Temple had a hip replacement, she asked Yepiz to take care of her.

"It was a great gift," said Temple, who was wearing a dark Indian dress to honor Yepiz. "She helped me from bed to the walker to the cane. She could be stubborn, too. But without that she wouldn't have survived. Then I lost track of her. Thank all of you who helped her."

Yepiz apparently got sick and moved to San Francisco. Her husband died eight months ago, someone said.

Daisy Yepiz died March 25, 2008

A Zimbabwean woman stood and said she had roomed with Yepiz in San Francisco, and she had been "like a mother to me." Yepiz had admonished her for fighting with her employer, reminding her she was "here illegally," and to be careful.

"She said to me, 'San Francisco is the only place that will take care of me — I have nothing now and I can't work.'" The woman added, "Thank you — she could die in a beautiful room."

When the woman moved out, Yepiz was praying, she said, and she never saw her again.

Entering the welfare system put "a very complex burden" on Yepiz because she was not a citizen and had no green card, a social worker said. As her shelter time drew near an end, and the worker tried desperately to get her housing, Yepiz was calm and cheerful.

"She was always reassuring us," said the social worker. "She was never down and had the most peace of mind of any of us. She respected the system."

Despite Yepiz's troubles, she received the city's full treatment.

The public administrator's office handles estates of deceased indigents and others who have no relatives here. In handling Yepiz's case, it worked through the Zimbabwe Embassy in Washington, D.C. It located her son Kelvin Shekede in the town of Gweru to send him the death certificate. Her daughter died years ago.

The public administrator planned to ship Yepiz's remains home but Lufthansa, the only airline flying to Zimbabwe, wanted $4,000. With the casket, fees and other costs, the total would be $11,000. But estate investigator Andres Garcia talked to the son and he gave permission to cremate the body instead and send on the ashes. That $2,260 cost is paid from Yepiz' small estate, Garcia said. Anything left goes to her son.

"Ms. Yepiz was lucky to have friends who cared about her," Garcia said. "They called us with information. It's nice to see that bonding, and it helps put a face on the people we deal with. I got to talk to the son, too.

"I'm glad this worked out. So many times we go into an apartment in the Tenderloin of someone young or old and there are no leads to find relatives."

Upon the arrival of the ashes, and after a proper ceremony, it is said in Zimbabwe's Shona tradition that Yepiz's spirit will become part of her ancestral tree. ●

— TOM CARTER

Didn't Want to Be a Burden
ROBERT CLARK

IN FAILING HEALTH, Robert Clark, a Lockheed sheet metal worker for 23 years, moved into the Civic Center Residence so he wouldn't be a burden to his family here in town, his friends said. He had multiple medical problems, including advanced diabetes, and died in his seventh-floor room eight months later at 72.

"He was so polite he was "almost courtly," social worker Barbara Fitzpatrick said at his memorial at the hotel. "He was very well liked, but he was quiet and stayed in his room a lot."

Clark had difficulty walking. He preferred shuffling along with one-inch steps to using a wheelchair, which he "hated," according to Johnny his friend of a year. "It would take him forever to walk to the corner, but he wouldn't touch his wheelchair."

Robert Clark died Dec. 5, 2006

Johnny said Clark was at the hotel not to "be a burden to his family — his beautiful wife and daughter." The two spent hours sitting in the hotel conference room admiring the coffered ceilings and talking about architecture.

"He was an educated man," Johnny said. "And when I look up there now I think of him looking down at me. You can't say anything bad about that man."

Fitzpatrick recalled the day Clark died.

"I went to his room to remind him of flu shots and he didn't answer," she said. "An hour later a young man from property management found him dead in his room. It's very upsetting. It's the third death we've had in two weeks."

"It's that time of year," said Rev. Glenda Hope, who officiated the service."The earth is dying. The darkness comes early and there can be a heaviness, especially if someone we know has died." ●

— TOM CARTER

Married 54 Years, Still in Love

ANTHONY GAGLIANO

TUESDAYS, Thursdays and Saturdays, Anthony Gagliano had one thing on his mind: seeing the love of his life, wife Janith, he called her "Kip," who moved into a rest home on 26th Avenue two years ago.

Dressed in his red robe, which he wore everywhere, the white-haired Gagliano, 5 feet tall and hunched, would go downstairs to the Antonia Manor lobby and shuffle to the front desk.

"You know what I want," he would declare, beaming to clerk Yoshida Ellis. "Call me a cab!"

He often carried fresh fruit or presents for Kip, who had lived with him at the Manor for 18 years. The rooms are so small, theirs adjoined on the seventh floor. Gagliano would keep his door open so he could hear if she needed anything.

Tony Gagliano died in July, 2004

Then he suffered chest pains. Taken to the hospital, he died there at age 80. At his memorial, Manor General Manager Peter Shanley said how moved he was when he found Gagliano's love letters in his room.

"Their love was so fresh," Shanley said. "They always joked so much. It was like they had just met. He was a blessed man."

"It was true love every day," said Ellis.

Gagliano retired as a North Beach bartender. His friendliness and ready smiles, his "presence," as his friends described it, had helped give Mike's Pool Hall and Enrico's a warmth beyond their cool reputations.

He met Kip in 1950 at Raposa, a long-gone Broadway bar. Married in Reno, their love lasted 54 years. They had no children. "He was the most considerate person I have ever known," Ellis said.

Alejandro Loma struggled behind his dark glasses but found the words: "He was my neighbor, a good neighbor. He always greeted me. He gave me food. He was a good man. His face is always full of smiles. I never thought he'd die. I am very sorry. I loved him. He was like a brother."

Russell Christopel met Gagliano at the Manor in 1984. They would talk about sports, especially horses. Gagliano had been playing the ponies since 1944, Christopel said. "If he made a bet, he'd ask me not to tell his wife because it would upset her."

Gagliano's friends all felt lucky to have known him. He seemed to have cast a larger ring of love than he might have imagined. One woman, new to the Manor, said she hadn't known him but attended anyway. "This is a tribute to him for his huge contribution in setting the tone for this place," she said. "It's a wonderful place to live." ●

— TOM CARTER

Full-Throated Voice for the Homeless

RONNIE EAGLES

EVEN WITHOUT TEETH, Ronnie Eagles, a former Coalition on Homelessness staffer, could belt out speeches to pierce the heart and inspire the homeless to believe that a better day is possible.

Stretching his pencil-thin frame to full 5-foot-4 stature, Eagles delivered his inventive punch line — "We want solutions, not persecutions!" — at rallies and press conferences, and zinged it as well at Police Commission and Board of Supervisors meetings.

"Yes, for a while he even did it without his front teeth — the uppers," fellow coalition worker Mara Raider, who attended Eagles' memorial at the Senator Hotel, said with a faint smile. Eagles' family in Oakland, where he was raised, had a service there a week ago.

Eagles, who lived a dozen satisfying years at the Senator, died unexpectedly of natural causes in his fifth-floor room. He was only 44. For many years he worked with Community Housing Partnership's maintenance crew, servicing the Senator, Iroquois and San Cristina hotels.

Several among the 13 mourners spoke of his infectious personality and skill cooking soul food. Two weeks before he died, he looked healthy as he served Thanksgiving dinner in the Senator — "with joy in his heart," Manager Isabella Marshall said. "He was well-known and loved."

"Ronnie had passion and was inspiring," a man said as he rose to his feet. "He taught me a lot about overcoming things to effect change."

Rae Suber, tenant services manager, sang "What a Friend We Have in Jesus" in "15 keys," she said. "And he would've told me that. But that song makes me think of Ronnie."

Ronnie Eagles died Dec. 9, 2005

Eagles was a Street Sheet vendor in the mid-'90s when he discovered the coalition's civil rights project and plunged into it, Raider said. He was at the Turk Street office daily, eventually became paid staff and soon showed his skill as a public speaker who could move people.

"He was very experienced and passionate and invaluable for me," Raider said. "He trained dozens of people to document civil rights violations."

After 1999, Eagles slacked off, Raider guesses because of burnout.

"But the way he talked — 'We need to be down there!' — it got me and others going."

"Yes," another mourner added, "he was all about the do." ●

— TOM CARTER

3 Die Days Apart

JAN CASTRO
BERNARD CLARK
FRANKLIN MOSBY

A CLOUD OF SORROW settled on the Jefferson Hotel at the ground zero block of Turk Street before Christmas when three residents died within a week of each other, one of them a warm-hearted maintenance man who lived there more than a dozen years and was a cherished regular at Brown Jug bar over on Hyde Street.

The hotel held a memorial for them in a bright, carpeted basement room set with handsome wood chairs and a white cloth-covered table. On it, three floral arrangements celebrated the lives of Jan Castro, 53; Bernard Clark, 38; and Franklin Mosby, 61.

Jan Castro died Dec. 4, 2005

Castro went to St. Francis Memorial Hospital on her birthday, Nov. 21, and died of pneumonia two weeks later.

"I had a denim skirt for her," said one of the dozen mourners. "She died before I could give it to her. Her death broke my heart; she was my friend."

Castro arrived at the hotel six months before to be close to a companion, Jeffrey Leggett, and soon began volunteering for the hotel's social activities.

ANALYSIS

Bernard Clark died Dec. 11, 2005

Clark had been a Jefferson Hotel resident less than a month when he went into an Oakland hospital where he died while on life support.

"Both Clark and Castro were expected to come back, and that's what makes it so hard," said Mariko Obrero, hotel case manager.

Mosby, 13 years at the SRO, died in his room of natural causes.

"The three losses have been very painful for our community," Obrero said.

Randy Burns sobbed and struggled as he spoke of Mosby, a drinking buddy for 20 years and a gay man like himself.

"He'd always say, 'Randy, be strong for gay people with AIDS.' He knew all the gay people who died of AIDS. I can't believe he's gone. I loved him so much. He was a very special person."

A neighbor of his on the second floor said Mosby always greeted him with: "Have a good day and enjoy yourself."

Obrero said Mosby had diabetes. But it didn't stop him from drinking daily at the Brown Jug where he became a close friend of Ralph Schaefer, owner, a bartender 37 years.

"He was in here every day for more than 15 years," Schaefer said as a country and western song blared from the bar's jukebox. When the door is open the place isn't so dark; two muted televisions compete at either end of the old-timey bar. A patron nursing a beer said he had known Mosby 30 years, and that he worked as a maintenance man and janitor at many TL bars, including the Ram's Head on Taylor and Leona's Cocktail Lounge on Turk.

Franklin Mosby died Dec. 9, 2005

"He was my handyman," Schaefer said. "He'd do plumbing and electrical, small things. I'd pay him. And when I'd have a bar party he'd always volunteer to do the cooking."

Seated at his regular spot — the third stool from the end of the bar near the door so he could look outside — Mosby was a soft touch for his acquaintances.

"People would come in and whisper in his ear, then he'd borrow $5 from me and give it away," Schaefer said. "He always paid me at the end of the month. But he never got his money back. He was a drinker. He couldn't remember everything."

When Mosby didn't show up at his seat one day, Schaefer sent three people at different times to the hotel to check on him. The latter was a Jefferson resident who persuaded management to open Mosby's door. They found him dead.

"We were close buddies," Schaefer said. "He was gay, you know. I'm going to get a brass plate engraved with his name and 'rest in peace' and put it on the bar at his seat.

"I got a whole barful of people I'd gladly change for him. That's the way I feel about it." ●

— TOM CARTER

Vietnam Vet and the Flower Peddler

CURTIS JONES and LUCIANO MORENO

THE FRIENDS of a Vietnam War POW and a Mission Street flower vendor remembered both in memorials at the Camelot Hotel where the two had landed within two months of each other. They died two days apart.

Luciano Moreno was born in El Salvador; he died of cancer at age 45. Curtis Jones, the POW, died of AIDS at 55. Both were in failing health when they moved into the Camelot just months ago; they went to the hospital about the same time and neither came back.

Moreno, cheerful and energetic, loved tacos and mole, especially during Cinco de Mayo, a friend recalled. Moreno's social worker, Lauren Wichterman, said that as a strolling flower vendor Moreno worked throughout the Mission and at S.F. General. He lived in an apartment building basement and was fighting cancer before moving to the Camelot. Chemotherapy debilitated him, she said, and he confronted his mortality.

"When he got sick he talked to me about dying; he was afraid of it," said Wichterman. "It touched me deeply." But Moreno came to realize "how much love was around him," she said, and it was a comfort when he went into the hospital. He died six days later.

Sandra Green arrived just as the service was concluding. She wore a bright red dress and carried a sheaf of drawings. She said she was Jones' common-law wife of six years. They had met when she was homeless. She was distraught but started telling his story.

Luciano Moreno died Feb. 8, 2006

Jones had suffered as an Army POW. "His thumbs were broken 20 times," Green said. His shoulders were fractured when he was "stuffed into a barrel." Lingering pain dogged him after the war. He screamed at night, she said, and turned to smoking crack to feel better than he ever felt before.

They separated after he was diagnosed with HIV because he didn't want to give her AIDS, she said. He wouldn't take his medicine, then stopped eating. She lived at the Columbia Hotel five blocks away, yet didn't know until three days before he died that his worsening condition had landed him in the VA Hospital.

When she went to see him, she said, he told her how much he loved her.

As mourners left, it was cold and drizzling outside. Green dabbed her eyes and opened the sheaf. Scores of her chalk drawings on 8-by-11 paper showed Jones, the love of her life, in the nude. "Most are X-rated," she said.

"I bought this dress for him, but he never saw me wear it. I didn't know where he was. Now, they won't let me in his room. But if I could just have something of his, anything, his pillow, anything with his smell on it." •

Curtis Jones died Feb. 6, 2006

— TOM CARTER

They Called Him 'Hollywood'
GLEN BURISE

GLEN BURISE had a spark. Everybody saw it. Maybe it was personality, though he wasn't boisterous, funny or overly playful, just kind of edgy. It made you look and consider him. And that's what he wanted.

That was the image held among the eight friends and acquaintances who gathered at Civic Center Residence for his memorial. The native San Franciscan, 6 feet tall, always smartly dressed, died of lung cancer at Laguna Honda Hospital at age 56. His trademark black hat was hanging from the wall at the head of his bed. His estranged daughter had visited him the night before.

Donald Beard, who said he met Burise when he was 14, told how he got his nickname. Glen so wanted to be like his late older brother, Fred, a colorful and well-known player in the heyday of the Fillmore jazz scene. But the younger brother couldn't quite pull it off, Beard said, and got called "Hollywood" for his efforts.

Burise moved into a fifth-floor unit in the 200-room residence a year ago. He was quiet and dignified and spoke like he had some education. He avoided petty fighting among the residents and brandished an occasional smirk to punctuate conversations. Over recent months, according to friends, he was in and out of the hospital, lost 40 pounds and had to wear white support stockings and blue hospital slippers down to the dining room, never complaining about his pain, deterioration or lost image.

He had another dimension, too.

"He expected you to look at him and see him, even in a crowd," said Carlita Barry.

"Here, where he lived a reduced life, he continued to be himself. He didn't dissolve or disappear. And it was refreshing to see. Congratulations to anyone who holds on to their personality. And he had a sense of humor, too."

Barry said that if Burise wasn't around for a typical bread donation delivery, he expected someone there to grab a sliced loaf for him because it was known that's what he wanted. And when cake was served he wanted his special piece, a corner with lots of frosting. And when he flashed his smirk, some found it a rather "charming" touch. He had a look, Barry added, that said: "Once I could have bought the cake and told you how to cut it."

Glen Burise died June 5, 2005

"Not many of us have that left here," she said. "We're beaten down. But he was sick and still remembered what he liked and insisted on it. He still had flash and a little style. Out of the 200 people in this building he expected to be seen and was disappointed if he wasn't."

The memorial took place in a vast, high-ceilinged room off the lobby called the library, though no books were visible. People sat in the middle of the room on a small circle of comfortable straight chairs, a donation from San Francisco State's dorms. TNDC, which owns Civic Center Residence, was renovating and the daytime throb of construction noises drowned out much of the conversation. So Barry and Beard consented to reminisce after the memorial — suddenly, the noise ended.

"He would have liked that," Barry said of the irony.

"And I'm sure when his feet hit the ground on the other side he lit up a cigarette, opened a can of beer and started looking for young women. Good for him. Congratulations." •

— TOM CARTER

The Model Tenant
RON MALIGON

IN SOME CORNER of the Philippines there is a great sadness over the death of Ron Maligon, who lived 10 years at the Ritz Hotel and died there when he was 57.

Ron Maligon died Aug. 2, 2004

Unlike many fellow residents, Maligon was independent; he worked five days week at the airport and liked his job. He chose to live quietly and frugally. That lifestyle earned the praises of the hotel clerk, manager and others. They said he was a model tenant who paid rent on time, never complained, was polite, quiet, helpful, giving and caring.

"I only saw him when he paid his rent," Manager Kelvin Nance said. "He was like an invisible person."

Six of Malignon's friends gathered around a long black table with a blue vase graced by white daisies in the first-floor kitchen overlooking Eddy Street to bid him good-bye. A reading from Scriptures fought with the clamor of traffic outside.

"He had none of the socio-psychological problems that many around him had and I enjoyed talking to him," recalled Otto Duffy, who knew him for 12 years. "He was a strong person. I figured with all the money he sent back to the Philippines, he'd go back there and retire."

But the money was for "many relatives," Assistant Manager Eric Asuncion said. "He was very generous." •

— TOM CARTER

Hard-Drinking Baseball Buff
RUDY JIMENEZ

RUDY JIMENEZ'S daily drinking buddies were a no-show at his memorial but he got a proper sendoff from people who didn't know him.

"He was a nice guy when he wasn't blasted and then he'd talk a bit about baseball," Ray Boscacci said to the small gathering at the West Hotel. "But when he was, which was 80% of the time, he wouldn't talk to you.

"Two or three friends of his would show up every day to go drinking with him. And he'd come downstairs in his wheelchair. I dunno, maybe he had the money."

The West's residents didn't see much of Jimenez, a two-year resident. Even when he was around and looking beat up — with black eyes, Boscacci remembered — he wouldn't talk about that either, or his suffering.

Jimenez had been in Laguna Honda Hospital since early spring. He died there in July. Liver failure, Boscacci and others figured, but the official cause of death was unknown. He was 60.

"I'm here because I saw his picture," said one man. "Although you don't know a person here, you say hello anyway — it might make someone's day."

A Polaroid picture of Jimenez with his room number on it was on a table with a candle and small bunch of flowers.

Rudy Jimenez died July 2007

Too many liquor stores are around with cheap booze, Boscacci said. "You can get a half pint of vodka for $2 and a quart of beer for $1."

Three groceries within a half block of the hotel sell alcohol. Two doors away, one sells hard liquor, too. That afternoon, during the memorial, a drinking crowd of a dozen was partying on the sidewalk in the middle of the block. ●

— TOM CARTER

Vietnam War Hero With Mystery Legacy
ROBERT DUSSAULT

A DOZEN FRIENDS bid farewell to Robert Frederick Dussault, a Vietnam War hero and former Union Street antique dealer, in a memorial at the Empress Hotel where his friendliness and generosity were highly regarded.

Dussault died of "natural causes." His friends said the ravages of old war wounds reduced him in recent years and hastened his death at 64.

They described the frail, 5-foot-10, five-year resident of the hotel as an intelligent man with a lovely soul who volunteered to help without being asked, was courteous, invariably had a kind word for folks and would do anything for a friend. But he deeply distrusted the government and impressed people by making his conspiracy theories seem so reasonable.

He also liked to give away pens and Post-its, they said, and seemed to especially frequent Copy Central stores.

"The pens he gave away were all from Copy Central," said one man with a grin, "and he said they were so good they wouldn't leak at 5,000 feet up in a plane."

Robert Dussault died Sept. 16, 2005

Kathleen Manning, Dussault's friend for 25 years, read an email she received from Orin Wells, one of his high school classmates. Dussault came from a well-to-do family in Massachusetts, Wells wrote, but his parents divorced and he ended up in Chico with his father. Not an athlete, yet "part of the in crowd," the letter said, he was elected senior class president.

Dussault attended UC Berkeley, married his high school sweetheart and joined the Navy, becoming a lieutenant in the SEALS. He was wounded in Vietnam and sent home for good, but he insisted on returning, and he did as "a river pilot," a move that ended his marriage, the letter said. His boat was strafed, he was wounded and lost the use of his right arm.

Manning met him in the 1970s when he had an antique shop on trendy Union Street and was also an art print dealer. But Dussault gave it all up to go live in Switzerland for 10 years, she said. He was "a changed man" when he returned in the early 1990s, physically reduced and health slipping, she said. His ribs easily broke from bone deterioration and my, she said, how he suffered.

Besides the memory of his good will he leaves at the hotel he loved, Dussault bequeathed a mystery. He was believed to have several storage rooms full of antiques. (His room, 602, remained locked, accessible only to medical examiners who will sort through his possessions and search for a will and information about next of kin, the manager said.)

Manning said Dussault told her he wanted his estate to go to disabled veterans, but she was certain he had no will. •

Navy Lt. Robert Dussault

— TOM CARTER

Died One After the Other

DONALD CONNELLY and HERBERT BROWN

TWO Civic Center Residence tenants died within a day of each other, one peacefully in his room, the other in the hospital after a long, painful struggle with cancer that had hobbled him.

Donald Connelly was 52 when he was found dead in his room. Cause of death is pending. Connelly had come from the Boyd Hotel on Jones Street next to St. Anthony's Dining Room less than a year ago. Little was known about him other than that he battled diabetes.

Donald Connelly died Sept. 30, 2011

Herbert Brown died the day before at UC Medical Center after being in and out of the hospital for cancer. He was 67.

"Herbert had cancer bad," said Donald Nadile, one of eight mourners at the memorial in the SRO's downstairs community room. "He said chemotherapy wasn't doing him any good."

Tanya Wells knew him all six years she's lived at TNDC's Civic Center Residence. "He had it rough in the beginning," Wells said. "He was a funny little guy, always rushing to the elevator in pain. I'd yell, 'Make it, Herbert, make it!'"

Herbert Brown died Sept. 29, 2011

Wells said the thin, 5-foot-6 Brown was always well-dressed and kept his hair combed. In recent months Brown walked bent over with a cane. Wells, a large woman with a pretty smile, walks with two canes herself.

Once she saw him in the hospital's emergency room when she was in for a shoulder problem. He smiled at her across the room when she said, "I'll see you back home."

Brown was home one week before returning to the hospital for the last time.

"He was a good person, but he couldn't take care of himself at the end," Wells said. "This last year he was more nourished than before, though. It was a change. He was accepting it. He decided to live his life as a sick person. He made the transition, and he smiled a lot. I miss him running around here." •

— TOM CARTER

A Well-Regarded Man
JOSEPH BARROW

ON A BRISK afternoon, a small group of friends and relatives gathered to mark the passing of San Francisco native Joseph Barrow, a former merchant seaman who is survived by his wife and three children who live in the Philippines.

Barrow collapsed in the elevator on the sixth floor of the Coast Hotel, where he'd lived quietly for six or seven years. Emergency medical staff were unable to revive him. "He didn't suffer," said Shelly Brown, the hotel's assistant support services manager. Barrow was 62.

"He was very well-mannered," Brown said. "It didn't seem like he belonged here. We talked about going to the doctor, and he told me, 'Don't hold me to that yet, we'll talk about it at our next meeting.' But our next meeting never came."

Case workers and fellow residents recalled a genial man held in warm regard by those who knew him. Neighbor Larry Taylor called him "a good guy. I miss seeing him getting off the elevator every morning to get his coffee. I called him my coffee-drinking buddy."

Anita, a hotel housekeeper, fought back tears remembering how Barrow would give her a box of candies every month for her kids. Robert Majitt said that life in their SRO "is a stressful environment sometimes, but I never saw it get to him. Here, it's easy to lose your temper, but I never saw Joe lose his."

Joseph Barrow died Feb. 8, 2011

Paulette Baker, Barrow's sister, said their family was raised in the Fillmore District, and that as a youngster Joe liked music and lifting weights. He attended Polytechnic High, which the city shut down years ago. His poor eyesight disqualified him from military service, but he worked as a merchant seaman for many years. "I don't think he liked it very well," his sister said. "He got off that boat and wouldn't even get on a ferry. He was done with boats."

He came ashore for good in the late '90s to help care for his aging parents in the Fillmore. He worked as a janitor at S.F. General Hospital, which was his job at sea, and as a property manager. Caring for the family became "a bit much" for him, Baker said, and she had little contact with him in recent years.

"There's always issues, but you leave the door open, keep the same number. You don't close your heart." He liked to watch TV and listen to music, she recalled. "James Brown, that was his guy. He liked soul."

Barrow was "basically a loner," she said, though he treasured his children. He displayed their pictures prominently in his room, and kept all their letters calling him Dad. His middle child, Christine, had recently given birth to his first granddaughter.

"His kids were the highlight of his being," Baker said. "I think every penny he got on the side he would send them. But this is where he chose to live," she said of the community of friends at the Coast, many of whom had signed cards that were on display.

"I will miss our little talks," one wrote. "Your smile was so warm," wrote another, and a third told how Barrow was "always very kind."

"I never saw him in anything other than the best moods," said Jon, a fellow resident. "He was always outgoing and about his business." He saw Barrow frequently sitting in the lobby, typing on his laptop.

Besides his sister, daughter and granddaughter, Barrow is survived by his oldest son, Joseph. Baker did not know whether the youngest son, Richard, is still alive.

— MARK HEDIN

Pioneer of Supportive Housing
LEROY LOOPER

FROM CITY HALL to San Quentin, representatives of the community cross-section that he'd served gathered at the Cadillac Hotel to honor Leroy Branch Looper, whose vision had transformed the site from a slated-for-demolition relic into a beacon of hope.

Looper, a former addict and convict who dedicated himself to helping others, died three days after quietly losing consciousness in his chair at McCormick and Kuleto's restaurant, just after he'd made a speech. He was 86.

Former Mayors Dianne Feinstein and Art Agnos sent huge floral displays. Mayor Ed Lee, Tenderloin police Capt. Joe Garrity, Supervisors Bevan Dufty and Malia Cohen, Assemblyman Tom Ammiano, state Democratic Party Chair John Burton, a bunch of musicians who'd performed at the "Concerts at the Cadillac" series, men Leroy had helped transition from prison, friends and family filled the hotel lobby to overflowing as they reminisced about Looper's remarkable life.

Leroy Looper died Sept. 11, 2011

He rose from a child of the underworld to become a leader in efforts to lift others from such circumstances, using his hard-earned street smarts to educate better-credentialed social workers in how that world actually works.

"Leroy had a charmed life," said Kathy Looper, his wife of 39 years. He was "a man who changed destiny in a lot of ways, not only his own but others' as well."

Looper's 1976 purchase and subsequent conversion of Eddy Street's rundown Cadillac Hotel into a supportive housing facility may prove to be his most significant and lasting accomplishment, though there were many.

He founded Reality House — drug detox and rehab free to addicts — in New York in the early 1960s. Kathy Looper said that until Reality House, drug programs were available only to whites. Looper left New York and opened Reality House West in San Francisco's Fillmore District in 1968.

"There was no other program like Reality House, there were no community-run drug treatment centers," said Kathy Looper, who was an S.F. State student seeking school credits while the campus was closed during the '68 student strike when she met her future husband at Reality House West.

But they didn't make history with the Cadillac until some years later. Kathy Looper described a "handshake deal" struck in 1976 with Cadillac Hotel owner John Foggy.

At the time, Richard Livingston was administrator of Reality House West. Livingston had been administrator at Youth Advocates when it made its transformation from Huckleberry's for Runaways to a system of residential services, so Livingston was experienced in nonprofit real estate.

Looper had told Foggy he wanted Reality House to become self-sufficient and the key was that hotel. Foggy operated the Cadillac at the time, but it was deteriorating. Only about 40 of its more than 150 rooms could be rented. When a room needed any repair, even just to fix a broken window, it was simply boarded up.

Kathy Looper and Brad Paul, then staff of the North of Market Planning Coalition, which was leading the way toward neighborhood improvement, believe that speculators — including Don Fisher of the Gap, who also had had a stake in the Cadillac — had bought the hotel in anticipation of rising real estate values. Zoning ordinances of the time — later revised after Looper, Paul and NOMPC made it an issue — allowed for much taller buildings so that the low-rise hotels and apartment buildings that characterized the Tenderloin's residential allure could eventually be demolished and replaced with much bigger — thus pricier — properties.

THAT'S WHAT occurred back in the 1960s in what is now the Yerba Buena area of South of Market. But the Cadillac was going to seed, the height limits had not been raised and the anticipated real estate boom had not yet arrived on Eddy Street.

As Paul tells it, Foggy asked Looper how much money he had to buy the building, and was told, "None! You're bleeding money. I'm not going to pay you for it, I'm just going to take over your mortgage."

Kathy Looper recalls that the mortgage, in fact, was $325,000, but that the price came to $525,000 as Foggy paid all the bills for the first two years after the Loopers took control. "He really went out of his way to be of help to us," she said. "He's a hero in this story."

"The timing was perfect," says Tenderloin Housing Clinic Executive Director Randy Shaw, who calls Looper his mentor. "1977 was also the year of the International Hotel, the demolitions of SROs South of Market ... the Cadillac became an important model" for the concept of supportive housing.

"Supportive housing didn't become a term until the mid- to late-'80s," Paul said. "Residential hotels were associated with flophouses or slums."

For a few years, Looper had a contract with the Bureau of Prisons for "keeping the foxes with the hens," Kathy Looper says. "Who would think of putting prisoners in with senior citizens?" But, at the Cadillac, she said, "It worked. They took care of each other, 'cause they're both wounded."

"Technically, the Cadillac was a federal prison," Paul explained. The deal was, as convicts got to within 90 days of parole, they could be placed in a program at the Cadillac to prepare them for re-entry into society, a key component that Looper had found missing in his earliest attempts at rehabbing drug users in New York. For the first month the ex-offenders were at the Cadillac, Paul said, they couldn't leave their third-floor quarters. In the second month, they could leave with a chaperone, and so on. Once they had completed job training, found employment and reconnected with their families, Kathy Looper said, they could be paroled.

THE PROGRAM ran successfully, Paul said, until its funding was cut early in the Reagan years. "People who graduated from the ex-offender program stayed on," Paul said, and, meanwhile, seniors, too, were living in the building as it was gradually renovated, including the restoration of its original facade, with labor from the ex-offenders, VISTA and CETA jobs programs, according to Kathy Looper, Paul and Livingston, now managing director of EXIT Theatre, which had its first office in a Cadillac storefront.

EXIT Theatre, which produces the annual San Francisco Fringe Festival, staged its first production, "Lives and Loves of the Gibbs Sisters," in the lobby of the hotel in late 1983, Livingston said, exemplifying how Looper encouraged community development. The Cadillac is a big building with a number of storefronts.

"He increased community services by giving them cheap rent in the Cadillac," Paul said. "He was all about using the building to build back the lives of the people who lived there and rebuilding the neighborhood."

Looper put a Sizzler restaurant in the Cadillac's corner storefront, in a breakthrough deal for the franchise chain that was engineered by Livingston. The Police Athletic League took over what had been the landmark of amateur boxing, Newman's Gym. Paul called it "like something out of a 1930 Jimmy Cagney movie." Later the space was home to a child care program.

Kathy Looper blamed the Sizzler's ultimate failure on changes in the neighborhood after the 1989 earthquake, but in its day it provided dozens of jobs and "a great meal for a great price," she said.

Rev. Glenda Hope had a computer training center in a storefront there, and the Vietnamese Youth Development Center got its start at the Cadillac, too. A donated 1884 Steinway grand piano sits in the lobby today and attracts musicians for regular no-cost concerts.

"Leroy was one of the first to organize activities," Paul said. "This is the model for supportive housing. A lot of it is old residential hotels fixed up ... the Senator, the Iroquois, how they're laid out and staffed.

"If you live in an apartment in the Tenderloin, you're pretty much alone," said Paul, a Cadillac resident for 3½ years. "Of all the places I've lived in my life — and there were many — it was where I felt most welcome and safest. You felt like there was always somebody that had your back."

"Leroy was an amazing guy," Paul said. "One of the most unforgettable people I ever met. He had so much knowledge and passion and cared so much about the people who lived there." Paul said Looper taught him many surprisingly simple secrets to succeeding where many have failed. One such tip was to merely push a broom.

"People think criminals are crazy," Looper told him. "They're not. They're businesspeople. When people are new to town they look around for where the city is telling them it's OK to operate. Vacant storefronts, graffiti and trash" do just that.

"When he first took over the Cadillac, he got a big push broom," Paul recalls. The dealers moved down the street." They'd return in a few hours, so Looper then began hosing down the sidewalk. That would keep them away for a few more hours. Before long, Paul said, merchants up and down the block were following suit and things started improving.

"He understood that was more important than having one more police cruiser."

AS IF the Cadillac Hotel wasn't enough, the Loopers also in the late '70s took on the Chateau Laura, a mental health facility housed in an aging mansion on the corner of Guerrero and Liberty streets in the Mission. In a 1987 profile in the New Yorker magazine, writer Bill Barich chronicled how the Loopers — Leroy, Kathy, their son and daughter and Leroy's two sons from a previous marriage — lived in the Chateau, which they renamed Agape after their daughter, while caring for their schizophrenic clients.

Kathy Looper says that, as they aged, the Loopers were less able to personally perform as many of the chores associated with running Chateau Agape. So they turned its operation over to the city, which promptly tripled the staffing levels, she said. When a client broke the no-smoking rules and a fire broke out, it ultimately spelled the end of Chateau Agape.

Looper's autobiography, which he wrote in the late 1970s and can be found online, tells of his formative years during the Great Depression, when he lived in Washington, D.C., and learned firsthand the ways of bootleggers, numbers runners, pimps, prostitutes and the people who cared for them, too — most specifically, his beloved Aunt Carrie.

"More than anything, I wanted to be a credit to my race," Looper wrote.

Looper was in reform school for petty theft when he was 8, went to jail and prison for drug possession and sales in his 20s, and eventually weaned himself from heroin in his 30s, while living in New York City. In doing so, he discovered that for many leaving heroin, himself included, alcohol proves to be a new challenge. He returned to New York's Riker's Island prison in a new capacity, as a counselor to inmates.

Looper's activities and accomplishments were too many to recount conclusively, but he co-founded the Concerned Business Persons, the Tenderloin AIDS Network, YouthBuild S.F. and YouthBuild U.S.A., the Tenderloin Crime Abatement Committee, San Francisco Alive's Tenderloin Cleanup Committee and the Tenderloin Community Fund. Paul also cited Looper's role in the Corporation for Supportive Housing, the Tenants Association in the Cadillac, work with Glide and St. Anthony's and NOMPC.

Besides his wife, Kathy, and children Camlo, Esan, Malik and Agape, Looper leaves eight grandchildren.

—MARK HEDIN

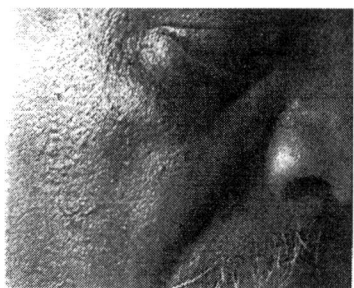

I Remember Hiram

BY ED BOWERS

Sept. 9, 2003, 1:30 a.m.
Hiram,
I have just returned from a bar.
On my answering machine is a
Message from Keith Savage
Informing me that you have
Died of a heart attack.

You're playing boogie woogie piano
On another planet now
And when you introduce yourself
As a negro no one knows what
You're talking about.
So just ask them if they want to purchase
One of your c.d.s for ten dollars
And leave it at that.

You lived in my neighborhood
The Tenderloin of San Francisco,
But now you're dead.

I saw you on Golden Gate ave.
Two weeks ago
As I was walking a manic-
depressive friend

To her psychiatric hotel
At Jones and Leavenworth.

All the streets here
Are spelled like names of prisons
Or heavens or hells.

They sound like jazz.
They sound like the blues piano
You played at the Brainwash
Less than a week ago.

The music in the smile
In your face looked too alive
To die.

Now,
When gazing carefully
Into the eyes of those
I pass on the street,
I also look for you.

Just because
No one can see a face
Doesn't mean
It's gone. ●

> "His ego was in his heart."

Last call at the 21 Club. Photo by Lenny Limjoco

San Francisco Study Center

BOARD OF DIRECTORS

JOHN BURKS, PRESIDENT
Chairman emeritus, Department of Journalism, San Francisco State University;
magazine writer and editor

LIBBY DENEBEIM, SECRETARY-TREASURER
Former president, San Francisco Board of Education; 1st Norma Satten Award winner

RICHARD LIVINGSTON, VICE PRESIDENT
Managing director, EXIT Theatre; publisher, EXIT Press

STAS MARGARONIS
Study Center co-founder, author, journalist, Santa Maria Shipping founder

REIKO HOMMA TRUE
Former director, S.F. Community Mental Health Services, consultant

BEN FONG-TORRES
Journalist, author, broadcaster, emcee, community advocate

JIM McWILLIAMS
San Francisco Mental Health Clients' Rights Advocates staff advocate

EDGAR MERCADO
Office of Self Help counselor, fitness program

TINA TONG YEE
Former city director of Client Relations and Cultural Competence,
nonprofit executive, consultant

STAFF

GEOFF LINK, EXECUTIVE DIRECTOR, CENTRAL CITY EXTRA EDITOR & PUBLISHER
MARJORIE BEGGS, SENIOR WRITER/EDITOR
KEVIN WALSH, FINANCE DIRECTOR
TOM CARTER, COMMUNITY REPORTER, CENTRAL CITY EXTRA
JOHN DAVID NUÑEZ, BOOKKEEPER
KEN HARPER, CONTRACTS ADMINISTRATOR
JONATHAN NEWMAN, MARK HEDIN, BRIAN RINKER, ED BOWERS — REPORTERS
LEONOR VERA, EDITORIAL ASSISTANT, RECEPTIONIST, BOOK DISTRIBUTION
BETH RENNEISEN, DESIGNER

San Francisco Study Center, a nonprofit founded in 1972, provides editorial, graphic
and fiscal sponsor services for other nonprofits, foundations and city departments.

944 Market Street, Suite 701, San Francisco, CA 94102   415.626.1650
www.studycenter.org

Ambassador Hotel plaque summarizes the SRO's history and marks its listing on the National Register of Historic Places.
Photo by Marjorie Beggs

INDEX OF THE DECEASED

Barrow, Joseph 125	Lutz, Eric 96
Bishop, Dewayne 33	MacKenzie, John 44
Bishop, Jason 43	Maguire, Gary 112
Bradshaw, Leo 62	Mai, Jimmy 31
Brooks, Robert Bruce 94	Maligon, Ron 122
Brown, Herbert 124	Mann, Patrick 17
Brunner, Phil 100	Martirosyan, Gyulli 21
Burise, Glen 121	McGee, Loraine 97
Carlos, Patricia 5	McHale, John 12
Carson, Ted 60	McKenney, John 'Mike' 23
Castro, Jan 119	Melone, John 70
Chikere, Linda 72	Merchant, Ernie 64
Clanton, Christopher 52	Miller, Lawrence 51
Clark, Bernard 119	Mobley, Charles 92
Clark, Robert 117	Moreno, Luciano 120
Clark, Rowena 45	Morgan, Londevette 6
Conley, Steve 14	Morris, Jesse 101
Connelly, Donald 124	Mosby, Franklin 119
Coomes, Marla 97	Mosley, Jason 91
Deaton, Jeff 115	Nunez, Carlos 64
DeFoe, Bernard 19	Pangle, Steven 98
Dias, Darwin 39	Parks, Ghia 96
Diaz, Feliciano 73	Parsons, Linda Slinkard 63
Dick, Michael 10	Phillips, Loretta Florence 7
Dillard, Terry 62	Pike, Samuel Robert 22
Dussault, Robert 123	Pineda, Samuel 52
Eagles, Ronnie 118	Pugliesi, Raymond 11
Eid, Abed 'Abe' 46	Prill, Anna 37
Entriken, Larry 24	Resto, Rita 35
Evans, Raymond 25	Ridolfi, Rose 61
Field, Kathy 113	Schwarz, Herbert Ivan 93
Fitzpatrick, Kathleen 50	Shelton, Anthony 78
Gagliano, Anthony 118	Shelton, Joseph William 111
Gannon, Kathleen 73	Silva Jr., Steven Alexxis 8
Gombos, James 18	Smith Jr., Garrison 41
Griffin, Lacy 76	Smith, Luke 13
Guzman, Louis O. 9	Smith, Robert 73
Hamilton, William 44	Soldivela, Joseph 75
Harmony, Lee 48	Stroface, Mark 73
Hevey, Christopher Marcus 40	Sturgis, Bruce 36
Hiram 129	Tao, Chui Y. 20
Horowitz, Preston 48	Taylor, John 49
Hunter, Brunette 'Nelly' 90	Tirado, George 34
Jackson, Joseph 68	Van Rijn, Michelle 95
Jenkins, Lee 77	Varnado, Sam 'Selfless' 66
Jimenez, Rudy 123	Walsh, Jerald 17
Jones, Curtis 120	Washington, Karen 69
Juve, James 78	Whitlock, Harvey 115
Kausman, Logan 'Cito' 89	Williams, James 114
Lane, James 'Pete' 46	Williams, Louis 60
Larsen, Jens 66	Wilson, Hank 79
Leach, Willie 25	Wood, Clyde 38
Lee, Byron 49	Yepiz, Daisy 115
Lee, Linda Rae 73	
Looper, Leroy 126	

ANALYSIS

Made in the USA
Charleston, SC
01 December 2012